BLOOMING

THROUGH THE ASHES

BLOOMING

THROUGH THE ASHES

An International Anthology on
Violence and the Human Spirit

Edited by

CLIFFORD CHANIN *and* AILI MCCONNON

RUTGERS UNIVERSITY PRESS
NEW BRUNSWICK, NEW JERSEY, AND LONDON

Library of Congress Cataloging-in-Publication Data

Blooming through the ashes : an international anthology on violence and the
human spirit / edited by Clifford Chanin and Aili McConnon.
p. cm.
Includes bibliographical references.
ISBN-978–0-8135–4212–6 (hardcover : alk. paper)
ISBN-978–0-8135–4213–3 (pbk. : alk. paper)
1. Violence—Literary collections. 2. Inspiration—Literary collections.
I. Chanin, Clifford. II. McConnon, Aili, 1980–
PN6071.V5B56 2008
808.8'03552—dc22
2007015500

A British Cataloging-in-Publication record for this book
is available from the British Library.

Visit our Web site: http://rutgerspress.rutgers.edu

Manufactured in the United States of America

CONTENTS

PROLOGUE

∾ SEAMUS HEANEY,
Poetry's Power against Intolerance—NORTHERN IRELAND

Nobel Laureate Seamus Heaney wrote (and later edited for this anthology) this essay for the *New York Times* in 2001, inspired by the aspirations of the imminent United Nations Conference Against Racism, held in South Africa. The conference eventually foundered on disputes over Israel and Palestine and, indeed, on how that issue obstructed consideration of others. Nonetheless, Heaney's essay stands as an eloquent plea for literature as "a *de profundis* on behalf of the desperate and deprived."

DUBLIN—Some lines from "Incantation," a poem by the late Czeslaw Milosz, express the fundamental belief upon which hope for the amelioration of our species must be based:

> Human reason is beautiful and invincible.
> No bars, no barbed wire, no pulping of books,
> No sentence of banishment can prevail against it.
> It puts what should be above things as they are.
> It does not know Jew from Greek nor slave from master.

It is thrilling to hear the ideal possibilities of human life stated so unambiguously and unrepentantly. For a moment, the dirty slate of history seems to have been wiped clean. The lines return to the bliss of beginnings. They tempt us to credit all over again liberations promised by the Enlightenment and harmonies envisaged by the scholastics, to believe that the deep well of religious and humanist value may still be unpolluted.

Yet there is also something problematic about what is being said. While the lines do have original force, the evidence of the ages is stacked against them. So it comes as no surprise to be told that in the original Polish, there is a certain frantic, even comic pitch to the meter and tone of "Incantation." Milosz's irony saves him and his poem from illusion and sentimentality; the fact that a tragic understanding coexists with the apparent innocence of his claims only serves to make those claims all the more unyielding and indispensable.

In the course of the past century, imaginative writers have grown more and more conscious of the darker levels to which human beings can descend, yet their art remains answerable to "what should be" as well as to "things as they are." And this means, I believe, that the example of writers has something to say to all who hunger and thirst for justice at the present time. Activists have different priorities than artists do, but they, too, are forced to acknowledge the prevalence of the atrocious while maintaining faith in the possibility of the desired. The artist's voice, in other words, is potent reinforcement in the campaign for human rights.

Campaigners in that cause will be in total sympathy with another famous utterance by Czeslaw Milosz. "What is poetry," he asks, "which does not save nations and peoples?" It was a question on my mind when I coined the phrase "the redress of poetry," by which I meant the need poets feel to align themselves with those who have been wronged, to repair and compensate for injustices suffered, to stay mindful of the miseries of the world. It is the serious artist's question to himself and the question he will usually hear when he comes in contact with the activist. And it is a question to be answered by posing another one: What is poetry that does not address itself to the individual consciousness, that does not convey an experience of verification at the personal level?

The fight against racism certainly must be waged by governments, as a highly organized, internationally coordinated, deliberately pursued effort of education and legislation. Nations and peoples must be recognized and represented equally, must be saved by just laws and civilized treatment— by committed actions. Nevertheless, the fight is also helped by every statement that strengthens an individual's moral sense and gratifies his or her sense of right, every utterance that reawakens the feeling of personal dignity or promotes a trust in human solidarity.

Much of the literature of the past century is a *de profundis* on behalf of the desperate and the deprived in gulag or ghetto or township or camp, but in spite of its desolate content that literature has been a positive influence: it has had the paradoxical effect of raising spirits and creating hope. We need only think of Aleksandr Solzhenitsyn to remind ourselves how the integrity of an individual writer can underwrite a whole culture of resolution and resistance. It can even underwrite a new idiom of affirmation, like the one employed in the United Nations declaration "Tolerance and Diversity: A Vision for the 21st Century."

The document is direct: "The horrors of racism—from slavery to holocaust to apartheid to ethnic cleansing—have deeply wounded the victim and debased the perpetrator. These horrors are still with us in various forms. It is now time to confront them and to take comprehensive measures against them." The document further declares that "we all constitute one human family" and asserts a new scientific basis for this belief by invoking the proof afforded by the mapping of the human genome. Yet the scientific reinforcement of the argument remains just that: reinforcement. Its primary strength comes from moral and philosophical sources, from the witness of heroic individuals to the belief that human reason is indeed beautiful and invincible.

When we see the signature of Nelson Mandela at the bottom of the declaration, it immediately acquires a kind of specific moral gravity, for the name Mandela, like the name Solzhenitsyn, is the equivalent of a gold reserve, a guarantee that the currency of good speech can be backed up by heroic action. There is nothing loose-mouthed involved. When Mr. Mandela's writing rises to a noble statement, that statement has been earned. It has behind it the full weight of a life endured for the sake of the principles it affirms.

Consequently, there is genuine healing power rather than mere rhetorical uplift in Mr. Mandela's espousal of the aims of the Durban conference, and the conference could well adopt as its sacred text something he wrote in his book, *Long Walk to Freedom:* "It was during those long and lonely years that my hunger for the freedom of my own people became a hunger for the freedom of all people, black and white. I knew as well as I knew anything that the oppressor must be liberated just as surely as the oppressed. I am not truly free if I am taking away someone else's freedom, just as surely as I am not free when my freedom is taken away from me. The oppressed and the oppressor alike are robbed of their humanity."

These lines, like those from "Incantation," have a radiance that is only enhanced by the tragic knowledge behind them, including the knowledge of how the oppressor is not free. With such personal, individual empathy, Mr. Mandela shows himself to be an artist of human possibility. He might well be called an activist, but he has a visionary understanding and would surely agree with the conviction that sustains Milosz's poem. It, too, could be adopted as a text by all who travel to Durban, for there is nothing improbable about the poem's luminous conclusion:

> Beautiful and very young are Philo-Sophia
> And poetry, her ally in the service of the good.
> As late as yesterday Nature celebrated their birth.
> The news was brought to the mountains by a unicorn and an echo.
> Their friendship will be glorious, their time has no limit.
> Their enemies have delivered themselves to destruction.

ACKNOWLEDGMENTS

The Legacy Project has been the beneficiary of support from many sources, particularly the Rockefeller Foundation and the Hamburg Institute for Social Research. This anthology could not have been written without the generous support of the Princeton Reach Out '56 Fellowship, whose aid meant that the Legacy Project could have a full-time literary editor, Aili McConnon, to co-author this project and bring it to fruition. The Rotary Club of New York was also generous in backing this project.

A special thank you to the following writers: Galway Kinnell, Breyten Breytenbach, Dunya Mikhail, Fadhil Al-Azzawi, Eva Hoffman, Zakes Mda, Khaled Mattawa, and Alfred Arteaga, for giving interviews to the Legacy Project on the larger themes of memory, loss, and recovery that are central to the anthology. Historians, human rights activists, and editors at Words Without Borders, the PEN American Center, and Human Rights Watch also provided very helpful input.

We are extremely grateful to the many scholars from universities around the world whose guidance shaped this anthology, some of whom include Lawrence Langer, Perry Link, Deborah McDowell, the late Sybil Milton, and Saul Sosnowski. This group recommended many literary selections in a series of meetings in 1996 supported by the Rockefeller Foundation in cooperation with the United States Holocaust Memorial Museum, under the direction of Wesley Fisher. Thanks also to Liz Appel, a PhD student in literature at Yale, who spent many hours helping interview writers, editing prose, and offering literary guidance.

We are indebted to the tireless efforts of Leah Smith and Maria Ali-Adib at the Legacy Project for their combination of organizational skills that kept such a multi-faceted project on track and editing insight.

Finally, we would like to thank our respective families for their support of the Legacy Project and this book in so many ways and at so many different times that it would be impossible to list them all here.

INTRODUCTION

The pieces first fell into place in Cambodia—at least some of them.

The purpose of the trip was to prospect for contemporary reflections on the Khmer Rouge and the killing fields: literature, paintings, music, dance. This was in 1999, more than two decades after the killing, but experts on Cambodia had been discouraging about the possibility of finding much. Explaining their doubts, they pointed to the continuing trauma that gripped Cambodian society. The culture, they said, did not encourage open expressions of mourning. The continuing presence of senior Khmer Rouge officials in the government made it dangerous to speak openly about the past. The population had been so profoundly depleted by violence that there still weren't enough artists, intellectuals, and academics to take on this work.

All true, it seemed. But wrong. The work was underway. It was just a matter of finding it. The combined efforts of Ly Daravuth, a Cambodian artist and academic, and Ingrid Muan, an American doctoral student living in Phnom Penh, made this possible. (Muan, who received her PhD in art history from Columbia University in 2000, died unexpectedly in January 2005. The Legacy Project was only one of the many beneficiaries of her exceptional generosity and her dedication to Cambodian art. She had a very large hand in bringing global attention to the work of Cambodian artists.) In addition to teaching, research, and art-making, Muan and Daravuth had founded the Reyum Gallery to show contemporary art. Having been given some advance warning, they had circulated word within Cambodia's small community of artists that the Legacy Project (whatever that was) had been inquiring about art that engaged the mass killing and the consequences for Cambodian society—and was coming to Cambodia to see it.

At this news, paintings began to appear. Some had been made years before, only to be put away. Others were still fresh, or in the final stages of composition. For some artists, this outside interest spurred them to begin thinking about making work that would address Cambodia's past.

In sum, instead of nothing, there was a critical mass of materials. Artists might not have been willing or able to show this work—there were political and economic incentives to make scenes of Angor Wat or elaborate advertising signboards instead. But they had been making the work all along. In 2000, these works were shown together, in an unprecedented exhibition at the Reyum Gallery.

The Cambodian story was really the last piece of the puzzle. Many societies had suffered a large-scale, man-made trauma during the twentieth century. For those closer to global culture—Germany, Argentina, South Africa—the evidence was clear: artists and writers and creative people of all genres were working openly on issues of history and memory. Now, in a place where there had been a pitiably small amount of outside interest, the same impulse could be found. As it turned out, there was virtually no society that had endured a major trauma that was not producing work of this kind.

But could these works be put together? Not in either a chronology or hierarchy of suffering, but rather as a means of understanding whether there was a common root to these creative inquiries, whether differences of history, culture, and geography—however much they might mean— were the only criteria for understanding this mass of materials.

And a mass of materials it was. Once we started looking, under the guidance of a global network of scholars and curators, the Legacy Project was inundated with documentation on thousands of works of literature, film, and visual art that engaged the past, many of which appear on our Web site: www.legacy-project.org. These works were not outliers, but were central to cultural development—not just in a few places, but pretty much everywhere.

What did all this mean? The Legacy Project was a nonprofit organization created to ask: If a society had endured large-scale, man-made violence, what would it have in common with other societies that had also faced such suffering? How could we identify whatever common responses they shared? How would these responses be expressed? As time and generations passed, would the differences in the actual historical occurrences be mitigated at all by any similarities in response? The anthology that you are holding is an attempt at gathering some answers to these questions.

At its core, violence is directed at the individual, even if the ambition of its perpetrators may be to extend their violence to as many individuals as they can. The individual nature of violence—one person taking steps that kill or injure another—should never be forgotten, even though modern weaponry can kill enormous numbers of individuals instantaneously, creating in its wake a kind of community of the dead. In spite of a geometric increase in the killing power of weapons (and also in the aspirations of many who use them), the fundamental character of death and mourning is individual. But at the scale of suffering that will be evoked in the following chapters, violence is also a social actor, reshaping the contemporary life of a society, altering its sense of its history and its prospects for the future. Violence at this scale moves out of the realm of the individual and establishes an autonomous presence in social life.

We understand this most easily in situations in which violence continues over an extended period of time. For example, the conflict in the former Yugoslavia combined the following deadly, self-reinforcing elements: social disorder, ethnic hostility, outside sponsors of this hostility, and a sense of history that emphasized earlier conflicts that were themselves premised on social disorder and ethnic hostility. In this context (and in many others), violence is a part of the social fabric, a logical recourse to avenge those who were killed through earlier enactments of a bloody dynamic. The logic of respite—or even of a final settlement of historical grievances—is, of course, available in charged circumstances, but to succeed it must overtake an often quite powerful momentum toward revenge and renewed conflict.

In retrospect, the route into violence seems obvious, and therefore easily avoidable. In advance, however, the affairs of individuals and societies seldom provide a clear path away from conflict. Many of the excerpts in this anthology describe critical moments when violence has just occurred, or when its impact is beginning to stretch into the future. Looking backwards in time, we know of the violence that will come and the cost it will exact. Yet, this retrospective knowledge still does not offer a clear way out of violence.

As individuals, the writers will have wished to avoid the terrible fates that they have described. Or perhaps they are reliving those moments just before the wave of violence crashed over them. In either case, few of them are able to offer an alternative to the violence they suffered, or suggest a way they could have avoided it. The machinery of violence, as described here, often has a life of its own, organizing the lives of both perpetrators and victims. In those horrible moments of deepest loss, one finds individuals entirely overwhelmed by the complete absence of any way out of the trauma they are facing. Quite literally, their lives are no longer in their own hands.

Such is the fate of many of the individuals whose plights are described in the following pages. In thinking about them, however, it is important to mark a generational distinction between us and them. This is not really a matter of age, nor even a matter of the difference between those who endure (and, one hopes, survive) such events and those who have no experience of the awful realities being described. Instead, it is a matter of how time affects human memory, and what it means to be a successor to the events described here, even if not a survivor of them. For if the actual encounter with such violence marks one as a survivor, then what is the status of those who come a generation or more after these histories and yet seek to find meaning in them? This status may perhaps be captured in the idea of successor generations, those born after a historic episode of violence, but whose generational life has been profoundly shaped by the consequences of this history.

The most prominent characteristic of a successor generation is that it represents a choice: the choice to make a common connection with the past. *Common* is the key word here, since the successor generation does not necessarily share the conventional ties of culture or geography to the historic event in question, or to its victims. And yet, in spite of this, the choice is made to engage with this distant history. And in its making, this choice takes history out of the realm of sectarian grievance.

This does not, of course, take history out of the realm of interpretation. Nor does it deny the possibility that history can still be understood in traditional ways. And it certainly does not minimize the importance of the work of historians in documenting and explaining the past—quite the contrary. However, this approach does reflect a view that the traumas of the past are somehow applicable to our well-being in the present. It views history as a platform for a convergence around certain ethical questions that have appeared in a wide range of historic events. It also gives priority to these ethical questions because their answers—though founded in the past—seem important for the present and the future.

In recent years, the concept of collective memory, as developed in the 1920s by Maurice Halbwachs (*On Collective Memory*, 1992) and elaborated by later scholars, has reemerged as a critical means of understanding how societies engage their history. For Halbwachs, memory could not be made coherent outside of a social context, since the accuracy of what we remember and its importance in our view of the world require affirmation from the society in which we live. For an individual, shared memories set the terms of his or her membership in a society.

In inherited social settings—that is, within the social groups into which we are born—the integration of personal and collective memory comes with relative ease. In considering the role of successor generations, we come to the question of how the identity of a new group may be formed around a collective memory of events that are already part of the collective memory of groups with more conventional historical ties to them. How do you make a collective memory out of someone else's history?

Literature plays a special role in this process. Its great variety reflects the enormous range of culture and experience that shapes unique, individual voices. And yet, time and again, these unique voices return to universal themes of human experience. Their differences do not disappear. Instead, their differences come to complement one another. From the vast horizon of human experience, they return to a common core. When focused on the meaning and impact of mass violence, they tell a common story of shock and loss and remembrance—in spite of their origins in different events. In this way, literature offers the possibility of taking these accounts of the past and making them into a collective narrative about the future.

Literature will be able to play this role only if the resulting narrative can incorporate accounts of different historical events into a coherent whole. This anthology intends to sketch at least the beginnings of such a coherent account. In each of its sections, another point in the arc of memory is presented. Overall, this arc moves from accounts of the actual moments of mass violence, through the initial reactions of individuals, then into the process by which these accounts become part of the collective memory of affected groups. By the end, however, we note another phenomenon: the appearance of remembrance as a more general social response to traumatic history, a response that incorporates the memories of survivors as well as the memories of their successors. And, it cannot be stressed enough, the identity of successors is increasingly determined not only by direct links of culture or genealogy to traumatic events. This identity is determined also by a choice to engage today with the consequences of the past. At its core, this is an identity of aspiration.

Whence this aspiration? The human quality of empathy has an ancient pedigree, and it certainly predisposes us try to understand one another. Literature plays a role in its development as well, since the telling of stories implies an interest in other lives that is more than simply instructive. As this anthology demonstrates, the telling of stories about traumatic violence is widespread, shared by the various societies that have suffered from it. As a social phenomenon, this aspiration is of more recent vintage. By now, it seems very much a part of the global world, in which encounters with distant peoples—and their histories—have become commonplace, particularly for younger people at ease with the technologies that place such encounters no more than a click away.

At its inception, though, lies a world-changing catastrophe. The Holocaust, a historic event spanning the twelve years of Nazi rule in Germany, may have ended in 1945. But the cost of this history was so great, and the enormity of its destructiveness made such a powerful case for ethical transformation, that the global community has struggled for some sixty years—five times the length of the actual event—with its legacy. The Holocaust historian Yehuda Bauer put it this way: "There is a growing realization that something unprecedented happened in the genocide of the Jews, something that is both so extraordinary and yet so indicative of the human condition in general, that a vague feeling exists that that is a matter that a person living in our generation has to know something about. It is something that if we are not careful could happen to all of us, not in the same way, not in similar circumstances, but possessed of the same quality perhaps and bringing similar dangers to all" ("We Are Condemned to Remember," *Jerusalem Post*, April 19, 2001).

From the newsreels of the extermination camps to the Nuremburg Trials and the codification of international conventions against genocide and in protection of human rights, the Holocaust reshaped international discourse about our mutual responsibilities as citizens of the world. That this discourse emerged only after it was too late to save the victims is tragic. That it should nonetheless create the aspiration to do better is, in spite of subsequent failures to do better, a sign that this aspiration has taken hold.

But there is more than the wish to do better, as important as that is. The post-Holocaust world—of the historical, the moral, and the possible—is profoundly different than the world as it was before the Holocaust. This is not because terrible things had not happened before; they certainly had. It is because these events were thought of separately, individually, not as different entries into a common historical category. What was different about the Holocaust—or, rather, the response to it—was that the Holocaust was the event that provoked the creation of this new category. Indeed, the word *genocide* was coined to describe the Holocaust, but was quickly extended—both legally and morally—into a standard against which one could judge events in the future: events that had the quality of genocide. So powerful was the concept of genocide that it was also extended back into time, so that events that had chronologically preceded the Holocaust—like the Armenian genocide or chattel slavery—were brought into this category and described in this new way.

Underneath this reconsideration of history lies a collective awareness that has been profoundly altered. The philosopher Berel Lang describes the pre-Holocaust world as "one from which genocide was absent, in which that occurrence was quite inconceivable." By contrast, he continues, "For the post-Holocaust generation . . . that absence was dismissed before they were born; they do not remember the world without it. The possibility of genocide and its present immanence has become a world inheritance" (Berel Lang, *The Future of the Holocaust: Between History and Memory* [Ithaca, NY: Cornell University Press, 1999], 4–5).

A world inheritance.

If this is so, then there is a powerful reason for new generations to think of themselves collectively and engage their shared aspirations through a better understanding of this legacy. This will not be easy. A shared aspiration will not necessarily mitigate political or other differences on how to respond to new crises that arise. Darfur is at the top of the agenda today, but Cambodia, Rwanda, and the former Yugoslavia provide recent examples of how difficult it is to move from shared aspiration to practical effect. In fact, the simple enumeration of this list demonstrates how far short the world has fallen in handling its inheritance.

While an anthology will not reverse this, it might begin to solidify an approach to literature that encompasses these different histories within a single strand of collective memory. To this end, the chapters of this anthology are organized thematically, rather than by event, as a speculation on how this codification might proceed. The concept for this ordering, along with some of the selected writings, was first developed in a series of meetings, directed by Wesley Fisher and supported by both the Rockefeller Foundation and the United States Holocaust Memorial Museum.

In all this, the challenge is to protect the authenticity of original voices, even while reading them as a collective testimony: the truth of the past balanced against the aspiration for the future. Fortunately, literature can manage this balance. The poet Robert Pinsky, writing in *Slate* after September 11, 2001, made it clear: "More often than not, the best poems about an event are written long before it happens. . . . [They] anticipated, in indelible form, things that many were saying or feeling."

PART I

TERROR AND TRAUMA

ONE

BEARING WITNESS

"To write poetry after Auschwitz is barbaric," wrote Theodo Adorno. With these words, written just a few years after the Second World War, the German social critic Theodor Adorno rejected making art after the Holocaust. For Adorno, the very act of creating art to express the pain of Auschwitz was a kind of betrayal. Artistic representation of the horror was not simply misguided—it was a barbaric reversal of standards, in which the aesthetic world superseded the moral. This reversal, where beauty trumps ethics, would faintly echo the crime itself, which emerged when the Nazis' subordinated morality to national, racial, and, at times, even aesthetic ideals.

Adorno's advice to refrain from filtering horror through the lens of art can also be understood in another way: as a call to silence in the face of a tragedy that goes beyond human comprehension. No words, no music, no images can properly express the loss. Better, it is argued, to acknowledge through silence our inability to understand, than to diminish the enormity of the crime by futile expressions of incomprehension. Yet should silence be the final word? Certainly, most people's immediate reaction to unexpected large-scale violence is stunned silence. In the wake of 9/11, British writer Martin Amis declared himself rendered wordless by the enormity of what had happened. Visiting the barricaded site six months after September 11, 2001, he wrote how he "experienced the direct and vital connection that no words and images had prepared [him] for. This was a crime scene, and the crime was a crime against humanity" (*Daily Telegraph*, September 11, 2002).

For many though, the need to break the silence after such calamities becomes increasingly urgent. The Cambodian artist Svay Ken began to

3

paint his series, *The History of My Family*, right after his family was re-united, after the end of the bloody Khmer Rouge rule in Cambodia in 1978. In 1948, Wanda Jakubowska, a Holocaust survivor, took a cast and crew onto the grounds of Auschwitz to film *Last Stop*, an account of her years as a prisoner in the extermination camp.

Sometimes the poems of others can break the silence as well. W. H. Auden wrote "September 1, 1939" in response to the onset of World War II in Europe. In the days and weeks that followed the attacks of 9/11 in New York, this poem was reprinted in newspapers across the United States and excerpted in many of the makeshift memorials that mushroomed through-out New York City. Four blocks from Ground Zero, Stuyvesant High School featured it prominently in a special issue of the school newspa-per, which the *New York Times* distributed to many of its metropolitan readers. "September 1, 1939" was also part of a variety of memorial ser-vices, including the *New Yorker*'s program *Beyond Words*, a title which high-lights the paradox of facing the unimaginable: an event that is, indeed, beyond words, even as words are all we have to communicate. And Auden's words written about World War II resonated with the outrage, grief, and fears of many New Yorkers after 9/11. Similarly, citizens around the world have reached into literature in the wake of destruction in order to begin to heal, carefully applying words to the wounds in an attempt to get closer to what cannot be fully expressed.

The writers in this first chapter are driven to speak about horrific events in spite of Adorno's injunction to silence. These writers address various global calamities that have taken the lives of millions of people in the twentieth and early twenty-first centuries. The Armenian poet Siamento writes about the Armenian genocide (1896, 1915–1918); the Cambodian memoirist Someth May discusses the Khmer Rouge's Killing Fields (1975–1978); Nobel Laureate Elie Wiesel writes about the Holocaust (1939–1945); German novelist Eric Maria Remarque addresses World War I (1915–1919); the American writer Anthony Swofford writes of the first Persian Gulf War (1990–1991); the Polish poet Zbigniew Herbert discusses German-occupied Poland during the World War II (1939–1945); and the American writer Debra Fontaine discusses 9/11 (2001). Yet the "writing of disaster," to use a term coined by the French writer Maurice Blanchot, is never easy. In the excerpts, each author struggles, in different genres and in different ways, with the need to speak, to tell the story of what has happened. At the same time, many feel they will never find the words to describe the horror they have witnessed.

In this first chapter, Siamento's, May's, and Wiesel's speakers are civilians caught up in calamity. Remarque's and Swofford's speakers are soldiers reflecting on battle. Herbert's and Fontaine's speakers are conscious chroniclers of violence.

The main thread that connects all the selections in this first chapter is the implicit understanding that unremembered calamities pave the way for new cases of violence. As Anglo-American poet W. H. Auden writes, "Those to whom evil is done. Do evil in return" (from his "September 1, 1939"). Violence can set in motion a tragic cycle. An exhibition in the U.S. Holocaust Memorial Museum pinpoints the importance of bearing witness. A quotation, attributed to Hitler, claims that his own proposed Final Solution will succeed—and that no one will care. He asks rhetorically, "Who speaks any longer of the Armenians?" By the 1930s, many had indeed forgotten or ignored the earlier mass killing of the Armenians in the Ottoman Empire. Today, while few have forgotten the Holocaust, it has still been followed by atrocities that include the Cambodian Killing Fields, the Balkan conflicts, and most recently the ongoing slaughter of civilians in Darfur. Without greater vigilance, genocide will continue to ravage the twenty-first century as it has scarred the twentieth.

❦ SIAMENTO, "The Dance"—TURKISH ARMENIA

Born Adom Yarjanian, Siamento was born in Eghine, at the edge of the Euphrates River in Turkish Armenia. In 1892, he left for Constantinople, where he started at Merdjanian College and then later went to Berbérian College. After the massacres of 1896, Siamento took refuge in Egypt and then moved to Paris, where he took classes at the Sorbonne. He later moved to Switzerland, where he connected with other Armenian writers and patriots in Geneva. Siamento visited the United States in 1910. In Armenia, he became a popular political activist and a poet.

Siamento's poem, "The Dance," written in the early years of the twentieth century, bears witness to the massacre of the Armenians by the Ottoman Empire of the Turkish government in 1896. Siamento's speaker describes this "incomprehensible" atrocity so that "people will understand the crimes men do to men," simultaneously burdened by the fact that witnessing this violence makes her want to dig out her eyes.

The first massacre in 1896 was followed by mass deportation, expropriation, abduction, torture, massacre, and starvation between 1915 and 1918. On April 24, 1915, Siamento was one of hundreds of intellectuals and political and spiritual leaders who were rounded up. He was held in detention until August, when he was murdered. In the same year the international community condemned the Armenian genocide as a crime against humanity. Thirty-three years later, in 1948, the UN Genocide Convention was adopted.

In a field of cinders where Armenians
were still dying,
A German woman, trying not to cry,
told me the horror she witnessed:
"This incomprehensible thing I'm telling you about,
I saw with my own eyes.
From my window of hell
I clenched my teeth
and watched with pitiless eyes:
the town of Barez turned
into a heap of ashes.
Corpses piled as high as trees.
From the waters, from the springs,
from the streams and the road,
the stubborn murmur of your blood
still revenges my ear.

Don't be afraid. I must tell you what I saw,
so people will understand
the crimes men do to men.
For two days, by the road to the graveyard . . .
Let the hearts of the whole world understand.
It was Sunday morning,
the first useless Sunday dawning on the corpses.
From dusk to dawn in my room,
with a stabbed woman,
my tears wetting her death.

Suddenly I heard from afar
a dark crowd standing in a vineyard
lashing twenty brides
and singing dirty songs.

Leaving the half-dead girl on the straw mattress,
I went to the balcony of my window
and the crowd seemed to thicken like a forest.
An animal of a man shouted, 'You must dance,
dance when our drum beats.'
With fury whips cracked
on the flesh of these women.
Hand in hand the brides began their circle dance.
Now, I envied my wounded neighbor
because with a calm snore
she cursed the universe
and gave her soul up to the stars . . .

In vain, I shook my fists at the crowd.
'Dance,' they raved,
'dance till you die, infidel beauties.
With your flapping tits, dance!
Smile and don't complain.
You're abandoned now, you're naked slaves
so dance like a bunch of fuckin' sluts.
We're hot for you all.'
Twenty graceful brides collapsed.
'Get up,' the crowds roared,
brandishing their swords.
Then someone brought a jug of kerosene.
Human justice, I spit in your face.
The brides were anointed.
'Dance,' they thundered—
here's a fragrance you can't get in Arabia.'
Then with a torch, they set
the naked brides on fire.
And the charred corpses rolled
and tumbled to their deaths . . .
Like a storm I slammed the shutters
of my windows,

and went over to the dead girl
and asked: 'How can I dig out my eyes,
how can I dig, tell me?'"

〜 SOMETH MAY,
    Excerpt from *Cambodian Witness*—CAMBODIA

Someth May was born in Phnom Penh, Cambodia in 1958.
He studied science at school and began a medical course in a
university. When the Khmer Rouge came to power in 1975, he
and his family were forced to flee Phnom Penh. They eventually
escaped to a refugee camp on the Thai-Cambodian border in
1979. Only four of Someth May's family of fourteen survived this
ordeal. Someth May started writing his autobiography in the
Khao-i-Dang camp and completed it while studying in England.
He then moved to the United States, where he worked as a janitor
for the *Washington Post*. He is now living in Washington and is
writing a second book.

    In his memoir *Cambodian Witness* (1986), the quest to reveal
the duplicity of his labor camp leader—who "had come across
like a benevolent father to us all when in fact he was really a
killer"—fuels Someth May to persevere against the horror and
uncertainty of the Khmer Rouge's labor camps of the 1970s. The
title of Someth May's memoir highlights the power of testimony.
May survived the Khmer Rouge's Killing Fields in order to tell
subsequent generations what he witnessed. Amidst the horror, he
concludes, "I thought that if I died I might find some peace, but
I had to stay alive. I had my responsibilities. . . . I wanted to tell
our story to my children, and to my grandchildren, like the
stories I had learnt as a child."

Now terror became the very theme of my daily life. If I walked past the
Khmer Rouge on the way to work, I didn't dare to look them in the eye.
In the field I worked on my own, and quite often spent the day without
saying a word to anyone except my family. The women worked separately
from the men, and the only chance of talking to my sisters was during
the lunch break. But the spiteful little boys were always within earshot.
Rations were cut down and our working hours increased. Sometimes we
were kept in the fields until eight in the morning.

There were now sixteen of us. The Khmer Rouge were killing the heads of the families. Malnutrition was destroying the youngest. Phan buried a second child. My cousins lost their only daughter. I was worried at the way my two youngest brothers grew thin. But most of all I was concerned to cover up our background. For, since my father's death, I was the head of the family.

Towards the end of November 1975, at the time when we would normally have been celebrating the festival of the spirits, we were told at a meeting that all the new residents would be moved to Battambang, at the other end of the country. There, said the village leader, we would have more food and less work. We were told to pack everything up and leave the next day. We returned the "weapons of the revolution"—our spades, mattocks, rakes, et cetera—and gathered our belongings.

That night something strange happened. The Khmer Rouge families paid us a visit, asking us if we wanted to exchange anything for rice, salt or palm sugar. We had nothing left to exchange. Everything had gone on food and medicines. The Khmer Rouge began chatting. They told us how upset they would be to see us go. They said how boring it was working in the paddy fields, and how difficult things would be when we had left. I realized that they must have known beforehand that we were not going to stay here very long. They had used us for all we were worth, sapping our strength and getting their hands on all our belongings. Now they were feeling sorry for themselves.

I didn't sleep. I couldn't help wondering whether we were really going to Battambang or not. Maybe we were going to our deaths like the heads of family. The other adults in the camp were busy preparing the food they had exchanged. At dawn, people pulled down their huts and burnt them in disgust. The Khmer Rouge were angry at this, but it was too late to stop it.

People paid a last tearful visit to the graves of their relatives. Among the crowd assembled for departure, some felt relieved to be off. They felt that if they stayed here any longer, it would be their turn next. But others who had relatives in the mysterious infirmary were distressed at the prospect of separation. We sat in the open field, waiting quietly.

A dozen trucks arrived, including one full of soldiers—new faces. They were smartly turned out, and the village and regional leaders treated them with respect. They took off their caps and bowed to them. The village leader made a speech praising our hard work and our devotion to the community. He said they would be sad to lose us. We had never given any cause for complaint. We were exemplary workers, just what society needed. The new faces looked searchingly at us. For exemplary workers, we were a sorry sight.

No family was allowed more than four pieces of luggage. The space in the trucks they said, was for people, not possessions. So, as we climbed into the trucks a great pile of bundles was left behind. We were packed tightly— I couldn't turn at all or make my way to the corner where my little brothers had been squeezed in beside my sisters. As we approached the road, revolutionary songs played over the radio. A wave of anger hit me.

Their songs told how the party had delivered the country from slavery, and how happy everybody was. I thought of the leader's speech and my blood boiled. He had come across like a benevolent father to us all when in fact he was really a killer. If I tried to resist, I knew that I would put my family in danger, as my father had said. All I could do was feign ignorance. This was easy enough, but it was hard to live under the rule of ignorant people. I thought that if I died I might find some peace, but I had to stay alive. I had my responsibilities. And besides, I wanted to see what would happen under the new regime. I wanted to tell our story to my children, and to my grandchildren, like the stories I had learnt as a child.

ᐁ ELIE WIESEL,
   Excerpt from *Night*—UNITED STATES

Elie Wiesel was born in Sighet, Transylvania, which is now Romania, in 1928. In 1944, he was deported to the Auschwitz concentration camp with his family, where his mother and sister perished. He later spent time in Buchenwald, where his father died of starvation. After the liberation of the camps in April 1945, Wiesel spent a few years in a French orphanage, later studied in Paris at the Sorbonne and then became a journalist. He met Nobel laureate Francois Mauriac, who contributed to Wiesel's decision to write of his experience in the concentration camps. Wiesel has published over thirty books and has been a visiting scholar and professor at Yale University, City University of New York, and Boston University. In 1978, Wiesel was appointed to chair the President's Commission on the Holocaust and in 1985 he was awarded the Congressional Gold Medal of Achievement. In 1986 he was awarded the Nobel Peace Prize. Soon after, he created the Elie Wiesel Foundation for Humanity, an organization combating intolerance and injustice through international dialogue and programs targeted to youth.

In Elie Wiesel's *Night* (1960), the character Moché miraculously survives the first round of deportation and slaughter of the Jews in Romania. He explains to the young narrator, "I wanted to come back to Sighet to tell you the story of my death." Yet those in his home community cannot believe the horrors he describes, such as babies thrown into the air and used for rifle practice by the Gestapo. They decide he must be mad and they treat Moché as an aberration, outside the cherished rhythm of normal life. The excerpt concludes with perhaps the most famous passage in *Night,* excerpted in many places, including the U.S. Holocaust Museum in D.C., when the narrator finally begins to comprehend the ineffable horror Moché tried to describe.

They called him Moché the Beadle, as though he had never had a sur-name in his life. He was a man of all work at a Hasidic synagogue. The Jews of Sighet—that little town in Transylvania where I spent my child-hood—were very fond of him. He was very poor and lived humbly. Gen-erally my fellow townspeople, though they would help the poor, were not particularly fond of them. Moché the Beadle was the exception. Nobody ever felt embarrassed by him. Nobody ever felt encumbered by his pres-ence. He was a past master in the art of making himself insignificant, of seeming invisible.

Physically he was as awkward as a clown. He made people smile, with his waiflike timidity. I loved his great, dreaming eyes, their gaze lost in the distance. He spoke little. He used to sing, or, rather, to chant. Such snatches as you could hear told of the suffering of the divinity, of the Exile of Providence, who, according to the cabbala, awaits his deliverance in that of man.

I got to know him toward the end of 1941. I was twelve. I believed pro-foundly. During the day I studied the Talmud, and at night I ran to the synagogue to weep over the destruction of the Temple.

One day I asked my father to find me a master to guide me in my stud-ies of the cabbala.

"You're too young for that. Maimonides said it was only at thirty that one had the right to venture into the perilous world of mysticism. You must first study the basic subjects within your own understanding."

My father was a cultured, rather unsentimental man. There was never any display of emotion, even at home. He was more concerned with others than with his own family. The Jewish community in Sighet held him in the greatest esteem. They often used to consult him about public matters and even about private ones. There were four of us children: Hilda, the eldest; then Bea; I was the third, and the only son; the baby of the family was Tzipora.

My parents ran a shop. Hilda and Bea helped them with the work. As for me, they said my place was at school.

"There aren't any cabbalists at Sighet," my father would repeat.

He wanted to drive the notion out of my head. But it was in vain. I found a master for myself, Moché the Beadle.

He had noticed me one day at dusk, when I was praying.

"Why do you weep when you pray?" he asked me, as though he had known me for a long time.

"I don't know why," I answered, greatly disturbed.

The question had never entered my head. I wept because—because of something inside me that felt the need for tears. That was all I knew.

"Why do you pray?" he asked me, after a moment.

Why did I pray? A strange question. Why did I live? Why did I breathe?

"I don't know why," I said, even more disturbed and ill at ease. "I don't know why."

After that day I saw him often. He explained to me with great insistence that every question possessed a power that did not lie in the answer.

"Man raises himself toward God by the questions he asks Him," he was fond of repeating. "That is true dialogue. Man questions God and God answers. But we don't understand His answers. We can't understand them. Because they come from the depths of the soul, and they stay there until death. You will find the true answers, Eliezer, only within yourself!"

"And why do you pray, Moché?" I asked him.

"I pray to the God within me that He will give me the strength to ask Him the right questions."

We talked like this nearly every evening. We used to stay in the synagogue after all the faithful had left, sitting in the gloom, where a few half-burned candles still gave a flickering light.

One evening I told him how unhappy I was because I could not find a master in Sighet to instruct me in the Zohar, the cabbalistic books, the secrets of Jewish mysticism. He smiled indulgently. After a long silence, he said:

"There are a thousand and one gates leading into the orchard of mystical truth. Every human being has his own gate. We must never make the mistake of wanting to enter the orchard by any gate but our own. To do this is dangerous for the one who enters and also for those who are already there."

And Moché the Beadle, the poor barefoot of Sighet, talked to me for long hours of the revelations and mysteries of the cabbala. It was with him that my initiation began. We would read together, ten times over, the same page of the Zohar. Not to learn it by heart, but to extract the divine essence from it.

And throughout those evenings a conviction grew in me that Moché the Beadle would draw me with him into eternity, into that time where question and answer would become *one*.

Then one day they expelled all the foreign Jews from Sighet. And Moché the Beadle was a foreigner.

Crammed into cattle trains by Hungarian police, they wept bitterly. We stood on the platform and wept too. The train disappeared on the horizon; it left nothing behind but its thick, dirty smoke.

I heard a Jew behind me heave a sigh.

"What can we expect?" he said. "It's a war . . ."

The deportees were soon forgotten. A few days after they had gone, people were saying that they had arrived in Galicia, were working there, and were even satisfied with their lot.

Several days passed. Several weeks. Several months. Life had returned to normal. A wind of calmness and reassurance blew through our houses. The traders were doing good business, the students lived buried in their books, and the children played in the streets.

One day, as I was just going into the synagogue, I saw, sitting on a bench near the door, Moché the Beadle.

He told his story and that of his companions. The train full of deportees had crossed the Hungarian frontier and on Polish territory had been taken in charge by the Gestapo. There it had stopped. The Jews had to get out and climb into lorries. The lorries drove toward a forest. The Jews were made to get out. They were made to dig huge graves. And when they had finished their work, the Gestapo began theirs. Without passion, without haste, they slaughtered their prisoners. Each one had to go up to the hole and present his neck. Babies were thrown into the air and the machine gunners used them as targets. This was in the forest of Galicia, near Kolomaye. How had Moché the Beadle escaped? Miraculously. He was wounded in the leg and taken for dead . . .

Through long days and nights, he went from one Jewish house to another, telling the story of Malka, the youngest girl who had taken three days to die, and of Tobias, the tailor, who had begged to be killed before his sons . . .

Moché had changed. There was no longer any joy in his eyes. He no longer sang. He no longer talked to me of God or of the cabbala, but only of what he had seen. People refused not only to believe his stories, but even to listen to them.

"He's just trying to make us pity him. What an imagination he has!" they said. Or even: "Poor fellow. He's gone mad."

And as for Moché, he wept.

"Jews, listen to me. It's all I ask of you. I don't want money or pity. Only listen to me," he would cry between prayers at dusk and the evening prayers.

I did not believe him myself. I would often sit with him in the evening after the service, listening to his stories and trying my hardest to understand his grief. I felt only pity for him.

"They take me for a madman," he would whisper, and tears, like drops of wax, flowed from his eyes.

Once, I asked him this question:

"Why are you so anxious that people should believe what you say? In your place, I shouldn't care whether they believed me or not . . ."

He closed his eyes, as though to escape time.

"You don't understand," he said in despair. "You can't understand. I have been saved miraculously. I managed to get back here. Where did I get the strength from? I wanted to come back to Sighet to tell you the story of my death. So that you could prepare yourselves while there was still time. To live? I don't attach any importance to my life any more. I'm alone. No, I wanted to come back, and to warn you. And see how it is, no one will listen to me . . ."

That was toward the end of 1942. Afterward life returned to normal. The London radio, which we listened to every evening, gave us heartening news: the daily bombardment of Germany; Stalingrad; preparation for the second front. And we, the Jews of Sighet, were waiting for better days, which would not be long in coming now . . .

Never shall I forget that night, the first night in camp, which has turned my life into one long night, seven times cursed and seven times sealed.

Never shall I forget that smoke. Never shall I forget the little faces of the children, whose bodies I saw turned into wreaths of smoke beneath a silent blue sky. Never shall I forget those flames which consumed my faith forever. Never shall I forget that nocturnal silence which deprived me, for all eternity, of the desire to live. Never shall I forget those moments which murdered my God and my soul and turned my dreams to dust. Never shall I forget these things, even if I am condemned to live as long as God Himself. Never.

ᕐ ERICH MARIA REMARQUE,
   Excerpt from *All Quiet on the Western Front*—GERMANY

Erich Maria Remarque was born in Osnabrück, Lower Saxony. Remarque's father, Peter Franz Remark, was a bookbinder. Remarque studied at the University of Münster but was drafted into the German army at the age of eighteen. He fought on the Western Front and was wounded several times. After his discharge, Remarque took a teacher's course offered to veterans by the government. He taught in a school for a year, and also tried being a stonecutter and a test-car driver. Remarque began his writing career as a sports journalist. His first novel, *All Quiet on the Western Front* (1929), translated from German by A. W. Wheen, touched a nerve in the era, sparked a storm of political controversy, and brought him fame. Its sequel, *The Way Back* (1931), dealt with the collapse of the German Army after the war.

In the 1930s the German government banned Remarque's books. The Nazis ordered stores to stop selling Remarque's books and *All Quiet on the Western Front* was among the first works they ordered to be publicly burnt in 1933. Nazi gangs disrupted the film's premiere. Remarque moved to Switzerland in 1932; he lost his citizenship in 1938 and in 1939 emigrated to the United States. In 1947 he became a citizen. There he made friends with Hollywood star Paulette Goddard, whom he married in 1958. Remarque had been married twice before, to Ilsa Jeanne Zamboul in 1923 and again in 1938. After the war Remarque eventually settled back in Switzerland. He died in Locarno on September 25, 1970.

Remarque offers us the perspective of a soldier in World War I in *All Quiet on the Western Front*. The narrator documents the corporeal toll of violence as he records a long list of injuries he sees in the German hospital where he is recuperating. The war hospital is where "one realizes for the first time in how many places a man can get hit." Yet this hospital also becomes a microcosm of all World War I war hospitals in Germany, France, Russia, and of any war hospital for that matter. The hospital illuminates how coping with the physical pain inflicted by war forms a common human thread that connects Remarque to all other soldiers, allies and enemies.

I am operated on and vomit for two days. My bones will not grow together, so the surgeons' secretary says. Another fellow's have grown crooked; his are broken again. It is damnable.

Among our new arrivals there are two young soldiers with flat feet. The chief surgeon discovers them on his rounds, and is overjoyed. "We'll soon put that right," he tells them, "we will just do a small operation, and then you will have perfectly sound feet. Enter them down, Sister."

As soon as he is gone, Josef, who knows everything, warns them: "Don't you let him operate on you! That is a special scientific stunt of the old boy's. He goes absolutely crazy whenever he can get hold of anyone to do it on. He operates on you for flat feet, and there's no mistake, you don't have them anymore; you have club feet instead, and have to walk all the rest of you life on sticks."

"What should a man do, then?" asks one of them.

"Say No. You are here to be cured of your wound, not your flat feet. Did you have any trouble with them in the field? No, well, there you are! At present you can still walk, but if once the old boy gets you under the knife you'll be cripples. What he wants is little dogs to experiment with, so the war is a glorious time for him, as it is for all surgeons.

"You take a look down below at the staff; there are a dozen fellows hobbling around that he has operated on. A lot of them have been here all the time since 'fourteen and fifteen.' Not a single one of them can walk better than he could before, almost all of them worse, and most only with plaster legs. Every six months he catches them again and breaks their bones afresh, and every time is going to be the successful one. You take my word, he won't dare do it if you say No."

"Ach, man," says one of the two wearily, "better your feet than your brain-box. There's no telling what you'll get if you go back out there again.

They can do with me just as they please, so long as I get back home. Better to have a club foot than be dead."

The other, a young fellow like ourselves, won't have it done. The next morning the old man has the two hauled up and lectures and jaws at them so long that in the end they consent. What else could they do?—They are mere privates, and he is a big bug. They are brought back chloroformed and plastered . . .

Gradually a few of us are allowed to get up. And I am given crutches to hobble around on. But I do not make much use of them; I cannot bear Albert's gaze as I move about the room. His eyes always follow me with such a strange look. So I sometimes escape to the corridor—there I can move about more freely.

On the next floor below are the abdominal and spine cases, head wounds and double amputations. On the right side of the wing are the jaw wounds, gas cases, nose, ear, and neck wounds. On the left the blind and the lung wounds, pelvis wounds, wounds in the joints, wounds in the kidneys, wounds in the testicles, wounds in the intestines. Here a man realizes for the first time in how many places a man can get hit.

Two fellows die of tetanus. Their skin turns pale, their limbs stiffen, at last only their eyes live–stubbornly. Many of the wounded have their shattered limbs hanging free in the air from a gallows; underneath the wound a basin is placed into which drips the pus. Every two or three hours the vessel is emptied. Other men lie in stretching bandages with heavy weights hanging from the end of the bed. I see intestine wounds that are constantly full of excreta. The surgeon's clerk shows me X-ray photographs of completely smashed hip-bones, knees, and shoulders.

A man cannot realize that above such shattered bodies there are still human faces in which life goes its daily round. And this is only one hospital, one single station; there are hundreds of thousands in Germany, hundreds of thousands in France, hundreds of thousands in Russia. How senseless is everything that can ever be written, done, or thought, when such things are possible. It must be all lies and of no account when the culture of a thousand years could not prevent this stream of blood being poured out, these torture-chambers in their hundreds of thousands. A hospital alone shows what war is.

I am young. I am twenty years old; yet I know nothing of life but despair, death, fear, and fatuous superficiality cast over an abyss of sorrow. I see how peoples are set against one another, and in silence, unknowingly, foolishly, obediently, innocently slay one another. I see that the keenest brains of the world invent weapons and words to make it yet more refined and enduring. And all men of my age, here and over there, throughout the whole world see these things; all my generation is experiencing these things with me. What would our fathers do if we suddenly stood up and came before them and proffered our account? What do they expect of us if a time ever comes when the war is over? Through the years our business has been killing—it was our first calling in life. Our knowledge of life is limited to death. What will happen afterwards? And what shall come out of us?

ᐁ Anthony Swofford,
Excerpt from *Jarhead*—UNITED STATES

Anthony Swofford was born in 1970, conceived nine months earlier while his father had a surprise week of R and R from service in Vietnam. Anthony Swofford served in the U.S. Marine Corps Surveillance and in a scout and sniper platoon during the Gulf War. After the war, he was educated at American River College; the University of California, Davis; and the University of Iowa Writer's Workshop. Swofford has taught at the University of Iowa and at Lewis and Clark College. His fiction and nonfiction have appeared in the *New York Times, Harper's Men's Journal,* the *Iowa Review,* and other publications. Anthony Swofford is currently a Michener-Copernicus fellow and lives in New York.

In his memoir *Jarhead* (2003), Swofford feels linked to his enemies, several dead Iraqi soldiers. He keeps their identifying dog tags with his own essential wartime belongings—his uniforms, medals, and badges—long after the conflict. Having fought each other, their identities are inextricably bound together. Since Swofford could have easily shared their mortal fate, he wishes they could have survived as he did because "the men who go to war and live are spared for the single purpose of spreading bad news when they return, the bad news about the way war is fought and why." Like Remarque's speaker, who counters the senselessness of war by recording it, Swofford explains, "I remade my war one word at a time, a foolish, desperate act."

Throughout the long drive to base I grasped the dog tags around my neck—not mine, but those that I'd ripped from the necks of three dead

Iraqi soldiers. Those dog tags remain in my ruck, in my basement, with my uniforms and medals and badges and ribbons and maps.

Stealing the tags was a crime. I sometimes wonder if the families of the dead men were notified of the deaths, or if the men are listed as missing in action on a stone wall in Baghdad. Probably the corpses were identified with dental records, and probably an Iraqi captain spent a few weeks after the war informing families of their loss, but maybe I am responsible for three Iraqi families living the horror of not knowing what happened to their sons and fathers. Now when I think of these men, I remember their dead faces, and I imagine them wearing their dead faces on a picnic with their families. I am sorry if the families don't know the men are dead, while I know for sure they are dead though not their names. Yes, I'm sorry the men are dead, for many reasons I am sorry, and chief among my reasons is that the men who go to war and live are spared for the single purpose of spreading bad news when they return, the bad news about the way war is fought and why, and whom for whom, and the more men who survive the war, the higher the number of men who might speak.

Unfortunately, many of the men who live through the war don't understand why they were spared. They think they are still alive in order to return home and make money and fuck their wife and get drunk and raise the flag.

These men spread what they call good news, the good news about war and warriors. Some of the men who spread good news have never fought—so what could they have to say about the purity of war and warriors? These men are liars and cheats and they gamble with your freedom and your life and the lives of your sons and daughters and the reputation of your country.

I have gone to war and now I can issue my complaint. I can sit on my porch and complain all day. And you must listen. Some of you will say to me: You signed the contract, you crying bitch, and you fought in a war because of your signature, no one held a gun to your head. This is true, but because I signed the contract and fulfilled my obligation to fight one of America's wars, I am entitled to speak, to say, *I belonged to a fucked situation.*

I am entitled to despair over the likelihood of further atrocities. Indolence and cowardice do not drive me—despair drives me. I remade my war one word at a time, a foolish, desperate act. When I despair, I am alone, and I am often alone. In crowded rooms and walking the streets of our cities, I am alone and full of despair, and while sitting and writing, I am alone and full of despair—the same despair that impelled me to write this book, a quiet scream from within a buried coffin. Dead, dead my scream.

What did I hope to gain? More bombs are coming. Dig your holes with the hands God gave you.

ZBIGNIEW HERBERT,
"Report from the Besieged City"—POLAND

Poet, essayist, playwright, and radio dramatist, Zbigniew Herbert was born in Lwow, Poland, in 1924. During World War II, Herbert studied literature, law, and philosophy. Herbert moved to Warsaw in 1950. His first book of poetry, *String of Light*, came out in 1956. For many years, he contributed regularly to several domestic and émigré journals. In December 1975, he was a signatory of the "Protest of 59" against the planned changes in the Polish constitution. He joined the editorial staff of the illegal magazine *Zapis* in 1981, and went to France in 1986, where he lived for several years afterwards. After returning to Poland, he lived in Warsaw until his death in 1998. Herbert won many Polish and foreign literary awards, including the Jerusalem Prize (1990). He is one of the most frequently translated Polish writers.

The speaker in Zbigniew Herbert's poem "Report from the Besieged City" (1982), originally written in Poland during World War II and translated here by John Carpenter and Bogdona Carpenter, is designated a chronicler because he is too old to bear arms. For this speaker, chronicling the violence becomes a way to contain his emotions and a way to "inform the world / that thanks to the war we have raised a new species of children / our children don't like fairy tales they play at killing."

Too old to carry arms and fight like the others—

they graciously gave me the inferior role of chronicler
I record—I don't know for whom—the history of the siege

I am supposed to be exact but I don't know when the invasion began
two hundred years ago in December in September perhaps yesterday at
    dawn
everyone here suffers from a loss of the sense of time

all we have left is the place the attachment to the place
we still rule over the ruins of temples spectres of gardens and houses
if we lose the ruins nothing will be left

I write as I can in the rhythm of interminable weeks
monday: empty storehouses a rat became the unit of currency
tuesday: the mayor murdered by unknown assailants
wednesday: negotiations for a cease-fire the enemy has imprisoned our
        messengers
we don't know where they are held that is the place of torture
thursday: after a stormy meeting a majority of voices rejected
the motion of the spice merchants for unconditional surrender
friday: the beginning of the plague saturday: our invincible defender
N.N. committed suicide sunday: no more water we drove back
an attack at the eastern gate called the Gate of the Alliance

all of this is monotonous I know it can't move anyone

I avoid any commentary I keep a tight hold on my emotions I write
        about the facts
only they it seems are appreciated in foreign markets
yet with a certain pride I would like to inform the world
that thanks to the war we have raised a new species of children
our children don't like fairy tales they play at killing
awake and asleep they dream of soup of bread and bones
just like dogs and cats

in the evening I like to wander near the outposts of the City
along the frontier of our uncertain freedom
I look at the swarms of soldiers below their lights
I listen to the noise of drums barbarian shrieks
truly it is inconceivable the City is still defending itself
the siege has lasted a long time the enemies must take turns
nothing unites them except the desire for our extermination
Goths the Tartars Swedes troops of the Emperor regiments of the
        Transfiguration
who can count them
the colors of their banners change like the forest on the horizon
from delicate bird's yellow in spring through green through red to
        winter's black

and so in the evening released from facts I can think
about distant ancient matters for example our
friends beyond the sea I know they sincerely sympathize
they send us flour lard sacks of comfort and good advice
they don't even know their fathers betrayed us
our former allies at the time of the second Apocalypse
their sons are blameless they deserve our gratitude therefore we are
    grateful
they have not experienced a siege as long as eternity
those struck by misfortune are always alone
the defenders of the Dalai Lama the Kurds the Afghan mountaineers

now as I write these words the advocates of conciliation
have won the upper hand over the party of inflexibles
a normal hesitation of moods fate still hangs in the balance

cemeteries grow larger the number of defenders is smaller
yet the defense continues it will continue to the end
and if the City falls but a single man escapes
he will carry the City within himself on the roads of exile
he will be the City

we look in the face of hunger the face of fire face of death
worst of all—the face of betrayal
and only our dreams have not been humiliated

ᗑ Debra Fontaine,
   "Witnessing"—united states

Debra Fontaine's essay "Witnessing" (2001) also speaks of the
bystander's responsibility to bear witness to horror. Her
recollections from September 11th, 2001 were forged from her
office window across the street from the burning towers, as she
watched people jumping from the upper floors. Early on, the
television networks made a decision to stop showing these searing
images. Yet Fontaine makes a case on behalf of witness, so the
victims would be accompanied in some way as they made their
fatal decisions.

World Financial Center

I was working at my job in the World Financial Center, just across the street from the two seemingly constant World Trade towers when the first plane hit. Feeling and hearing the force of the impact, my co-workers and I initially thought the first plane was a freak accident. We ran from the huge conference room window that faced the two towers, to the kitchenette and TV news, and then back again; fear, speculation, and rational explanations were flying.

But then, incredulously, while looking out [the] window at the damage and carnage the first plane had inflicted, I saw the second plane abruptly come into my right field of vision and deliberately, with shimmering intention, thunder full-force into the South Tower. It was so close, so low, so huge and fast, so intent on its target that I swear to you, I swear to you, I felt the vengeance and rage emanating from the plane.

Through that huge window and the space of the street between us, in those short seconds, its insanity seared me. It was completely overwhelming. I remember a tremendous, boiling, exploding ball of fire. I saw people jumping, falling, burning. My mouth agape, I stared at it all through wide, weeping eyes.

A co-worker said, "Don't look, how can anyone watch this?" But I ask, How could you not? How could you not watch these poor kinsmen, who unknowingly woke up damned that clear, beautiful yesterday morning, just hours away from a direction that no one could imagine, faced with an impossible final decision/fate: stay and burn . . . or . . . jump and fly?

Fly through a scorched sky engulfed in flames and smoke, debris and bodies . . . into a clear and cool, inviting blue sky with papers, papers languidly floating everywhere, a macabre ticker tape parade.

They deserved to be witnessed in their decision, their fate, in their final moment. They deserved to be witnessed in how they died, and to not be alone in that harsh, reeling, astonishing death.

We should all have witnessed them. We should all have stood at attention with not just one hand raised in a final, resigned salute, but with both of our hands at our throats, over our mouths, tearing our garments, making our own noises with their fall while we watched, and seen them, seen them, every last one of them.

TWO

ISOLATED AND APART

How do writers and civilians respond amid large-scale violence that defies comprehension and goes beyond the borders of the expected? In the wake of World War I, T. S. Eliot wrote, "These fragments I have shored against my ruins" in his poem "The Waste Land." Many of the authors in this chapter are writing amidst large-scale violence and express a strong sense that the world in front of their eyes is surreal and nightmare-like. In the selections in this chapter, "the sense of isolation increases the pitch of trauma," as the Polish Canadian writer Eva Hoffman said in an interview with the Legacy Project. This chapter brings together the American journalist Michael Herr, writing during the Vietnam War (1965–1975); the Russian Nobel prize–winning writer Aleksandr Solzhenitsyn, discussing Stalin's forced labor camps (1930s); the Indian writer and activist Begum Anis Kidwai, touching on the India-Pakistan Partition (1947); and the American writer Paul Morris, reflecting on September 11, 2001.

Yet in the very act of writing about these events the writers escape their isolation to connect with an audience, even though it may only be imagined. They are also starting to break down the event, to transform it, to get through to some deeper meaning about what has happened. Furthermore, for those generations that follow, this writing gives an immediate sense of what it was like to encounter such chaos. In an interview with the Legacy Project in April 2005, the contemporary Iraqi poet Dunya Mikhail described literature that addresses immediate violence as a type of X-ray: "For a sick patient, it helps to have X-rays of their wounds and medical problems. This literature is an X-ray of the times these people lived through. Literature traces the intimate details that historical documents cannot."

⤳ MICHAEL HERR,
   Excerpt from *Dispatches*—UNITED STATES

Michael Herr was born in 1940 in Syracuse, New York. After graduating from Syracuse University, Herr moved to New York City, where he worked at *Holiday* magazine and wrote articles and film criticism for *Mademoiselle,* the *New Leader,* and other periodicals. In 1967, he persuaded Harold Hayes, the editor of *Esquire* magazine, to send him to Vietnam. He stayed there for over a year and witnessed some of the most intense fighting of the war. Herr had no specific assignment in Vietnam and traveled widely. He initially intended to write a monthly column from Vietnam; but, in fact, Herr published only a few Vietnam pieces in *Esquire*. His novel *Dispatches* (1977) was his first longer attempt to gather his war experiences. For this book he used years of notes from his frontline reporting and turned them into what many people consider one of the best accounts of the Vietnam War. Herr has since written other novels and was a co-screenwriter on Francis Ford Coppola's film *Apocalypse Now.* He received both Academy Award and Writers' Guild nominations for his screenplay of *Full Metal Jacket.*

   The marine in this excerpt from Herr's memoir *Dispatches* stutters and seems near the breaking point of sanity. Other marines hold onto a thin thread of sanity by telling Herr, an American journalist in Vietnam, to record their experience for others and to tell it "as it is." As a correspondent, Herr has a strange relationship with the soldiers or "grunts." Some admire him; others despise him. In this selection he describes the surreal disarray in Vietnam as "grunts were telling their officers to go die, to go fuck themselves, to go find some other fools to run up those streets awhile." Some wish him dead because they hate him for volunteering to come into the mad world of war when they had no choice.

We could hear the sound of our Chinook coming in now, and we were checking to see if we had all of our gear, when I took a sudden terrible flash, some total dread, and I looked at everyone and everything in sight to see if there was some real source. Stone had been telling the truth about this being my last operation, I was as strung out as anybody on a last operation, there was nothing between here and Saigon that didn't scare me now, but this was different, it was something else.

"Fuckin' heat . . . ," someone said. "I . . . oh, man, I just . . . can't . . . fuckin' . . . make it!"

It was a Marine, and as soon as I saw him I realized that I'd seen him before, a minute or so ago, standing on the edge of the clearing staring at us as we got ourselves ready to leave. He'd been with a lot of other Marines there, but I'd seen him much more distinctly than the others without realizing or admitting it. The others had been looking at us too, with amusement or curiosity or envy (we were splitting, casualties and correspondents this way out, we were going to Danang), they were all more or less friendly, but this one was different, I'd seen it, known it and passed it over, but not really. He was walking by us now, and I saw that he had a deep, running blister that seemed to have opened and eaten away much of his lower lip. That wasn't the thing that had made him stand out before, though. If I'd noticed it at all, it might have made him seem a little more wretched than the others, but nothing more. He stopped for a second and looked at us, and he smiled some terrifying, evil smile, his look turned now to the purest hatred.

"You fucking guys," he said. "You guys are crazy!" . . .

There was the most awful urgency to the way he said it. He was still glaring, I expected him to raise a finger and touch each of us with destruction and decay, and I realized that after all this time, the war still offered at least one thing that I had to turn my eyes from. I had seen it before and hoped never to see it again, I had misunderstood it and been hurt by it, I thought I had finally worked it out for good and I was looking at it now, knowing what it meant and feeling as helpless under it this last time as I had the first.

All right, yes, it had been a groove being a war correspondent, hanging out with the grunts and getting close to the war, touching it, losing yourself in it and trying yourself against it. I had always wanted that, never mind why, it had just been a thing of mine, the way this movie is a thing of mine, and I'd done it; I was in many ways brother to these poor, tired grunts, I knew what they knew now, I'd done it and it was really something. Everywhere I'd gone, there had always been Marines or soldiers who would tell me what the Avenger had told Krynksi, *You're all right, man, you guys are cool, you got balls.* They didn't always know what to think about you or what to say to you, they'd sometimes call you "Sir" until you had to beg them to stop, they'd sense the insanity of your position as terrified volunteer-reporter and it would seize them with the giggles and even respect. If they dug you, they always saw that you knew that, and when you choppered out they'd say goodbye, wish you luck. They'd even thank you, some of them, and what could you say to that?

And always, they would ask you with an emotion whose intensity would shock you to please tell it, because they really did have the feeling that it wasn't being told for them, that they were going through all of this and that somehow no one back in the World knew about it. They may have been a bunch of dumb, brutal killer kids (a lot of correspondents privately felt that), but they were smart enough to know that much. There was a Marine in Hue who had come after me as I walked toward the truck that would take me to the airstrip, he'd been locked in that horror for nearly two weeks while I'd shuttled in and out for two or three days at a time. We knew each other by now, and when he caught up with me he grabbed my sleeve so violently that I thought he was going to accuse me or, worse, try to stop me from going. His face was all but blank with exhaustion, but he had enough feeling left to say, "Okay, man, you go on, you go on out of here you cocksucker, but I mean it, you tell it! You tell it, man. If you don't tell it . . ."

What a time they were having there, it had all broken down, one battalion had taken 60% casualties, all the original NCO's were gone, the grunts were telling their officers to go die, to go fuck themselves, to go find some other fools to run up those streets awhile, it was no place where I'd have to tell anyone not to call me "Sir." They understood that, they understood a lot more than I did, but nobody hated me there, not even when I was leaving. Three days later I came back and the fighting had dropped off, the casualties were down to nothing and the same Marine flashed me a victory sign that had nothing to do with the Marine Corps or the fading battle of the American flag that had gone up on the Citadel's south wall the day before, he slapped me on the back and poured me a drink from a bottle he'd found in one of the hootches somewhere. Even the ones who preferred not to be in your company, who despised what your work required or felt that you took your living from their deaths, who believed that all of us were traitors and liars and the creepiest kinds of parasites, even they would cut back at the last and make their one concession to what there was in us that we ourselves loved most: "I got to give it to you, you guys got balls." Maybe they meant just that and nothing more, we had our resources and we made enough out of that to keep us going, turning the most grudging admissions into decorations for valor, making it all all right again.

But there was often that bad, bad moment to recall, the look that made you look away, and in its hateful way it was the purest single thing I'd every known. There was no wonder left in it anywhere, no amusement, it came out of nothing so messy as morality or prejudice, it had no motive, no conscious source. You would feel it coming out to you from under a poncho hood or see it in a wounded soldier staring up at you from a chopper floor, from men who were very scared or who had just lost a friend, from some suffering apparition of a grunt whose lip had been torn open by the sun, who just couldn't make it in the heat.

At first, I got it all mixed up, I didn't understand and I felt sorry for myself, misjudged. "Well fuck you too," I'd think. "It could have been me just as easily, I take chances too, can't you see that?" And then I realized that that was exactly what it was all about, it explained itself as easily as that, another of the war's dark revelations. They weren't judging me, they weren't reproaching me, they didn't even mind me, not in any personal way. They only hated me, hated me the way you'd hate any hopeless fool who would put himself through this thing when he had choices, any fool who had no more need of his life than to play with it in this way.

"You guys are crazy!" that Marine had said, and I know that when we flew off of Mutter's Ridge that afternoon he stood there for along time and watched us out of sight with the same native loathing he'd shown us before, turning finally to whoever was around, saying it maybe to himself, getting out what I'd actually heard said once when a jeep load of correspondents had just driven away, leaving me there alone, one rifleman turning to another and giving us all his hard, cold wish:

"Those fucking guys," he'd said. "I hope they die."

ALEKSANDR SOLZHENITSYN,
Excerpt from *The Gulag Archipelago*—RUSSIA

Aleksandr Solzhenitsyn was born in Kislovodsk, Russia, and studied mathematics at the University of Rostov-na-Donu. He also took correspondence courses in literature at the Moscow State University. Solzhenitsyn fought in the Second World War and was arrested in 1945 for writing a letter criticizing Joseph Stalin. Stalin had any person he distrusted removed from posts of authority; many were jailed, sent to the forced-labor camps of the Gulag, or executed. In the darkest years of the terror, from 1937 to 1938, the political police rounded up several million people; as many as 1 million people were shot, while another 2 million are estimated to have died in the camps, in addition to the 5 million to 7 million who perished in the state-made famine between 1932 and 1935. Solzhenitsyn spent eight years in prisons and labor camps, followed by three years in enforced exile.

Rehabilitated in 1956, Solzhenitsyn began writing. His 1962 novel, *One Day in the Life of Ivan Denisovich*, based in part on his prison experiences, made him an instant celebrity. Yet censorship of cultural activity in the Soviet Union tightened, and after a publication of short stories in 1963, Solzhenitsyn was no longer officially published. He resorted to circulating his work in the form of *samizdat* (self-published) literature or literature published illegally, in addition to publishing his work abroad. In 1970, Solzhenitsyn was awarded the Nobel Prize for Literature, but he declined to go to Stockholm to receive his prize because he was worried he would not be readmitted to the Soviet Union. Solzhenitsyn's *The Gulag Archipelago*, which documented the Soviet prison system, terrorism, and secret police, was first published in France in 1973 and soon after was published in English. In 1974, Solzhenitsyn was deported to West Germany and deprived of his Soviet citizenship. Subsequently, he settled in the United States. In 1991, Soviet Officials dropped charges of treason against him, and Solzhenitsyn returned to live in Russia in May of 1994.

In *The Gulag Archipelago*, Aleksandr Solzhenitsyn captures the sense of the surreal at the precise moment when state violence interrupts one's regular life and consumes it. He describes the Gulag as an archipelago, an island, which emphasizes its separation from the regular world. The most surreal aspect of being arrested and transported to the Gulag was public erasure. Victims were erased from public records and pictures as if they had never existed in the first place.

How do people get to this clandestine Archipelago? Hour by hour planes fly there, ships steer their course there, and trains thunder off to it—but all with nary a mark on them to tell of their destination. And at ticket windows or at travel bureaus for Soviet or foreign tourists the employees would be astounded if you were to ask for a ticket to go there. They know nothing and they've never heard of the Archipelago as a whole or of any one of its innumerable islands.

Those who go to the Archipelago to administer it get there via the training schools of the Ministry of Internal Affairs.

Those who go there to be guards are conscripted via the military conscription centers.

And those who, like you and me, dear reader, go there to die, must get there solely and compulsorily via arrest.

Arrest! Need it be said that it is a breaking point in your life, a bolt of lightning which has scored a direct hit on you? That it is an unassimilable spiritual earthquake not every person can cope with, as a result of which people often slip into insanity?

The Universe has as many different centers as there are living beings in it. Each of us is a center of the Universe, and that Universe is shattered when they hiss at you: *"You are under arrest."*

If *you* are arrested, can anything else remain unshattered by this cataclysm?

But the darkened mind is incapable of embracing these displacements in our universe, and both the most sophisticated and the veriest simpleton among us, drawing on all life's experience, can gasp out only: "Me? What for?"

And this is a question which, though repeated millions and millions of times before, has yet to receive an answer.

Arrest is an instantaneous, shattering thrust, expulsion, somersault from one state into another.

We have been happily born—or perhaps have unhappily dragged our weary way—down the long and crooked streets of our lives, past all kinds of walls and fences made of rotting wood, rammed earth, brick, concrete, iron railings. We have never given a thought to what lies behind them. We have never tried to penetrate them with our vision or our understanding. But there is where the *Gulag* country begins, right next to us, two yards away from us. In addition, we have failed to notice an enormous number of closely fitted, well-disguised doors and gates in these fences. All those gates were prepared for us, every last one! And all of a sudden the fateful gate swings open, and four white male hands, unaccustomed to physical labor but nonetheless strong and tenacious, grab us by the leg, arm, collar, cap, ear, and drag us in like a sack, and the gate behind us, the gate to our past life, is slammed shut once and for all.

That's all there is to it! You are arrested!

And you'll find nothing better to respond with than a lamblike bleat: "Me? What for?"

That's what arrest is: it's a blinding flash and a blow which shifts the present instantly into the past and the impossible into omnipotent actuality.

That's all. And neither for the first hour nor for the first day will you be able to grasp anything else.

Except that in your desperation the fake circus moon will blink at you: "It's a mistake! They'll set things right!"

And everything which is by now comprised in the traditional, even literary, image of an arrest will pile up and take shape, not in your own disordered memory, but in what your family and your neighbors in your apartment remember: The sharp nighttime ring or the rude knock at the door. The insolent entrance of the unwiped jackboots of the unsleeping State Security operatives. The frightened and cowed civilian witness at their backs. (And what function does this civilian witness serve? The victim doesn't even dare think about it and the operatives don't remember, but that's what the regulations call for, and so he has to sit there all night long and sign in the morning. For the witness, jerked from his bed, it is torture too—to go out night after night to help arrest his own neighbors and acquaintances.)

The traditional image of arrest is also trembling hands packing for the victim—a change of underwear, a piece of soap, something to eat; and no one knows what is needed, what is permitted, what clothes are best to wear; and the Security agents keep interrupting and hurrying you:

"You don't need anything. They'll feed you there. It's warm there." (It's all lies. They keep hurrying you to frighten you.)

The traditional image of arrest is also what happens afterward, when the poor victim has been taken away. It is an alien, brutal, and crushing force totally dominating the apartment for hours on end, a breaking, ripping open, pulling from the walls, emptying things from wardrobes and desks onto the floor, shaking, dumping out, and ripping apart—piling up mountains for litter on the floor—and the crunch of things being trampled beneath jackboots. And nothing is sacred in a search! During the arrest of the locomotive engineer Inoshin, a tiny coffin stood in his room containing the body of his newly dead child. The *"jurists"* dumped the child's body out of the coffin and searched it. They shake sick people out of their sickbeds, and they unwind bandages to search beneath them.

Nothing is so stupid as to be inadmissible during a search! For example, they seized from the antiquarian Chetverukhin "a certain number of pages of Tsarist decrees"—to wit, the decree on ending the war with Napoleon, on the formation of the Holy Alliance, and a proclamation of public prayers against cholera during the epidemic of 1830. From our greatest expert on Tibet, Vostrikov, they confiscated ancient Tibetan manuscripts of great value; and it took the pupils of the deceased scholar thirty years to wrest them from the KGB! When the Orientalist Nevsky was arrested, they grapped Tangut manuscripts—and twenty-five years later the deceased victim was posthumously awarded a Lenin Prize for deciphering them. From Karger they took his archive of the Yenisei Ostyaks and vetoed the alphabet and vocabulary he had developed for his people—and a small nationality was thereby left without any written language. It would take a long time to describe all this in educated speech, but there's a folk saying about the search which covers the subject: *They are looking for something which was never put there.* They carry off whatever they have seized, but sometimes they compel the arrested individual to carry it. Thus Nina Aleksandrovna Palchinskaya hauled over her shoulder a bag filled with the papers and letters of her eternally busy and active husband, the late great Russian engineer, carrying it into *their* maw—once and for all, forever.

For those left behind after the arrest there is the long tail end of a wrecked and devastated life. And the attempts to go and deliver food parcels. But from all the windows the answer comes in barking voices: "Nobody here by that name!" "Never heard of him!" Yes, and in the worst days of Leningrad it took five days of standing in crowded lines just to get to that window. And it may be only after half a year or a year that the arrested person responds at all. Or else the answer is tossed out: "Deprived of the right to correspond." And that means once and for all. "No right to correspondence"—and that almost for certain means: "Has been shot."

That's how we picture arrest to ourselves.

The kind of night arrest described is, in fact, a favorite, because it has important advantages. Everyone living in the apartment is thrown into a state of terror by the first knock at the door. The arrested person is torn from the warmth of his bed. He is in a daze, half-asleep, helpless, and his judgment is befogged. In a night arrest the State Security men have a superiority in numbers; there are many of them, armed, against one person who hasn't even finished buttoning his trousers. During the arrest and search it is highly improbable that a crowd of potential supporters will gather at the entrance. The unhurried, step-by-step visits, first to one apartment, then to another, tomorrow to a third and a fourth, provide an opportunity for the Security operations personnel to be deployed with the maximum efficiency and to imprison many more citizens of a given town than the police force itself numbers.

In addition, there's an advantage to night arrests in that neither the people in neighboring apartment houses nor those on the city streets can see how many have been taken away. Arrests which frighten the closest neighbors are no event at all to those farther away. It's as if they had not taken place. Along that same asphalt ribbon on which the Black Marias scurry at night, a tribe of youngsters strides by day with banners, flowers, and gay, untroubled songs.

But those who *take,* whose work consists solely of arrests, for whom the horror is boringly repetitive, have a much broader understanding of how arrests operate. They operate according to a large body of theory, and innocence must not lead one to ignore this. The science of arrest is an important segment of the course on general penology and has been propped up with a substantial body of social theory. Arrests are classified according to various criteria: nighttime and daytime; at home; at work, during a journey; first-time arrests and repeats; individual and group arrests. Arrests are distinguished by the degree of surprise required, the amount of resistance expected (even though in tens of millions of cases no resistance was expected and in fact there was none). Arrests are also differentiated by the thoroughness of the required search; by instructions either to make out or not to make out an inventory of confiscated property or seal a room or apartment; to arrest the wife after the husband and send the children to an orphanage, or to send the rest of the family into exile, or to send the old folks to a labor camp too.

⌒ BEGUM ANIS KIDWAI,
    Excerpt from "In the Shadow of Freedom"—INDIA

    Begum Anis Kidwai, an Indian Muslim, lost her husband to
    communal violence in 1947, the year of the India-Pakistan
    Partition that separated India and Pakistan along religious lines:
    Hindus in India, Muslims in Pakistan. Devastated, Kidwai became

a social worker, working with Partition victims in the Muslim camps in Delhi.

In the excerpt from her essay, Kidwai comes face to face with the clash between the anticipated, idealized freedom and the alienating daily violence, during which "the corpse of freedom was being trampled upon." The desperation she witnesses mounts to nearly unbearable levels, and she contemplates suicide as an option to exit the madness surrounding her.

Independence Day

Now I recall our first Independence Day. From Calcutta to eastern and western Punjab, the country was in a fog rent with sighs and shrieks. We had freedom drenched in blood and gore. The corpse of independence was being trampled upon. Women were being robbed of their virtue and Government House echoed with the victims' cries. Nevertheless we strove to be happy. Despite everything, the yoke of slavery had been cast off. Later, perhaps, the ghost of communalism would also depart. No doubt the country had been divided, but perhaps, both communities would be happy in their own parts of the country.

But no. Disappointment and hopelessness overwhelmed us, we felt alienated. Even on such a happy occasion, our hopes were turned to dust. I covered most of the city on foot, rickshaw and car but I came back in the same mood. There was no happiness anywhere.

My heart sank, as if someone was strangling my happiness. The tricolor did not tug at the heart. The cries of "Inquilab Zindabad" had no emotional impact. Our blood was no longer hot. The signboards, slogans, and posters inscribed in Hindi looked as though they were mocking us.

At that moment India was going back to the past, with people donning tilaks on their foreheads. And I wondered why they had sent for Brahmins from Banaras. Why were they looking for a "Qazi" (reciter of the Quran)? What will bhikshus do in Government House? I felt suffocated. Lost in these thoughts I reached Government House. Momentarily I experienced a sense of pride. The national flag flew on the stately entrance which provided free passage to the common folk. Now, everything here was ours and our comrades in the national struggle lived in it.

But soon my heart sank again. A language was being spoken there which was stranger to us than English, a language in the words of Josh (Malihabadi):

Jis ko dewon ke siva koi samajh na sake
Zayr mashq hai who andaze bayan ay saqi.
(What cannot be understood except by giants,
O'Saqi, that is the current style of expression.)

The chowkis on the right side of the dais were adorned with Buddhist priests. Many languages were spoken. English, Sanskrit, Arabic, chaste Hindi. But not a word in our precious language (Urdu), each expression of which "sends a hundred flowers in bloom."

So much was said. But we could make nothing of it. (. . .) like me, were many others who had witnessed the scene with dry throats and bewildered eyes. They returned feeling that their backs were broken. Even the first Governor of free India, Mrs. Sarojini Naidu, could not read the oath (in Hindi) correctly.

Had we waited for this kind of future all these years? Who wanted to dig up the dead culture from the past? Who wanted the Government to take on the contract of religions in place of its responsibility for democracy?

The scene was painful—heartbreaking. Our hair stood on end, watching this spectacle of Brahmanism. We saw a glimpse of the future. Those who had been mere spectators of our struggle for twenty years were pleased and taunted us. "See, were we not saying that as soon as we get power, there will be Hindu Raj in India? That is why it has become essential for us to create Pakistan." In fact, it is this mentality which has created Pakistan.

Another gentleman remarked, "I have already written an article showing that Brahmanism has always dominated India. Buddhism spread and reached its zenith, but Brahmanism suppressed it so well that there's hardly a trace left in this country. How well Islam showed in this land! But it also got caught in the coils of Brahmanism, and lost its individuality. Christianity too bowed to Brahmanism in the shape of the Theosophical Society. Brahmanism will dominate this country. Gandhiji may knock his head against it, or your people may wail against it, but India cannot be rid of it."

It needed enormous patience. We were numbed. There was no glimpse of hope, no light ahead. And we were wondering how workers, peasants and the poor would get out of this morass. We would have to look for a way out. We had seen through the veil of the Congress, and would have to raise the curtain drawn over reality. Prognosticators could see in which direction the wind was blowing. The Muslim Leaguers were pleased that they were not alone in being shorn; others were too. The progressives (of the left) were wondering whether those tried soldiers who had won the battle against the British would serve the country's new objectives and whether they should bolster their strength or try to weaken them. Young men thought of a new battle front in which they would have to face their own people instead of aliens. A handful of them would have to wade through blood to build a new India. But who knew that the biggest price would have to be paid by the Father of the Nation himself.

September came again (in 1947). Hardly 15 days had gone by since Indian freedom, then beating and killing began in Delhi. The tricolors on houses and shops had hardly become grimy when they began to be streaked with blood. A flood of confusion and disorder from Punjab swamped Delhi, Mussoorie and Dehradun. One day in a gathering (around Gandhiji), someone remarked that the Ganga of communal riots was flowing throughout the whole country. Gandhiji laughed and said: "But its Gangotri is the Punjab."

The telephones were dead. The mail stopped. Trains stopped. Bridges were demolished. Human beings crawled like insects in lanes and fields, dying, were trampled upon and robbed. There was such a stampede. God's invisible stick was driving them here and there. Probably, India had never witnessed such a storm of murder and mayhem in her history. Carthage used to enslave the inhabitants of the country it conquered and set them to bake bricks. India too had witnessed the great battle of Mahabharata. Nadir Shah had sacked Delhi for three days. But these were of days, when even a province and district had the status of a country. Not more than twenty thousand people died in these large massacres. But what we saw with our own eyes might not have happened since the beginning of civilization.

In Lucknow, men, women and children, weeping bitterly, would beg me to telephone Delhi and get news of their relations. "For God's sake, arrange for our family members to get out of Mussoorie. If any of them has been left alive in Dehradun, find out their whereabouts." I used to pester my brother-in-law in Delhi.

Every morning I used to take a walk for a mile or two along La Montessori Road after prayers, alone. Who could accompany me so early in the morning? But at that time, there was no menace. However, as September began, the atmosphere began to weigh me down. I would pass by groups of four or five taking their morning walk, and having heated discussions on the politics of Punjab and India.

One day, seeing them carrying sticks and clubs, noticing the expression on their faces and overhearing their angry voices, I felt that peace in Lucknow was also going to be disturbed. People at home had been warning me not to go out on such lonely strolls, but I never heeded them. Sensing this change in the atmosphere, I had to stop my morning walks.

In the city, peace committees had been formed, in various quarters to try and prevent the breakdown of peace. Thank God they succeeded in these efforts, and Lucknow was able to preserve its reputation for civilized living. But news of disturbances exploding elsewhere were enough to destroy our peace of mind. We were less worried about our relations in Delhi as they were living under some protective arrangements. But anxieties about Mussoorie had robbed us of sleep at night. We believed that Shafi [Anis Kidwai's husband, Shafi Ahmed Kidwai, was administrator of the Mussoorie Municipal Board at that time] with his characteristic obstinacy would not leave Mussoorie. In fact, if prevailed upon to leave, he would become even firmer in his resolve.

At these times, as one gathered from his letter, he was headlong into providing relief and succor to those uprooted by the riots. In this situation, he was not prepared to come away. His brothers were worried.

He was expected on 21 September in Lucknow on some official business but soon he called them to postpone this date. And the date kept on being extended. Earlier he was worried about the safety of some of his relations, friends and employees in Dehradun. But when the riots caught up with Mussoorie, he was calm:

Mushkilain mujh par pari itni
Ki asan ho gayen.
(I suffered so many hardships
that I became immune to them.)

He would never write to me about his condition and would instead enquire about the safety of a whole lot of people. Once he wrote to me: "I am missing my eldest daughter very much, send me her address so that I may write to her." He enquired about me and the children, as if all of us were in peril while he was safe.

But one day a letter came from him in which he related the whole story of Mussoorie. He said, "While I am writing to you, I hear the din of the populace down below, the sounds of firing and the shrieks and wails of the victims. Houses and shops are on fire, shops are being looted and the police are watching the spectacle. This is happening in broad daylight."

In the next letter, he wrote that he had closed his office and was confined to the house for the last three days. "It is raining hard. The men who ply horses and mules could not escape the bestiality of the attackers. The jamadars have covered their corpses with grass and straw."

The next letter was at the peak of the disturbances. Those happenings broke his heart. He wrote: "Since 1921, I have seen several phases of the country, witnessed the soul-stirring period of Hindu-Muslim unity and also seen British atrocities during various Congress movements. I have seen the tumultuous period of 1942 with its upsurge of passion for achieving freedom, and the frenzy of the Muslim League during the elections. And now I am watching the madness of the majority community. Those days have passed. These will pass too. But I will remember the partiality and the insensitivity of Government officials."

In his letter of 27 September, he wrote: "The telegraph lines have been cut. A telegram from the Government dispatched on 12 September reached Mussoorie only on the 22 September. One cannot get through to Delhi on the telephone. Four or five days ago, I thought of talking to Pantji (Pandit Govind Ballabh Pant) about the state of affairs here but I could not get the telephone line to Lucknow. Both the telephone and the telegraph are useless."

On his way to the office in Mussoorie, he would see corpses on the road. But who was there to bury them? He was the only Muslim walking the streets of Mussoorie. There were only some jamadars available to drag the corpses off the roads or throw them into ditches, covering them with earth or stones so that they were secure from vultures and kites, and would keep the city air clean. Probably, no municipal administrator had faced such a gruesome responsibility.

When I thought of all this I felt like committing suicide. He was facing alone the responsibility which belonged to both of us. And here I was sitting secure in Lucknow. Greatly agitated, one day I started from home with the intention of going to Mussoorie. I had gone up to Nazarbagh when my younger brother caught up with me and asked me not to go as no train could reach Mussoorie safely, "Don't go now. You can go sometime later." He was anxious about my safety. But I wish I had gone on that day.

Shafi would write to me, "You should not worry about me. Despite the rain, I am attending the office except for one day a week." His Muslim employees had been sent to refugee camps. The Hindus did not feel obliged to come to the office. But as soon as the riots subsided, he felt it essential to keep his office open for the sake of riot relief activities. On

28 September, he wrote a long letter to his brother (Rafi Ahmed Kidwai) and another to a friend. The contents of both letters were the same. That detailed letter was lost. After Shafi's murder, when someone asked him about it, he said he had sent the letter to the District Magistrate of Dehradun. We did not see that letter again and one does not know why the District Magistrate even postponed the enquiry over his murder after seeing that letter. Why? Only the District Magistrate could throw light on it. But we have seen the letter he wrote to the friend. In it he said: "I go to office every day. People consider this a rash step. But had I let fear overcome me, some accident would have befallen me by now."

ᦁ PAUL W. MORRIS,
Excerpt from "Waking Up"—UNITED STATES

Paul W. Morris was born in 1971 in New Haven, Connecticut. He received bachelor's and master's degrees from Hampshire College in Amherst, Massachusetts, in 1995. A former editor at Viking Penguin and *Tricycle: The Buddhist Review,* Morris has written about religion and culture for the *Village Voice* and *Yoga Journal,* among other publications. His essays have appeared in various anthologies. He has been a co-editor of *KillingTheBuddha.com* since 2002 and is currently the director of special projects at *BOMB Magazine,* an arts and culture quarterly. He lives in New York City.

In his essay "Waking Up," Paul Morris recalls the nightmare-like quality of September 11, 2001, particularly in the heart of the chaos in downtown Manhattan as the World Trade Center towers collapsed, thousands fled uptown, and some of those who were trapped in the Twin Towers jumped to their death. Morris's piece is also punctuated by ellipses and fragments of phrases that people uttered as they attempted to describe what they were seeing. He concludes that incomprehensible events such as 9/11 enforce of the truth of impermanence. The lingering smell of smoke, which contained debris from the towers and the victims, served as a physical reminder of this truth.

The sound and the smoke . . . the terror of the crowds rushing past . . . a dark cloud billowing toward me in a wave of debris, determined, absolute . . .

Searching for a meaning in this memory, I look at other stories born on September 11 and see a shared vocabulary that is at once horrifying and epiphanic: "It was the apocalypse." "Like a revelation." "I thought I died and went to heaven." "There was only darkness." "I saw the light." "Then it hit me." "The world came crashing down." "My eyes were opened." "Everything looked different." "It was unreal." "It felt like I was dreaming." "I awoke into a nightmare."

Taken from first-person accounts, this is the language of enlightenment. In its syntax, we hear the words of awakening, of the struggle to see again after a blinding flash of insight. It is Saul's conversion on the road to Damascus. It is Arjuna's moksha in the *Bhagavad Gita*. For me, it was a Buddhist lesson in impermanence that I wish I could unlearn. Or at least relearn, like during a meditation retreat, or through a course lecture, or even in one of the books on Buddhism that line my window ledge. As it happened, the lesson I learned that Tuesday morning occurred on the streets below my apartment, just blocks from Ground Zero.

The explosions arrive in swift succession during a hurried morning routine, the first as I'm getting out of the shower, and then again, inconceivably louder, as I'm preparing to leave my apartment. I crane my neck and see burning papers littering the sky seventy stories up. To the west, I glimpse a side of the south tower, on fire and smoking.

I ride down in the elevator with a neighbor who is groggy and half-dressed.

"What's going on?" he asks. "I was asleep when an explosion woke me up."

When I tell him what I know so far, what we all know by now, from the limited and confused news reports I have already heard—that two airline jets crashed, intentionally, into both towers of the World Trade Center—he says nothing. We exit the elevator in silence and walk out of our building into chaos.

On the corner of Broadway and Fulton Street, windows all along the block have been blown out by concussion force. Gazing upward, I see what I saw on the television, the towers ablaze, the same, yet different. From where I stand I observe balloons of flames twenty floors high roiling over each other, more orange than I thought possible. I smell the acrid black smoke pouring out, bleeding a deep scar east across the azure sky. It's so bright out that it's hard to determine where the heat is coming from, the sun or the fires, and if there is any difference at all. The exit wounds made by the planes look like two dark eyes gone frighteningly askew, and I stare back at them, uncomprehendingly. Later, people will say it was like a movie, like a war zone, like a natural disaster. But right now there are no metaphors. It's like nothing that has ever happened. And, as it's happening, there is nothing to understand.

Coming back to Earth, I look at the people looking up, as if a closer inspection will reveal some deeper meaning. A woman walks past, covering her mouth, gasping.

"Oh God," she moans, "I saw bodies falling."

"They were jumping," adds another dazed woman.

"It's a nightmare," someone else says. "I have to wake up. Somebody wake me up."

Somewhere south of Chambers Street, I'm on a corner standing in a group of people, crowded around a guy with a walkman, waiting for news. Behind me, somebody is talking about a heap of twisted metal that was a jet engine a block away, and two guys holding briefcases march off for a closer look.

"They hit the Pentagon," the guy with the walkman finally says, his eyes fixed on the burning towers above us.

There is a pause as this information begins to sink in, as we weigh it against what we already know. Before we are allowed to mourn, though, a man announces, "Good! I'm glad they hit Washington, now they'll have to do something about these lunatics! It's about time they woke up!"

"It's the Palestinians, I know it," another man is saying and an argument erupts.

I'm waiting for more news to come over the radio, bracing myself for the next disaster. Anything can happen, I think. I have to be prepared. That's when the city shudders. I look up to see the top fifty stories of the south tower begin to slide off, down, and to the east. Then the rest falls in a deafening and unending crash, blanketing the corner where I had, minutes earlier, been standing, annihilating the rescue workers and vehicles that were still there. I hear the cacophony of cries: "Oh my God!" "It's coming this way!" "Run!"

And I run.

I have a recurring dream in which I'm running away from danger, but I'm not getting anywhere. The ground beneath me is like a treadmill preventing me from moving ahead, as though there were some invisible gravity holding me still. It's absurd and frustrating. No matter how hard I run, I can't go forward. When I finally wake up, I'm anxious, frightened.

Running north on Church Street, there is no clear or straight path.

People are everywhere, moving in every direction. Many, like me, are racing uptown. Some dart east or west. A few don't move at all, paralyzed by their disbelief. Zigzagging through the crowds, I have the sense that I'm going nowhere, that the cloud is getting closer instead of moving father away. I want to wake up, but there is no waking.

As I cross Canal Street, my run turns into a tired stride, a slow-motion sleepwalk through a shattered city. Suddenly, something tears through the sky, three, two, one block away—and I instinctively duck behind a van as an F-16 flies into view overhead. I feel foolish in the eyes of commuters flowing out of the subways, unaware of the world that awaits them. We are all coming at this from different perspectives, I think, but we share a common nightmare. Maybe if I get inside, I can reverse the dream, erase what I have witnessed, delude myself into believing that the people are still alive, that the planes never hit.

I'm almost at Houston Street, heading on auto pilot to a friend's office to make a phone call, type an e-mail, get a news update, do something, anything to escape the inevitability of what has happened from dawning on me. I'm entering the building when the north tower disappears from sight. I don't look back. I'm awake now, and I've already seen too much of what is no longer there.

After a week spent displaced on the upper west side, I'm finally able to go home, back to the ruins of my neighborhood. For days now, I have been trying to sift through the experiences of that morning, excavating my grief from the helplessness that overwhelms me. I feel shell shocked, incapable of being outside for extended periods; every loud truck that passes, every siren that blares is like a sharp whack bringing me back to the present, to the harsh reality of what has happened.

I expect the worst on the way down to my apartment, imagining it carpeted with debris, glass shards blown everywhere, furniture soaked from the previous night's rainstorm. It looks like a bomb went off, I muse darkly upon entering, only because this is exactly how I left it, neglected and in disarray, but for the smell of burnt plastic. Pale sunlight streams in through windows now spotted with filth and ash. A thin layer of chalky dust covers the window ledges and the books that line them. I wonder, even more darkly, how much of that dust is comprised of the towers, how much of the people who didn't get out, of the firefighters who rushed in; how much of it is the airplanes, the passengers and crews, and how much the hijackers themselves, all of them, blown apart in a storm of whirling atoms. I wonder: How much equanimity can I bear?

I find refuge in a teaching by an 8th-century Zen master of the T'ang Dynasty named Quingyuan, who described the process of his own enlightenment in *The Compendium of Five Lamps:* "Thirty years ago, before I practiced [Zen], I saw that mountains are mountains and rivers are rivers. However, after having achieved intimate knowledge and having gotten a way in, I saw that mountains are not mountains and rivers are not rivers. But now that I have found rest, as before, I see mountains as mountains and rivers as rivers."

To the pre-enlightened eyes, in other words, the physical world is just that, physical and nothing more. A mountain is just a mountain. At the moment of enlightenment, there is a new perspective, a deeper understanding of the world as it truly is: The mountain is merely an illusion, a construct of our own preconceptions. Afterwards, the eyes adjust to take in everything, the physical world as well as the world of impermanence. When the enlightened mind can hold both perspectives simultaneously, there are mountains again. There, and not there. Inspired by the simplicity of Quingyuan's teaching, sixties folk-singer Donovan distilled this koan even further when he sang,

First there is a mountain. Then there isn't. Then there is.

Buried beneath the seeming incomprehensibility of these lyrics lies a sophisticated lesson still pertinent today.

Especially today. It strikes me as a kind of Zen reasoning that the Trade Towers are no longer visible precisely because their very visibility made them targets. They were attacked not only because of what they represented economically and politically. They were attacked because of what they stood for metaphorically. They were as much a part of this country's geography as they were of my own neighborhood's. In the news of the past week, they have been referred to as "America's Pyramids" and "New York City's compass."

As early as 1976—three years after the completion of the second tower—Hollywood magic sent a giant gorilla climbing up them in a remake of the original King Kong. Even then, the towers were established symbols of both technological progress and financial prowess. They could be seen from around the world. At that height, King Kong's confusion was unmistakable. That's why he is up there in the first place, straddling the financial district, an ape foot squarely planted atop each tower, snarling and swatting at fighter jets. Kong's confusion is our confusion. His anger, our anger.

It is the hijackers' anger as well. King Kong represents the monkey mind Buddhists describe, the incessant internal banter that, if allowed to run rampant, perpetuates the cause and effect of suffering, of which we are all clearly implicated. And the towers he climbs are the mountains of our own delusion. Now that they are gone, all that is left is a palpable fear, the terror associated with moments of awakening.

Listening to the news report that "Everything has changed," I hear an old truth of impermanence. If the disaster on September 11 has transformed my perception at all, then I am still waiting to see how my eyes will adjust to the potential insight gained. For the enlightened mind, the vision is clear: The suffering of thousands of people is no different than the suffering of the hijackers; the destruction of the towers is proof that nothing remains unchanged. When I consider the sheer loss of life and degree of devastation, however, I know that I do not yet have Quingyuan's clarity of mind for seeing past distinctions.

This, then, is where practice begins. Here, at the place of impact, the center of gravity from which all things radiate. There is a Ground Zero inside me wherever I go. It is the home I return to and the nowhere I can never outrun. When I sit in silence, breathing deeply, I try not to think about whom and what I am inhaling, and if it even matters. I breathe in, and the city breathes out.

It's late now. My street is quiet. Only emergency vehicles are allowed this far downtown, and the urgency of their sirens has been long since negated. The smell of scorched debris is beginning to subside. It occurs to me that maybe it's only making way for something worse, the stench of decomposition. Up the block, I can hear the rumble of heavy machinery, the low, steady thunder of a lightning flash that will sound for months to come.

THREE

Coping Mechanisms

Breyten Breytenbach, a South African writer, would have never survived his seven years in an Apartheid-era prison if it were not for reading and writing. For the first two years, he was kept in isolation and the only texts he could read were the little squares of newspaper that were folded into cones which held his daily sugar ration. Sometimes the newspaper squares contained a death notice, sometimes an advertisement. Ultimately, Breytenbach built a "kaleidoscope ensemble" of what was going on in the world because even the slightest hint—perhaps a weather report or a drop in food prices—resonated immediately.

After two years, a second trial, and a petition organized by a group of writers and others, Breytenbach gained permission to write. Writing helped Breytenbach track the changes that he was undergoing in prison. He was deteriorating, the writer said in an interview with Legacy Project in December 2004, but he didn't have a yardstick like family or friends to measure this change against. "Writing is also literally a way of translating, integrating and digesting the unacceptable around you," said Breytenbach. "If it hadn't been for writing, I would have been destroyed totally, there is no doubt about it."

When a calamity turns victims' world upside down, some cope by acknowledging this topsy-turvyness in some manner. In certain cases, writing, theater, or creating art allows victims to maintain a link with normalcy and remake what has been unmade by terror and continuing uncertainty. In New York, after September 11, 2001, makeshift literary memorials centering on phrases or poems mushroomed around the city: on the sidewalks, in bus shelters, and in restaurants. "It was nearly an instinctive level of speech, a New York pavement patois, to try to articulate and reconstruct the inexplicable," said Breytenbach, who was teaching in New York at the time of the attacks.

In other cases, laughter functions as a pressure valve, not to express irreverence, but as a way to acknowledge the absurdity of the situation. The South African novelist and playwright Zakes Mda spoke with the Legacy Project about seeing a play at the Market Theatre in Johannesburg. Scenes of brutality against black South Africans elicited laughter from the black audience members. But Mda explained the reason for this perhaps counter-intuitive response: "We laughed when these things were happening in real life to us, so when we see them re-enacted on the stage, the recognition itself brings about that laughter. That's how we used to cope with such situations."

This chapter brings together the Argentine writer Julio Cortázar, addressing creative ways citizens coped with Latin American repression in the second half of the twentieth century; the South African playwright Athol Fugard, depicting daily life on Robben Island, where Nelson Mandela, among others, was imprisoned during Apartheid (1948–1990s); Yvonne Vera, writing about the Zimbabwean Civil War (1971–1979); the Chinese writer Wang Meng, discussing techniques people used to survive the Cultural Revolution in China (1966–1976); the South African novelist Zakes Mda, writing about daily violence in post-Apartheid South Africa of the 1990s; the human rights activist and writer Kay Boyle, examining how families coped with political violence in the Spanish Civil War (1936–1939); and the Hungarian Nobel Laureate Imre Kertész, remembering how he coped with life in the concentration camps during the Holocaust in World War II (1939–1945).

∾ JULIO CORTÁZAR,
"Graffiti"—ARGENTINA

Argentine writer Julio Cortázar was born in Brussels in 1914, the first year of World War I. When he was four years old his family moved back to Argentina. In addition to writing, Cortázar was a secondary-level teacher, university professor, publisher, translator, and human rights activist at different times throughout his career. He moved to France in 1951 in opposition to the Péron regime and remained active in Latin American politics, visiting Cuba in

1961 and Nicaragua in 1983. During the majority of his years in France he worked for four months each year for UNESCO as a translator from French and English into Spanish and devoted the rest of the year to writing and other hobbies such as the jazz trumpet. He published poems and plays in the 1930s and '40s but achieved his first major success with a book of stories, *Bestiario*, in 1951. His novel *Rayuela* (1963; translated by Gregory Rabassa as *Hopscotch*, 1966) was widely praised and earned Cortázar an enthusiastic international audience. He traveled widely but was based in France until his death in 1984.

Cortázar's short story "Graffiti" (1981), translated by Gregory Rabassa, depicts how two people subtly resist a repressive regime through a playful game of graffiti, drawing sketches in public spaces around town to communicate with one another. The graffiti are all visual images except on one occasion when the narrator's companion writes the phrase: *"It hurts me too."* Cortázar draws attention to this phrase—it is the only time italics are used throughout the story. This phrase also underscores how writing allows these two people to connect, escape their individual isolation, and cope with both the danger and the boredom of life in a city rife with fear, a curfew, and "a menacing prohibition against putting up posters or writing on the walls."

So many things begin and perhaps end as a game, I suppose that it amused you to find the sketch beside yours, you attributed it to chance or a whim and only the second time did you realize that it was intentional and then you looked at it slowly, you even came back later to look at it again, taking the usual precautions: the street at its most solitary moment, no patrol wagon on neighboring corners, approaching with indifference and never looking at the graffiti face-on but from the other sidewalk or diagonally, feigning interest in the shop window alongside, going away immediately.

Your own game had begun out of boredom, it wasn't really a protest against the state of things in the city, the curfew, the menacing prohibition against putting up posters or writing on walls. It simply amused you to make sketches with colored chalk (you didn't like the term graffiti, so art critic–like) and from time to time to come and look at them and even, with a little luck, to be a spectator to the arrival of the municipal truck and the useless insults of the workers as they erased the sketches. It didn't matter to them that they weren't political sketches, the prohibition covered everything, and if some child had dared draw a house or a dog it would have been erased in just the same way in the midst of curses and threats. In the city people no longer knew too well which side fear was really on; maybe that's why you overcame yours and every so often picked the time and place just right for making a sketch.

You never ran any risk because you knew how to choose well, and in the time that passed until the cleaning trucks arrived something opened up for you like a very clean space where there was almost room for hope. Looking at your sketch from a distance you could see people casting a glance at it as they passed, no one stopped of course, but no one failed to look at the sketch, sometimes a quick abstract composition in two colors, the profile of a bird or two entwined figures. Just one time you wrote a phrase, in black chalk: *It hurts me too.* It didn't last two hours, and that time the police themselves made it disappear. Afterward you went on making only sketches.

When the other one appeared next to yours you were almost afraid, suddenly the danger had become double, someone like you had been moved to have some fun on the brink of imprisonment or something worse, and that someone, as if it were of no small importance, was a woman. You couldn't prove it yourself, but there was something different and better than the most obvious proofs: a trace, a predilection for warm colors, an aura. Probably since you walked alone you were imagining it out of compensation; you admired her, you were afraid for her, you hoped it was the only time, you almost gave yourself away when she drew a sketch alongside another one of yours, an urge to laugh, to stay right there as if the police were blind or idiots.

A different time began, at once stealthier, more beautiful and more threatening. Shirking your job you would go out at odd moments in hopes of surprising her. For your sketches you chose those streets that you could cover in a single quick passage; you came back at dawn, at dusk, at three o'clock in the morning. It was a time of unbearable contradiction, the deception of finding a new sketch of hers beside one of yours and the street empty, and that of not finding anything and feeling the street even more empty. One night you saw her first sketch all by itself; she'd done it in red and blue chalk on a garage door, taking advantage of the worm-eaten wood and the nail heads. It was more than ever she—the design, the colors—but you also felt that that sketch had meaning as an appeal or question, a way of calling you. You came back at dawn, after the patrols had thinned out in their mute sweep, and on the rest of the door you sketched a quick seascape with sails and breakwaters; if he didn't look at it closely a person might have said it was a play of random lines, but she would know how to look at it. That night you barely escaped a pair of policemen, in your apartment you drank glass after glass of gin and you talked to her, you told her everything that came into your mouth, like a different sketch made with sound, another harbor with sails, you pictured her as dark and silent, you chose lips and breasts for her, you loved her a little.

Almost immediately it occurred to you that she would be looking for an answer, that she would return to her sketch the way you were returning now to yours, and even though the danger had become so much greater since the attacks at the market, you dared go up to the garage, walk around the block, drink endless beers at the café on the corner. It was absurd because she wouldn't stop after seeing your sketch, any one of the women coming and going might be her. At dawn on the second day you chose a gray wall and sketched a white triangle surrounded by splotches like oak leaves; from the same café on the corner you could see the wall (they'd already cleaned off the garage door and a patrol, furious, kept coming back), at dusk you withdrew a little, but choosing different lookout points, moving from one place to another, making small purchases in the shops so as not to draw too much attention. It was already dark night when you heard the sirens and the spotlights swept your eyes. There was a confused crowding by the wall, you ran, in the face of all good sense, and all that helped you was the good luck to have a car turn the corner and put on its brakes when the driver saw the patrol wagon, its bulk protected you and you saw the struggle, black hair pulled by gloved hands, the kicks and the screams, the cut-off glimpse of blue slacks before they threw her into the wagon and took her away.

Much later (it was horrible trembling like that, it was horrible to think that it had happened because of your sketch on the gray wall) you mingled with other people and managed to see an outline in blue, the traces of that orange color that was like her name or her mouth, her there in that truncated sketch that the police had erased before taking her away, enough remained to understand that she had tried to answer your triangle with another figure, a circle or maybe a spiral, a form full and beautiful, something like a yes or an always or a now.

You knew it quite well, you'd had more than enough time to imagine the details of what was happening at the main barracks; in the city everything like that oozed out little by little, people were aware of the fate of prisoners, and if sometimes they got to see one or another of them again, they would have preferred not seeing them, just as the majority were lost in the silence that no one dared break. You knew it only too well, that night the gin wouldn't help you except to make you bite your hands with impotence, cry, crush the pieces of colored chalk with your feet before submerging yourself in drunkenness.

Yes, but the days passed and you no longer knew how to live in any other way. You began to leave your work again to walk about the streets, to look fleetingly at the walls and the doors where you and she had sketched. Everything clean, everything clear; nothing, not even a flower sketched by the innocence of a schoolboy who steals a piece of chalk in class and can't resist the pleasure of using it. Nor could you resist, and a month later you got up at dawn and went back to the street with the garage. There were no patrols, the walls were perfectly clean; a cat looked at you cautiously from a doorway when you took out your chalk and in the same place, there where she had left her sketch, you filled the boards with a green shout, a red flame of recognition and love, you wrapped your sketch in an oval that was also your mouth and hers and hope. The footsteps at the corner threw you into a felt-footed run, to the refuge of a pile of empty boxes; a staggering drunk approached humming, he tried to kick the cat and fell face down at the foot of the sketch. You went away slowly, safe now, and with the first sun you slept as you hadn't slept for a long time.

That same morning you looked from a distance: they hadn't erased it yet. You went back at noon: almost inconceivably it was still there. The agitation in the suburbs (you'd heard the news reports) had taken the urban patrols away from their routine; at dusk you went back to see that a lot of people had been seeing it all through the day. You waited until three in the morning to go back, the street was empty and dark. From a distance you made out the other sketch, only you could have distinguished it, so small, above and to the left of yours. You went over with a feeling that was thirst and horror at the same time; you saw the orange oval and the hanging eye, a mouth smashed with fists. I know, I know, but what else could I have sketched for you? What message would have made any sense now? In some way I had to say farewell to you and at the same time ask you to continue. I had to leave you something before going back to my refuge where there was no mirror anymore, only a hollow to hide in until the end in the most complete darkness, remembering so many things and sometimes, as I had imagined your life, imagining that you were making other sketches, that you were going out at night to make other sketches.

∾ ATHOL FUGARD,
   Excerpt from *The Island*—SOUTH AFRICA

Athol Fugard was born in 1932, to an English father and Afrikaner
mother. He grew up in Port Elizabeth, the Cape Province city
where most of his plays are set. In 1958, Fugard moved to
Johannesburg, where he worked as a court clerk. In that same
year, he organized a multiracial theater for which he wrote,
directed, and acted. Fugard's attacks on Apartheid attracted the
attention of the South African government. After his play *Blood
Knot* (1961) was produced in England, the government withdrew
his passport for four years. In 1962, he supported an international
boycott against the South African practice of segregating theater
audiences, which led to further restrictions. Many of Fugard's
plays have subsequently been made into films. Fugard also acted
in the 1982 film *Gandhi*, the 1984 film *The Killing Fields*, about
the Khmer Rouge in Cambodia, and played a guest role as a mad
lighthouse keeper in *One Life to Live*. Athol Fugard now splits his
time between South Africa and living abroad.

   The Island (1973) addresses the boredom of life on Robben
Island, where stone breaking, collecting seaweed, and working
in the lime quarry were the main occupations of prisoners.
Fugard co-wrote the play with John Kani and Winston Ntshona,
former prisoners. When it first opened in Cape Town in 1973
and then in London, it was revolutionary because it gave a
symbolic voice to the many exiles whom the government had
isolated and imprisoned in an attempt to mute them. Unbe-
knownst to many outsiders, the prisoners organized shows for
each other, which included poems and short plays, to pass the
time. *The Island* centers on a two-man version of *Antigone*,
which the two prisoners—played by Kani and Ntshona—are
rehearsing. Creating theater allows them to roam in an imaginative
landscape since movement in their physical landscape was so
restricted. Fugard also reveals the toll of imprisonment through
a prisoner who has not been able to resist and has become an
automaton by his work breaking stone. Winston tells John in fear,
"He's forgotten himself. He's forgotten everything . . . why he's
here, where he comes from. That's happening to me John. I've
forgotten why I'm here."

The cell, later the same night. Both men are in bed. Winston is apparently asleep. John, however, is awake, rolling restlessly from side to side. He eventually gets up and goes quietly to the back for a drink of water, then back to his bed. He doesn't lie down however. Pulling the blanket around his shoulders he starts to think about the three months. He starts counting the days on the fingers of one hand. Behind him Winston sits up and watches him in silence for a few moments.

WINSTON [*with a strange smile*]. You're counting!

JOHN [*with a start*]. What! Hey, Winston, you gave me a fright, man. I thought you were asleep. What's the matter? Can't you sleep?

WINSTON [*ignoring the question, still smiling*]. You've started counting the days now.

JOHN [*unable to resist the temptation to talk, moving over to Winston's bed*]. Ja.

WINSTON. How many?

JOHN. Ninety-two.

WINSTON. You see!

JOHN. [*excited*]. Simple, man. Look . . . twenty days left in the month, thirty days in June, thirty-one in July, eleven days in August . . . ninety-two.

WINSTON [*still smiling, but watching John carefully*]. Tomorrow?

JOHN. Ninety-one.

WINSTON. And the next day?

JOHN. Ninety.

WINSTON. Then one day it will be eighty!

JOHN. *Ja!*

WINSTON. Then seventy.

JOHN. Hey, Winston, time doesn't pass so fast.

WINSTON. Then only sixty more days.

JOHN. That's just two months here on the Island.

WINSTON. Fifty . . . forty days in the quarry.

JOHN. Jesus, Winston!

WINSTON. Thirty.

JOHN. One month. Only one month to go.

WINSTON. Twenty . . . [*holding up his hands*] then ten . . . five, four, three, two . . . tomorrow!

[*The anticipation of that moment is too much for John.*]

JOHN. NO! Please, man, Winston. It hurts. Leave those three
    months alone. I'm going to sleep!
[*Back to his bed where he curls up in a tight ball and tries
    determinedly to sleep. Winston lies down again and stares up
    at the ceiling. After a pause he speaks quietly.*]
WINSTON. They won't keep you here for the full three months.
    Only two months. Then down to the jetty, into a ferry-boat . . .
    you'll say goodbye to this place . . . and straight to Verster
    Prison on the mainland.
[*Against his will John starts to listen. He eventually sits upright and
    completely surrenders himself to Winston's description of the last
    few days of his confinement.*]
Life will change for you there. It will be much easier. Because
    you won't take Hodoshe with you. He'll stay here with me, on
    the Island. They'll put you to work in the vineyards at Victor
    Verster, John. There are no quarries there. Eating grapes,
    oranges . . . they'll change your diet . . . Diet C, and exercises
    so you'll look good when they let you out finally. At night you'll
    play games . . . Ludo, draughts, snakes and ladders! Then one
    day they'll call you into the office, with a van waiting outside to
    take you back. The same five hundred miles. But this time
    they'll let you sit. You won't have to stand the whole way like
    you did coming here. And there won't be handcuffs. Maybe
    they'll even stop on the way so you can have a pee. Yes, I'm
    sure they will. You might even sleep over somewhere. Then
    finally Port Elizabeth. Rooihel Prison again, John! That's very
    near home, man. New Brighton is next door! Through your cell
    window you'll see people moving up and down in the street,
    hear the buses roaring. Then one night you won't sleep again,
    because you'll be counting. Not days, as you are doing now, but
    hours. And the next morning, that beautiful morning, John,
    they'll take you straight out of your cell to the Discharge Office
    where they'll give you a new khaki shirt, long khaki trousers,
    brown shoes. And your belongings! I almost forgot your
    belongings.
JOHN. Hey, by the way! I was wearing a white shirt, black tie, grey
    flannel trousers . . . brown Crockett shoes . . . socks? [*A little
    laugh*] I can't remember my socks! A check jacket . . . and my
    watch! I was wearing my watch!

WINSTON. They'll wrap them up in a parcel. You'll have it under your arm when they lead you to the gate. And outside, John, outside that gate, New Brighton will be waiting for you. Your mother, your father, Princess and the children . . . and when they open it . . .

[*Once again, but more violently this time, John breaks the mood as the anticipation of the moment of freedom becomes too much for him.*]

JOHN. Stop it, Winston! Leave those three months alone for Christ's sake. I want to sleep. [*He tries to get away from Winston, but the latter goes after him. Winston has now also abandoned his false smile.*]

WINSTON [*stopping John as he tries to crawl away*]. But it's not finished, John!

JOHN. Leave me alone!

WINSTON. It doesn't end there. Your people will take you home. Thirty-eight, Gratten Street, John! Remember it? Everybody will be waiting for you . . . aunts, uncles, friends, neighbours. They'll put you in a chair, John, like a king, give you anything you want . . . cakes, sweets, cool drinks . . . and then you'll start to talk. You'll tell them about this place, John, about Hodoshe, about the quarry, and about your good friend Winston who you left behind. But you still won't be happy, hey. Because you'll need a fuck. A really wild one!

JOHN. Stop it, Winston!

WINSTON [*relentless*]. And that is why at ten o'clock that night you'll slip out the back door and make your way to Sky's place. Imagine it, man! All the boys waiting for you . . . Georgie, Mangi, Vusumzi. They'll fill you up with booze. They'll look after you. They know what it's like inside. They'll fix you up with a woman . . .

JOHN. NO!

WINSTON. Set you up with her in a comfortable joint, and then leave you alone. You'll watch her, watch her take her clothes off, you'll take your pants off, get near her, feel her, feel it . . . Ja, you'll feel it. It will be wet . . .

JOHN. WINSTON!

WINSTON. Wet *poes*, John! And you'll fuck it wild!

[*John turns finally to face Winston. A long silence as the two men confront each other. John is appalled at what he sees.*]

JOHN. Winston? What's happening? Why are you punishing me?

WINSTON [*quietly*]. You stink, John. You stink of beer, of company, of *poes*, of freedom . . . Your freedom stinks, John, and it's driving me mad.

JOHN. No, Winston!

WINSTON. Yes! Don't deny it. Three months time, at this hour, you'll be wiping beer off your face, your hands on your balls, and *poes* waiting for you. You will laugh, you will drink, you will fuck and forget.

[*John's denials have no effect on Winston.*]

Stop bullshitting me! We've got no time left for that. There's only two months left between us. [*Pause.*] You know where I ended up this morning, John? In the quarry. Next to old Harry. Do you know old Harry, John?

JOHN. Yes.

WINSTON. Yes what? Speak, man!

JOHN. Old Harry, Cell Twenty-three, seventy years, serving Life!

WINSTON. That's not what I'm talking about. When you go to the quarry tomorrow, take a good look at old Harry. Look into his eyes, John. Look at his hands. They've changed him. They've turned him into stone. Watch him work with that chisel and hammer. Twenty perfect blocks of stone every day. Nobody else can do it like him. He loves stone. That's why they're nice to him. He's forgotten himself. He's forgotten everything . . . why he's here, where he comes from. That's happening to me John. I've forgotten why I'm here.

JOHN. No.

WINSTON. Why am I here?

JOHN. You put your head on the block for others.

WINSTON. Fuck the others.

JOHN. Don't say that! Remember our ideals . . .

WINSTON. Fuck our ideals . . .

JOHN. No Winston . . . our slogans, our children's freedom . . .

WINSTON. Fuck slogans, fuck politics . . . fuck everything, John. Why am I here? I'm jealous of your freedom, John. I also want to count. God also gave me ten fingers, but what do I count? My life? How do I count it, John? One . . . one . . . another day comes . . . one . . . Help me, John! . . . Another day . . . one . . . one . . . Help me, brother! . . . one . . .

[*John has sunk to the floor, helpless in the face of the other man's torment and pain. Winston almost seems to bend under the weight of the life stretching ahead of him on the Island. For a few seconds he lives in silence with his reality, then slowly straightens up. He turns and looks at John. When he speaks again, it is the voice of a man who has come to terms with his fate, massively compassionate.*]

Nyana we Sizwe!

[*John looks up at him.*]

Nyana we Sizwe . . . it's all over now. All over. [*He moves over to John.*] Forget me . . .

[*John attempts a last, limp denial.*]

No, John! Forget me . . . because I'm going to forget you. Yes, John, I will forget you. Others will come in here, John, count, go, and I'll forget them. Still more will come, count like you, go like you, and I will forget them. And then one day, it will all be over.

[*A lighting change suggests the passage of time. Winston collects together their props for Antigone.*]

Come. They're waiting.

JOHN. Do you know your words?

WINSTON. Yes. Come, we'll be late for the concert.

～ YVONNE VERA,
   Excerpt from *The Stone Virgins*—ZIMBABWE

Yvonne Vera was born in September 1964 in Bulawayo, in what was then Southern Rhodesia (now Zimbabwe), the year before the Unilateral Declaration of Independence was issued, which triggered a bitter civil war between the white minority government and fighters for independence. After completing her secondary schooling in Zimbabwe, Vera moved to Canada, where she enrolled at York University, Toronto, Canada. At York she gained a BA, a master of arts, and a doctorate, all in English literature. She is the author of many short stories and novels. Both *Nehanda* (1993) and *Without a Name* (1994) were short-listed for the Commonwealth Award in the Africa Region, and her work *Under the Tongue* was awarded this prestigious prize in 1997.

In this same year she was appointed director of the National Gallery of Zimbabwe in Bulawayo. Vera died from meningitis in 2005.

Yvonne Vera examines someone who has been hollowed out by struggling to survive the Zimbabwean Civil War in her novel *The Stone Virgins* (2002). The character Sibaso knows only life amidst war and writes, "During a war, we are lifeless beings. We are envoys, our lives intervals of despair." Sibaso is fascinated by dead spiders and eats them. He examines one spider, noting its "joints upon its legs are mere full stops, abbreviations for a death. Its outline is a parenthesis." Vera's choice of the words "outline" and "parenthesis" further suggest how war hollows out those who live through it, leaving behind shells.

His name is Sibaso, a flint to start a flame. Him. Sibaso. I follow him closely. My life depends on it. I follow the shape of his body. I follow his arms. He has killed Thenjiwe. He is in the midst of that death.

I listen, unsure of any of his words, what he means, what he needs, claims, pardons, affirms, but the rise of his voice could mean anything, and silence, an assertion of death.

"Is there anyone here besides yourself? Who else lives here? Do you expect someone? Are you with someone?"

He whispers in my ear, as though someone else will hear his deep secret and uncover his camouflage.

I dare not move. Is he asleep? Is he in an embrace of the past? He knows how to sleep in the midst of any reality, of several realities. He can inflict harm as easily as he can retrieve it. He has lived to tell many illicit versions of the war, to re-create the war. Here he is. Him.

"Spider legs," he insists. In my fear of him, I envy this kind of perfect truth, which sounds exactly like a well-constructed lie. While he closes his eyes, I have the sensation that I am drowning, and see a multitude of spider legs stretch into the darkness. "That is the other strange fact about spiders, their ability to walk on water while humans drown," he says.

Sibaso had eaten handfuls of spider legs throughout the war. He knew where spiders went to die. He knew their alcove of death. "Is this not a great secret to know?" he asks.

There is a tragic innocence that knows nothing but death, that survives on nothing but death.

. . .

My name is Sibaso. I have crossed many rivers with that name no longer on my lips, forgotten. It is an easy task to forget a name. Other names are assumed, temporary like grief; in a war, you discard names like old resemblances, like handkerchiefs torn, leave them behind like tributaries dried. During a war, we are lifeless beings. We are envoys, our lives intervals of despair. A part of you conceals itself, so that not everything is destroyed, only a part; the rest perishes like a cloud.

Independence, which took place only three years ago, has proved us a tenuous species, a continent that has succumbed to a violent wind, a country with land but no habitat. We are out of bounds in our own reality.

During a war, it is better to borrow a name, to lend an impulse to history. It is necessary to supply a motive to time, moment by moment, to offer a stimulus. Life has to be lived, even if not believed. A man must grow openly like a tree, with nothing between his cry and the elements. Instead, it is a war, and a man becomes a stalker, always a step behind some uncanny avenue of time, and he follows all its digression, its voyage into tragic places. He finds himself in dark places, unlit sites, dark and grim. A shadow when he walks, a shadow when he sleeps. His mind is perforated like a torn net and each event falls through it like a stone. When he stands, his head hits against something heavy—he discovers that history has its ceiling. He is surprised. He has to crouch, and his body soon assumes a defensive attitude; he possesses the desire to attack. If he loses an enemy, he invents another. This is his purge. He is almost clean. He seems to have a will, an idea that only he can execute. Of course, this idea involves desecration, the violation of kindness. It is a posture both individual and wasteful. He cannot escape. He is the embodiment of time.

There is a type of spider that turns to air, its life a mere gasp. This type of spider gathers all its kin before an earthquake, sending its messages through the air. Together, the spiders gather into a cubicle of time, a bowl in a peeling rock, a basin where the earth has been eaten by rain; this takes place before an earthquake, before the advance of an enemy, and war. Spider after spider piles into a mound, into a self-inflicted ruin, seeking another form of escape. Then the top of the spider mound is sealed with spit, thick and embroidered like lace, bright with sun rays, and rainbows arching like memories. A stillness gathers before an earthquake, before war. There is a stillness such as has not been witnessed before, and a new climate in that trapped air. Turning, again and again, till something is freed, like a kindness. A spider falls like a pendulum stilled. This is not hibernation for a death: the bodies take flight, free as time. The body vanishes, from inside out, the inside pouring like powdered dust, the legs a fossil. This is the end of creation, the beginning of war.

I have harvested handfuls of spider legs while they remained interlocking like promises, weightless, harmless needles. Time's shadow: life's residue. I blow life's remains off my hand like a prediction. On my hand is a dark melody, shapes that curl and twist into thin marks, like tiny words on a page, a hand written pamphlet, some spilled ink on an ancient rock. I wipe my palm clean. Our country needs this kind of hero who has a balm for his own wounds carried between lip and tongue, between thumb and forefinger, between the earth and the soles of his feet, who is in flight towards an immaculate truth.

I have seen a spider dancing with a wasp. This type of spider hangs from asbestos ceilings in every township home. Most men watch the motions of such a spider. Every survivor envies a spider dancing with a wasp.

∽ WANG MENG,
   Excerpt from *The Anecdotes of Section Chief Maimaiti*—CHINA

Wang Meng was born in 1934 in Beijing. As a high school student, he took an active part in the revolutionary movement led by the underground organization of the Chinese Communist Party, which he eventually joined in 1948. Soon after 1949, Meng began working at the headquarters of the Communist Youth League of China. In 1955 he published "The Young Newcomer in the Organization Department," a realistic portrayal of the clash between youthful, idealistic revolutionaries and older, entrenched party bureaucrats. He was labeled "rightist" in 1957, during the Great Leap Forward, in which China stepped up its industrial output to rival the greatest European producers. In 1958, the Chinese Communist Party combined agricultural collectives into gigantic communes, and millions of peasants and city workers were ordered to abandon their fields and factories in order to run primitive backyard furnaces. Meng was sent to labor for seven years on a farm in the Xinjiang Province, where he learned to speak, read, and write in Uighur; his excerpt addresses Uighur black humor. Within a couple of years, the Great Leap had proved an economic disaster, and it led to a massive famine from 1960 to 1962, during which time more than 20 million people died. In

1985, Meng became a member of the Central Committee Party, and later he was appointed culture minister. He resigned from this official post in 1989 because he refused to criticize the students and workers who protested for democracy at Tiananmen. He is now vice chairman of the Chinese Writers Association.

In *The Anecdotes of Section Chief Maimaiti* (1984), Wang Meng presents a sharp contrast between two twin brothers who were pummeled, thrashed, and forced to do grueling manual labor during the Great Proletariat Cultural Revolution in 1960s China. The toll of this violence visibly marks the body of Chief Saimaiti, who is hunched over, clutches a bottle of nitro-glycerin medicine and in whose pupils flickers "the gloomy reflection of a vanquished spirit." In contrast, his brother Chief Maimaiti is brimming with vigor, he smiles and "imparts a joy and mischievousness absent of guile." When asked how Maimaiti has emerged unscathed, he replies, "All it boils down to is that he's forever pulling a long face; as for me, there's not been one day pass by without my cracking a joke."

There are six necessities for the maintenance of life: air, sunlight, water, food, friendship, and a sense of humor. The exhaustion of tears leads to joy. A sense of humor is but the sense of superiority in wisdom.

I. Why Does Youth Spring Eternal for Section Chief Maimaiti?

On the warm and agreeable day of May 6, 1979, when the willows were still a fresh and delicate green, for the first time in over ten years I met with Section Chief Maimaiti and his twin brother at the Crossroads Muslim canteen in Arumqi, Sinkiang. I had a look at Maimaiti:

Although unfeeling Time has grooved ridges and troughs on his face,
A full head of black hair does his ever brimming vigor reveal.
His flushed shiny visage resembles a croissant just pulled from the oven;
Smiling to his heart's content, he imparts a joy and mischievousness
    absent of guile.

Now for a look at Saimaiti, his brother:

His rickets-afflicted spine's just like a quivering drawn bow,
The gloomy reflection of a vanquished spirit flashes in his dark pupils;

His unexplained sighs make one think he has the grippe,
He always clutches a medicine bottle with nitro-glycerin filled.

All sorts of feelings welled up in my heart as we exchanged salaams and sundry greetings. Whereupon I ventured a query: "Now during these past years, you've . . ."

SAIMAITI: I met with calamities.
MAIMAITI: I also met with calamities.
SAIMAITI: As soon as the events without historical precedent
    took place, I became a "black-ganger" and was locked up in a
    "cow shed."
MAIMAITI: I was also ferreted out and locked up in 1966.
SAIMAITI: I was pummeled.
MAIMAITI: I was thrashed.
SAIMAITI: I went up mountain paths lugging stones.
MAIMAITI: I went down mine shafts lugging coal.
SAIMAITI: After I was labeled a counterrevolutionary element my
    wife divorced me.
MAIMAITI: After I was labeled a "Three-Antis" element, my wife
    remarried and took our kids with her.

A schlemielish mess to have turned out this way! You could say that the two men's experiences were like eight ounces and half a pound, not varied at all. I couldn't help but ask in alarm. "Since you two's encounters were so similar as this, why does Maimaiti's youth spring eternal, yet Saimaiti's countenance droop so decrepitly?" Saimaiti slammed his fists down against his thighs and moaned and groaned, his eyes swimming with tears.

Maimaiti smiled slightly in reply. "All it boils down to is that he's forever pulling face; as for me, there's not been one day pass by without my cracking a joke."

V. Why Didn't Section Chief Maimaiti Shut the Door at Night?

In the ranks of the evil gang, Maimaiti was the one whose bed was next to the door. When other people closed the door, he'd always push it back open. People would then tell him that the class struggle was penetrating and complex, and that one couldn't say for sure whether there might be criminals, thieves, or robbers in the vicinity. Moreover, though their social position was that of an evil-ganger, most of them nevertheless wore wrist-watches and had money and ration tickets in their pockets. Because of this, while sleeping at night it would presumably be best to shut the door tightly and latch it securely.

Maimaiti took exception to this argument, saying, "Criminals, thieves, and robbers are people, but we are demons" (the Uighurs translate "cow ghosts and snake spirits" as "Satan" the arch-demon). "How could it be that people would not fear demons, while demons would fear people?"

When an overseer caught wind of Maimaiti's words, he called the Uighur in for an upbraiding.

OVERSEER: You've been spreading poisonous ideas!

MAIMAITI: I wouldn't dare!

OVERSEER: You aren't satisfied with your gang being labeled cow ghosts and snake spirits!

MAIMAITI: No, I'm satisfied; my heart's content.

OVERSEER: You're reactionary!

MAIMAITI: Therefore I'm a demon.

OVERSEER: You've always been reactionary!

MAIMAITI: I've always been a demon.

OVERSEER: Why are you so reactionary?

MAIMAITI (*Lowers his head and mumbles in a secretive and pitiable tone*): I fell under the influence of Liu Shaoqi.

OVERSEER: (*Suddenly breaks into a smile upon hearing Liu Shaoqi's name*): That's the way to make a clean breast of things! There's leniency for those who make frank confessions. By cleaning up your own problems, you can hasten the day when you return to the ranks of the People!

〰 ZAKES MDA,
Excerpt from *Ways of Dying*—SOUTH AFRICA

Zanemvula, or Zakes, Mda was born in the Eastern Cape in 1948 and spent his early childhood in Soweto. He finished his school education in Lesotho, where he had joined his father in exile. He is a writer, painter, composer, and film producer. His novels, including *Ways of Dying*, have won a number of awards, including the Commonwealth Writers' Prize for the Africa Region and the Zora Neale Hurston/ Richard Wright Legacy Award. Mda now divides his time between South Africa and the United States, working as a professor of creative writing at Ohio University, a beekeeper in the Eastern Cape, a dramaturge at the Market Theatre in Johannesburg, and a director of the Southern Africa Multimedia AIDS Trust in Sophiatown.

Mda touches on the theme of laughter in the midst of despair in his novel *Ways of Dying* (1995) as the characters cope with the prevalent violence and death in post-Apartheid South Africa. Toloki, a professional mourner, is in daily contact with death and grieving people. He shares some of these stories with his friend Noria, and the narrator sums up the value of laughter as he writes, "Laughter is known to heal even the deepest of wounds."

The stories of the past are painful. But when Toloki and Noria talk about them, they laugh. Laughter is known to heal even the deepest of wounds. Noria's laughter has the power to heal troubled souls. This afternoon, as the two of them sit in front of the shanty, exhausted from building last nights creation, and refreshing themselves with stories of the past and soured porridge, Toloki lavishly bathes his soul in her laughter.

"Well, Noria, I think I must go back to my headquarters now. My clients must be looking for me."

"How do they usually find you, Toloki?"

"Oh, at other funerals. Those who know where I live usually leave a message in my trolley."

"Toloki, you have helped me so much. I really don't know how to thank you enough."

"Your laughter is enough thanks for me, Noria."

"No, Toloki, it is not thanks enough. It would mean that we have not grown from the days when I gave pleasure, and was paid with favours. Remember, I am going to pay you back."

"I understand why it is important for you to pay me back, Noria. I do not object."

"Am I going to see you again, Toloki?"

"For surely you will, Noria. I'll visit you now and then, if you don't mind, that is."

"Of course not, I would like to see you again, silly."

They walk together to the taxi rank in the middle of the settlement. As usual, Toloki is the centre of attraction. Heads peer inquisitively from the small doors of shanties. Passers-by gawk at them.

"Why do you prefer to use taxis? Trains are cheaper."

"Indeed they are cheaper. But these days there is a lot of death in the trains."

Noria laughs. She agrees that people die everyday in the trains, but jokingly asks if Toloki is afraid to die, even though his daily work involves death. Toloki returns the laughter, and says that it is true that death is his constant companion, but where one can avoid one's own death, one must do so. He has a mission in the world, that of mourning for the dead. It is imperative that he does his utmost to stay alive, so that he can fulfill his sacred trust, and mourn for the dead.

"Fortunately my mourning for the dead makes it possible for me to avoid death by using alternative transport."

"It is a pity that the people who die everyday in the trains die because they want to earn a living for their children. They have no means of using alternative transport. Thank God some have survived, and live to tell the story."

She tells him the story of one of the residents of the settlement who escaped death by a hair's breadth only last week. He was waiting at the station when a group of men believed to be migrants from the hostels got off the train. As usual they were armed with sticks, and spears, and battle-axes, and homemade guns. He tried to board the train, but some of the men pulled him down onto the platform by his jacket. They demanded to know what ethnic group he belonged to. He told them, and it happened to be the same clan the men belonged to. They said that if he was a member of their ethnic group, then why was he not with them? Another one shouted, "This dog is lying! He does not belong to our people. He is of the southern people who are our enemies!"

A man wielding a knife rushed towards this resident of the settlement, and was about to stab him. But the resident escaped and ran along the platform shouting for help. He ran towards a group of security guards, whom he thought would come to his rescue. To his amazement, the security guards turned on their heels and fled. The resident jumped onto the railway line and hid under a train. He clung for dear life to the axles with both hands and feet, suspending his body between the railway sleepers and the bottom of the train floor.

The migrants jumped onto the railway line to look for him. They started shoving spears and pangas underneath the train. Fortunately he was protected by the train wheels, and the weapons could not reach him. After a while the migrants left, and the train driver came to his rescue. He told the terrified man to get into the driver's cabin, as some of the migrants were still milling about on the platform. The driver then drove the train to another station, where the resident realized for the first time that he had been stabbed in the eye.

"He is one-eyed now, but at least he is still alive."

"He was fortunate that the white man who drove the train saved him. Other people are not that fortunate."

Toloki tells her of another train incident, which also happened last week, where the victim was not as fortunate as this resident. A young man and his wife were in the train. She was holding their one-day-old baby. They had come from the hospital where the wife had just given birth the previous night. Three gangsters walked into the carriage and demanded that the woman give her baby to her husband and follow them. These were not migrants from hostels this time, but the very youths who live with us in the townships and in the settlements. The children we gave birth to, who have now turned against the community, and have established careers of rape and robbery.

The couple begged and pleaded. They explained that the woman had just given birth, and the baby was only a few hours old. But the gangsters showed no mercy. They insisted that the woman come with them. And she did. Not a single one of the other passengers lifted a finger to help. The next day, she was found dead in the veld. The gangsters had taken turns raping her, and had then slit her throat. Toloki knew her story because he had mourned at her funeral.

Toloki and Noria walk quietly until they reach the taxi rank. Her eyes are glassy with unshed tears.

"Mothers lose their babies, Toloki, and babies lose their mothers."

"Death lives with us everyday. Indeed our ways of dying are our ways of living. Or should I say our ways of living are our ways of dying?"

"It works both ways. Good-bye, Toloki."

"Good-bye, Noria."

"Just one more thing: please take a bath. Just because your profession involves death, it doesn't mean that you need to smell like a dead rat."

Toloki laughs good-naturedly, and promises that before he visits her again, he will take a shower at the beach. He boards the taxi with happy thoughts, and waves to Noria as it drives away.

∾ KAY BOYLE,
Excerpt from *Decision*—UNITED STATES

Born in St. Paul, Minnesota, in 1902, Kay Boyle grew up in
Cincinnati, Ohio. She studied architecture at Parson's School of
Fine and Applied Arts in New York and elsewhere, took courses at
Columbia, and studied violin briefly at the Cincinnati Conservatory
of Music. She married French-born engineer Richard Brault in 1922
while helping to edit the experimental literary magazine *Broom*.
She moved to France with her husband the following year, and
she lived mostly in France from 1923 to 1941, where she was well
known among the American expatriate community. She was a
journalist for the *New Yorker* in the 1940s, documenting the fall of
France. She was briefly imprisoned for protesting the Vietnam War
and founded the San Francisco chapter of Amnesty International
in the 1980s. Over the course of her life, Kay Boyle had three husbands and six children. She died in Mill Valley, California, in 1992.

Laughter functions as a subtle form of resistance and as a coping
mechanism for the characters in Kay Boyle's novella *Decision*
(1982). Señora García goes with her children to visit their father
and her husband, imprisoned during the Spanish Civil War of
1936–1939. They have traveled a great distance and scrounged up
food from their meager rations and through the black market.
They wait with steadily increasing anticipation only to discover
the inmates have gone on a hunger strike to protest their captors.
In response, the jailors decide to cancel the visitation for the day.
Señora García and the others stand dazed, unable to accept the
disappointing information. Finally, a butterfly distracts Señora
García's daughters, who begin laughing. Señora García finally joins
in, touching the locket around her neck, which holds a picture
of her husband's face: "her fingers clung to it as she stood there
laughing as if nothing as ludicrous as this had ever, in her lifetime,
taken place." It is as if she connects with her husband and his
protest through this gesture. In this moment she uses laughter to
downplay her disappointment to the guards and to re-establish
control.

The warm light breeze came through the open windows from the blazing
world without and lifted the tendrils of Señora García's hair at her temples

and her brow. She leaned forward from her seat to touch the children's pinafores and smooth their hair ribbons in her fingers, saying their names—"Manolita, Juanita"—like the notes of a stringed instrument plucked softly on the rushing air.

"Manolita, my Juanita," she said, her eyes admiring their dark locks, their delicate brows, and their pale creamy skins. "My little Juanita, my Manolita, my loves."

The bus was full, for as women of another country will press into a motion-picture theater of an afternoon, taking their children with them, so these women had crowded into their seats, some dressed as city women are, and some in bright colored skirts with artificial flowers in their hair. Infants vowed to pink or blue rode in their arms, and children slept on the seats beside them in the heat, but the women's faces were lifted, not in submission to a silver screen on which passed the shadows of a Bergman or a Cary Grant, but afternoon after hot afternoon, and month after month, their eyes were turned in patience to the current stage on which the drama of the prisoners might be played.

"Manolita had rheumatism all one year, so I took the vow then," Señora García said, and the bus went swiftly across the parched land. "I promised the Virgin that if she were cured, I would wear the Habit of Jesus until it fell to pieces and could no longer be worn. And that night, when I lit the candles, Manolita sat up in bed with no more pain, and she was cured." She leaned quickly forward in the swaying bus, and her gypsy-nimble fingers touched Manolita's ear. "Dirt in it," she said. "You can only see it in the sun." Sleep had begun to drift across the children's faces, weighting their lids so that the dark lashes hung heavily on them and drew them closed. "Our little Papa will be happy to see Juanita and Manolita," Señora García said, and now her hand moved to the locket that hung around her neck, and her sharp narrow thumb-nail pried the two laminae apart. "Here is Eleuterio," she said, and she tipped the locket on her breast so that I might see the tense small face, tight-lipped, tenacious as a fist, with the broad dome of the forehead overhanging it. Because of the height of brow, the eyes seemed placed in the exact middle of the skull, black, bead-like, intent, and yet they met one's own with a deep unbroken look of love. "Our Papa has only one arm, gone beneath the shoulder," Señora García said, and her nail showed the place in the locket where his right arm should be. "He lost it at Toledo. He was in the Republican army then," she said, and the silver bangles on her arm made light temporal music as she snapped the locket closed again.

Our bus was not the first to reach the gate of Carabanchel that after-noon. There were others drawn up, empty now, on the white road before the long, low adobe portico where the women waited with their children and their baskets in the shade. Over the tiled roof of the portico, the still unfinished portions of the prison could be seen—red brick walls, strong in color, standing in jagged malediction against the sky's deep violent blue. Señora García and I crossed the road, bearing the basket between us, and Manolita and Juanita came behind, the bags of oranges in their arms. We took our place in line behind the other women, and Manolita and Juanita moved forward step by patient step with us, asking no favor as children of another country might, voicing no word of protest against the man-dates of this world of adult incarceration and adult penalty.

"After we give our names," Señora García said, speaking as if in secret to me among the others, "it will be twenty minutes before the men come up from their cells and into the public reception place. They wait for the visitors there, the ones who have been called, behind a double ring of bars—like a bull ring," she said, telling this softly to me as if none of the others there must know. "The visitors are in the arena, and the men wait in the stalls. And although your man seems near to you beyond the bars, nearly close enough to touch, you have to shout your questions very loud to him above the sound of the other people's voices, or else he cannot hear." Her eyes were filling with pleasure again as the line advanced more quickly, and she turned and put her hand out to the little girls. "And I will ask him about Manuel at once," she whispered to me, "and if he says Man-uel was brought here with him, then we will ask them to let us see him. And if Eleuterio says he is not here, then Eleuterio will tell us where to go." *However it turns out, we will have played the trick on them*, she may have stopped herself from saying, and she put her dark thin beautiful face against my shoulder, laughing as wantonly as a gypsy who has just picked their pockets clean. "And whatever there is to do next, I will help you, I will go with you wherever it is," she said.

We were close to the wicket now, and her eyes were alive again with the strange dark look of delight. *In twenty minutes I shall see Eleuterio's face,* she kept herself from saying; *I shall hear his voice above the other voices.* She had come to the wicket, and she opened her identity paper out flat on the wood, and she ran her tongue along her lip as if her mouth were dry. And then we both turned and drew Manolita and Juanita close to the ledge, the bags of oranges in their arms, so that their faces might be seen as well.

"To see my husband, Eleuterio García," she said, and her voice and her hand did not tremble, but the blood had bleached from her nails as she held to the counter watching the guard behind the wickets scan the records for his name. And then, as the pen moved over the square of paper, writing the pass out, the blood ebbed darkly back under the small flakes of her nails again.

It was my turn now, and I stood before the wicket in a dress that was not mine, and I passed the papers that did not bear my name across the wood and under the wire to him, and the guard looked up into my face. Beyond, Señora García and the children waited with the others where the examination of the baskets took place. The mother had a comb in her fingers, and she did not turn her eyes to look at me, but she leaned over her two daughters, combing out their hair.

"I have brought some food to my cousin, Eleuterio García," I said to the man behind the wicket.

His face was a sad face, lonely-eyed, bony, long, and it hung between the heavy braid epaulettes like a horse's head in weariness between the shafts. It might have been he who was committed to solitary confinement in this cage, condemned by his own impotence, his own indecision, to the abjectness of being guard instead of prisoner, with the names he sought on record those of his jailers, and freer, more ruthless in their judgment of franchise than he. His blunt pencil was on the name of Eleuterio García still, and now he took the pen up, and wrote the second paper out.

At the end of the portico was the door, with another guard standing by it, and the visitors moved slowly toward it, one behind the other, and through it, their passes in their hands. Once I had followed them through, I faced with the others the wide dusty expanse, part vacant lot, part roadway, which lay the length of the prison wall. The parched earth that stretched away was rutted by cart wheels that had passed there in a wetter season, the deep troughs of them baked hard as sculpture now, wiped clean as asphalt of vegetation. Across this ground the narrow railway tracks ran from the strip of shade cast by the portico to the corner of the prison wall, and there passed through the open gateway and out of sight to a terminus that lay beyond. The coupled cars which had begun to roll slowly down the tracks were packed high with the baskets of bread and fruit, the hampers, the bundles which the visitors had loaded onto their double tiers.

"Manolita, Juanita, quick, quick, the oranges!" Señora García cried out, and we ran after the slowly moving miniature train. We lifted the basket up onto the last of the double-decked cars, and, still running, the children set the bags of oranges upright beside the basket, and then we paused a moment, watching the train go.

Before us, the women and children moved in scattered procession across the wasteland of heat and light, some walking singly, some hand in hand, following the way which the train took towards the gateway standing open in the prison wall. We began to walk now, and the children followed us, over the dust, in the direction in which the others walked. And beside us, over the prison wall, were the new buildings taking shape, the new facades reaching upwards toward completion under the blue candescent sky. Brick by brick, and with trowelful after trowelful of slapped wet cement, were the prisoners erecting their own sepulchers, as if sealing themselves alive within them as they worked.

"It is going to be seven times larger than its present size," Señora García said. "Eleuterio worked two years on it, he and Manuel and Alfonso together. That is the work political prisoners do."

We passed through the open gateway, as the others did, moved with a stream of people to the door of the building on the right, showed our passes to the third guard stationed there, and entered the bare low-ceilinged crowded room. And here Señora García turned quickly to the children.

"Let me see your hair, let me fix your ribbons, Manolita," she said. "We'll see Papa in a minute." She took a handkerchief from the pocket of her purple cassock dress, and wet the corner of it with her tongue. "Come to me, Juanita; dirt all around your mouth," she said. And she took the comb out in her narrow nimble fingers again, and drew it through their hair.

The heat lay like a blanket on the people crowded in the room; you could not get from under it, you could not cast it away. *In fifteen minutes,* the voices said, and the soiled colored handkerchiefs were lifted to wipe the sweat from necks and brows, and the mouths were smiling; *in fifteen minutes the door will open.* The low wide room was drained by a corridor at one end, and the double doors at the end of that corridor would be flung open when the time had come, and the women carrying their infants in their arms, and with their children at their skirts, moved down the bottleneck in hope. *In fifteen minutes, only fifteen minutes,* said Señora García's bright lively eyes.

It could not be said when the other whisper began to run from mouth to mouth, from ear to ear in the crowded room, but from instant to instant the sound of it ran faster, louder, and the heads turned uneasily on the shoulders, and the look in the faces altered as the whispered words came clear. *Hunger,* the telegraphic message went; *the political prisoners are on strike. On hunger strike.* And the women lifted their infants higher on their shoulders, and looked into one another's eyes.

"Our men are on strike," said a woman close to me in the press of the room. "Our men are on strike," said the other voices.

The political prisoners are on hunger strike, the words rang louder, clearer. *They are to be punished. There will be no visitors allowed today.*

"But perhaps some of them will be allowed to come up!" said Señora García, rejecting the unconditional terms of it. "Perhaps not all of them will be punished!" But a small white bloodless ring of pain or fear was cast around her mouth.

And now the women with their children pressed forward down the corridor, as those who are left above will press to the entrance of a mine, hearing the far deep muffled detonations of disaster. Whatever time was, or had been once, or whatever its customary demands might be, there was no recognition of it left as they moved forward to the brink, asking mutely that word be given of the men trapped below. It might have been an hour that passed, or two or three, in which only one infant roused from sleep and cried in hunger for a little while. *Ah, hunger, hunger,* said the disembodied voices, sounding the note of mourning now. *Our men are on hunger strike! We have brought food to them, food scraped out of a week's or two weeks' ration, bartered for on the black market, a trainload of food, and they cannot open their mouths and eat!*

They could not have seen the guard step from the blazing sunlight of the courtyard into the room, for their backs were turned to him, but a ripple of cognizance ran through the waiting women when he came. They turned their faces, dry-eyed and drawn and weary in the heat, to where he stood dwarfed and puny on the threshold, reaching up on his toes to see across their heads.

"The visitors!" he called out to the packed sweltering room. "The visitors will leave the hall and go out through the gate by which they entered! They will surrender their passes to the guard outside! All visits have been cancelled for today!"

"All visits, all?" said Señora García, refusing it still. She had made her way near to him, drawing the children behind her.

"All. There are no exceptions being made," he said, and he took off his official hat and mopped his streaming brow.

And patiently the women turned, and in patience took this other direction, moving submissively out into the brilliant day again. They stood there, their eyes dazzled for a moment as are the eyes of women who have stepped in stupor from a motion-picture theater, and they looked about for the train of food.

"Where are we going?" Juanita cried out in sudden distress.

"We must get the basket and the oranges," Señora García said.

"We must take the food back with us. We cannot leave it here." *The prisoners are on hunger strike,* went the whisper along the walls and through the dust, but the women's mouths were silent. "When Manuel was at Alcala, his wife hardly ate, all those years she hardly ate," said Señora García scarcely aloud, and now something which could not be precisely named had begun shaking like the cold in her flesh. "She brought everything to him," she said, "three times a week, in the afternoons like this—*And hunger, hunger, hunger,* repeated the hot dry wind as it blew through the women's hair.

We were standing on the outskirts of the crowd, a little apart from the others, when the butterfly came towards us down the current of the air. It was not a large butterfly, but one with pure white wings, and it fluttered forward and alighted on Manolita's hand. It trembled there for a moment before beginning its promenade from Manolita's wrist up to her elbow, its wings upright and quivering variably, like the sails of a sloop tacking to the breeze. And then its clinging feet advanced up Manolita's small bare arm, the face quite visible, twisted and venomous as an old man's face, the legs arching like a circus pony's as it climbed. When the minutely feathered feet entered the hollow of Manolita's arm, she began to laugh with pleasure in her smooth pale cheeks. And Juanita too burst with laughter, and Señora García touched the locket, which hung around her neck, and her fingers clung to it as she stood there laughing as if nothing as ludicrous as this had ever, in her lifetime, taken place.

 IMRE KERTÉSZ,
 Excerpt from *Fatelessness*—HUNGARY

Imre Kertész was born in Budapest in 1929 into a Jewish family. At the age of fifteen, he was deported to the Auschwitz-Birkenau concentration camp and then transferred to Buchenwald, from which he was liberated in 1945. After the war, Kertész returned to Hungary and worked initially as a journalist and translator. Barred from a journalistic career in the early 1950s by the

Communist regime, he earned his living translating German writers into Hungarian. In 1975, he published *Fatelessness,* based on his experiences in Auschwitz and Buchenwald. The Swedish Nobel committee cited this specific text in their press release for his award in 2002: "The reader is confronted not only with the cruelty of atrocities but just as much with the thoughtlessness that characterised their execution. Both perpetrators and victims were preoccupied with insistent practical problems, the major questions did not exist. Kertész's message is that *to live is to conform.*" Kertész published *Fiasco* in 1988 and *Kaddish for a Child Not Born* in 1990, viewed as the second and third texts in the trilogy that *Fatelessness* began.

In the novel *Fatelessness* (1975), here translated by Tim Wilkinson, the narrator remembers how he and others coped with the incredible boredom of life in the concentration camps in Germany. In his Nobel speech, Kertész discussed his narrator: "Instead of a spectacular series of great and tragic moments, he has to live through everything which is oppressive and offers little variety, like life itself."

Since I was really starting to feel my leg by the time I got to the station, and since, among the many streetcars there, one with the number I knew from the old days just happened to be swinging in ahead of me, I got on. On the open platform of the streetcar, a gaunt old woman with a queer, old-fashioned lace trimming on her dress edged away a bit to the side. Soon a man in cap and uniform came along and asked me to show my ticket. I told him I didn't have one. He suggested I buy one, so I said I had just got back from abroad and didn't have any money. He inspected my jacket, me, then the old woman as well, before informing me that there were travel regulations, they weren't his rules but had been brought in by his superiors. "If you don't buy a ticket, you'll have to get off," he declared. I told him my leg was hurting, at which, I couldn't help noticing, the old woman abruptly turned away to face the outside scene, yet somehow, I had no idea why, with such an affronted air it was as if I had insulted her personally. However, at that moment, with a commotion already audible from some way off, a burly man with dark, matted hair burst through the doorway from the inside compartment. He was in an open-necked shirt and light linen suit, with a black box slung from a strap on his shoulder and an attaché case in his hand. "What's all this?" he was shouting, and then ordered, "Give him a ticket!" handing, or rather thrust-ing, a coin at the conductor. I tried to thank him but he cut me off and, casting a furious look around, said, "More to the point, some people ought to be ashamed of themselves," but the conductor was by then passing into the carriage while the old woman carried on gazing out into the street. His face calmer, he then turned toward me. "Have you come from Ger-many, son?" "Yes." "From the concentration camps?" "Naturally." "Which one?" "Buchenwald." Yes, he had heard of it; he knew it was "one of the pits of the Nazi hell," as he put it. "Where did they carry you off from?" "From Budapest." "How long were you there?" "A year in total." "You must have seen a lot, young fellow, a lot of terrible things," he rejoined, but I said nothing. "Still," he continued, "the main thing is that it's over, in the past," and, his face brightening, he gestured to the houses that we hap-pened to be rumbling past and inquired what I was feeling now, back home again and seeing the city that I had left. "Hatred," I told him. He fell silent at that but soon volunteered that, sadly, he had to understand why I felt that way. In any case, "under the circumstances," he reckoned, hatred too had its place, its role, "even its uses," adding that he supposed we could agree on that, and he was well aware whom I must hate. "Every-one," I told him. He fell silent, this time for a longer period, before start-ing up again: "Did you have to endure many horrors?" to which I replied that it all depended what he considered to be a horror. No doubt, he de-clared, his expression now somewhat uneasy, I had undergone a lot of deprivation, hunger, and more than likely they had beaten me, to which I said, "Naturally." "Why, my dear boy," he exclaimed, though now, so it seemed to me, on the verge of losing his patience, "do you keep on say-ing 'naturally,' and always about things that are not at all natural?" I told him that in a concentration camp they *were* natural. "Yes, of course, of course," he says, "they were *there,* but . . . ," and he broke off, hesitating slightly, "but . . . I mean, a concentration camp in itself is *unnatural,*" finally hitting on the right word as it were. I didn't even bother saying any-thing to this, as I was beginning slowly to realize that it seems there are some things you just can't argue about with strangers, the ignorant, with those who, in a certain sense, are mere children so to say. In any case, suddenly becoming aware that we had reached the square, still standing there, only a bit bleaker and less well tended, and that this was where I needed to get off, I told him as much. He stuck with me, however, and, pointing across to a shaded bench that had lost its backboard, suggested we sit down for a minute.

He seemed somewhat uncertain at first. The truth was, he remarked, only now were the "horrors really starting to come to light," and he added that "for the time being, the world stands uncomprehending before the question of how, how it could have happened at all." I said nothing, but at this point he turned around to face me fully and suddenly asked, "Would you care to give an account of your experiences, young fellow?" I was somewhat dumbfounded, and replied that there was not a whole lot I could tell him that would be of much interest. He smiled a little and said, "Not me—the whole world." Even more amazed, I asked, "But what about?" "The hell of the camps," he replied, to which I remarked that I had nothing at all to say about that as I was not acquainted with hell and couldn't even imagine what that was like. He assured me, however, that it was just a manner of speaking: "Can we imagine a concentration camp as anything but a hell?" he asked, and I replied, as I scratched a few circles with my heel in the dust under my feet, that everyone could think what they liked about it, but as far as I was concerned I could only imagine a concentration camp, since I was somewhat acquainted with what that was, but not hell. "All the same, say you could?" he pressed, and after a few more circles I replied, "Then I would imagine it as a place where it is impossible to become bored," seeing as how that had been possible in the concentration camp, even in Auschwitz—under certain conditions of course. He fell silent for a while before going on to ask, though rather as if it were now somehow against his better judgment: "And how do you account for that?" After brief reflection, I came up with "Time." "What do you mean, time?" "Time helps." "Helps? . . . With what?" "Everything," and I tried to explain how different it was, for example, to arrive in a not exactly opulent but still, on the whole, agreeable, neat, and clean station where everything becomes clear only gradually, sequentially over time, step-by-step. By the time one has passed a given step, put it behind one, the next one is already there. By the time one knows everything, one has already understood it all. And while one is coming to understand everything, a person does not remain idle: he is already attending to his new business, living, acting, moving, carrying out each new demand at each new stage. Were it not for that sequencing in time, and were the entire knowledge to crash in upon a person on the spot, at one fell swoop, it might well be that neither one's brain nor one's heart would cope with it. I tried to enlighten him somewhat, upon which, having meanwhile fished a tattered pack from his pocket, he offered me one of his crumpled cigarettes, which I declined, but then, having taken two deep drags, he set both elbows on his knees and leaned his upper body forward, not so much as looking at me, as he said in a somehow lackluster, flat tone, "I see." "On the other hand," I continued, "the flaw in that, the drawback you might say, is that the time has to be occupied somehow." For instance, I told him I had seen prisoners who had already been—or to be more accurate were still—in concentration camps for four, six, even twelve years. Now, those people somehow had to fill each one of those four, six, twelve years, which in the latter case means twelve times three hundred and sixty-five days, which is to say twelve times three hundred and sixty-five times twenty-four hours, and twelve times three hundred and sixty-five times twenty-four times . . . and so on back, every second, every minute, every hour, every day of it, in its entirety. From yet another angle though, I added, this is exactly what can also help them, because if the whole twelve times three hundred and sixty-five times twenty-four times sixty times sixty-fold chunk of time had been dumped around their necks instantaneously, at a stroke, most likely they too would have been unable to stand it, either physically or mentally, in the way they actually did manage to stand it: That, roughly, is the way you have imagined it." At this, still in the same position as earlier, only now instead of holding the cigarette, which he had meanwhile discarded, with his head between his hands and in an even duller, even more choking voice, he said: "No it's impossible to imagine it." For my part, I could see that, and I even thought to myself: "So, that must be why they prefer to talk about hell instead."

Soon after that, though, he straightened up, looked at his watch, and his expression changed. He informed me that he was a journalist, "for a democratic paper" moreover, as he added, and it was only at this point that it came to me which figure from the remote past, from this and that he had said, he reminded me of: Uncle Willie—albeit, I conceded, with about as much difference and indeed, I would say, authoritativeness as I could detect in, let's say, the rabbi's words and especially his actions, his degree of obstinacy, were I to compare them with those of Uncle Lajos. That thought suddenly reminded me, made me conscious, really for the first time in fact, of the no doubt shortly impending reunion, so I did not listen too closely to what the journalist said after that. He would like, he said, to turn our chance encounter into a "stroke of luck," proposing that we write an article, set the ball rolling on a "series of articles." He would write the articles, but basing them exclusively on my own words. That would allow me to make some money, the value of which I would no doubt appreciate at the threshold of my "new life"—"not that I can offer

very much," he added with a somewhat apologetic smile, since the paper
was a new title and "its financial resources are as yet meager." But anyway,
the most important aspect right now, he considered, was not that so much
as "the healing of still-bleeding wounds and punishment of the guilty."
First and foremost, however, "public opinion has to be mobilized" and
"apathy, indifference, even doubts" dissipated. Platitudes were of no use
at all here; what was needed, according to him, was an uncovering of the
causes, the truth, however "painful the ordeal" of facing up to it. He dis-
cerned "much originality" in my words, all in all a manifestation of the
age, some sort of "sad symbol" of the times, if I understood him properly,
which was "a new, individual color in the tiresome flood of brute facts,"
as he put it, after which he asked what I thought of that. I noted that before all else I needed to attend to my own affairs, but he must have misunderstood me, it seems, because he said, "No, this is no longer just your
own affair. It's all of ours, the world's." So I said, yes, that might well be,
but now it was high time for me to get back home, at which he asked
me to "excuse" him. We got to our feet, but he was evidently still hesitating, weighing something up. Might we not launch the articles, he wondered, with a picture of the moment of reunion? I said nothing, at which,
with a little half smile, he remarked that "a journalist's craft sometimes
forces one to be tactless," but if that was not to my liking, then he, for his
part, had no wish "to push" the matter. He then sat down, opened a black
notebook on his knee, speedily wrote something down, then tore the page
out and, again rising to his feet, handed it to me. His name and the address
of the editorial office were on it; after he had said farewell with a "hoping
to see you soon," I felt the cordial grip of his hot, fleshy, slightly sweaty
palm. I too had found the conversation pleasant and relaxing, the man
likable and well meaning. Waiting only until his figure had disappeared
into the swarm of passersby, I tossed the slip of paper away.

A few steps later I recognized our house. It was still there, intact, trim
as ever. I was welcomed by the old smell in the entrance hall, the decrepit
elevator in its grilled shaft and the old, yellow-worn stairs, and farther
up the stairwell I was also able to greet the landing that was memorable
for a certain singular, intimate moment. On reaching the second floor, I
rang the bell at our door. It soon opened, but only as far as an inner lock,
the chain of one of those safety bolts, allowed, which slightly surprised
me as I had no recollection of any such device from before. The face peer-
ing at me from the chink in the door, the yellow, bony face of a roughly
middle-aged woman, was also new to me. She asked who I was looking

for, and I told her this was where I lived. "No," she said, "*we* live here," and would have shut the door at that, except that my foot was preventing her. I tried explaining that there must be a mistake, because this was where I had gone away from, and it was quite certain that we lived there, whereas she assured me, with an amiable, polite, but regretful shaking of the head, that it was me who was mistaken, since there was no question that this was where they lived, meanwhile striving to shut—and I to stop her from shutting—the door. During a moment when I looked up at the number to check whether I might possibly have confused the door, I must have released my foot, so her effort prevailed, and I heard the key being turned twice in the lock of the slammed door.

On my way back to the stairwell, a familiar door brought me to a stop. I rang, and before long a stout matronly figure came into view. She too, in a manner I was now getting accustomed to, was just about to close the door when from behind her back there was a glint of spectacles, and Uncle Fleischmann's gray face emerged dimly in the gloom. A paunch, slippers, a big, ruddy head, a boyish hair-parting, and a burned out cigar stub separated themselves from beside him: old Steiner. Just the way I had last seen them, as if it were only yesterday, on the evening before the customs post. They stood there, mouths agape, then called out my name, and old Steiner even embraced me just as I was, sweaty, in my cap and striped jacket. They led me into the living room, while Aunt Fleischmann hurried off into the kitchen to see about "a bite to eat," as she put it. I had to answer the usual questions as to where, how, when, and what, then later I asked my questions and learned that other people really were now living in our apartment. "What else?" I inquired. Since they somehow didn't seem to get what I meant, I asked "My father?" At that they clammed up completely. After a short pause, a hand—maybe Uncle Steiner's, I suppose—slowly lifted and set off in the air before settling like a cautious, aging bat on my arm. From what they recounted after that, all I could make out, in essence, was that "unfortunately, there is no room for us to doubt the accuracy of the tragic news" since "it is based on the testimony of comrades of misfortune," according to whom my father "passed away after a brief period of suffering . . . in a German camp," which was actually located on Austrian soil, oh what's the name of it, dear me . . . , so I said "Mauthausen"—"Mauthausen!" they enthused, before recovering their gravity; "Yes, that's it." I then asked if they happened by any chance to have news of my mother, to which they immediately said but of course, and good news at that: she was alive and well, she had come by the house only a couple of months ago, they had seen her with their own eyes, spoken to her, she had asked after me. What about my stepmother, I was curious to know, and I was told: "She has remarried since, to be sure." "To whom, I wonder?" I inquired, and they again became stuck on the name. One of them said "Some Kovács fellow, as best I know," while the other contradicted: "No, not Kovács, more like Futó." So I said "Sütő," at which they again nodded delightedly, affirming just as before: "Yes, of course, that's it: Sütő." I had much to thank her for, "everything, as a matter of fact," they went on to relate: she had "saved the family fortune," she "hid it during the hard times," was how they put it. "Perhaps," mused Uncle Fleischmann, "she jumped the gun a little," and old Steiner concurred in this. "In the final analysis, though," he added, "it's understandable," and that in turn was acknowledged by the other old boy.

After that, I sat between the two of them for a while, it having been a long time since I had sat on a comfortable settee with claret red velvet upholstery. Aunt Fleischmann appeared in the meantime, bringing in a decoratively bordered white china plate on which was a round of bread and dripping garnished with ground paprika and finely sliced onion rings, because her recollection was that I had been extremely fond of that in the past, as I promptly confirmed I still was. The two men meanwhile recounted that "it wasn't a picnic back here either, to be sure." From what they related I gained an impression, the nebulous outlines of some tangled, confused, undecipherable event of which I could basically see and understand little. Instead, all I picked out from what they had to say was the continual, almost tiresomely recurrent reiteration of a phrase that was used to designate every new twist, turn, and episode: thus, for instance, the yellow-star houses "came about," October the fifteenth "came about," the Arrow-Cross regime "came about," the ghetto "came about," the Danube-bank shootings "came about," liberation "came about." Not to mention the usual fault: it was as if this entire blurred event, seemingly unimaginable in its reality and by now beyond reconstruction in its details even for them, as far as I could see, had not occurred in the regular rhythmic passage of seconds, minutes, hours, days, weeks, and months but so to say all at once, in a single swirl or giddy spell somehow, maybe at some strange afternoon gathering that unexpectedly descends into debauchery, for instance, when the many participants—not knowing why—all of a sudden lose their sanity and in the end, perhaps, are no longer aware of what they are doing. At some point they fell silent, then, after a pause, old Fleischmann suddenly asked: "And what are your plans for the future?" I was mildly astonished, telling him I had not given it much thought. At that, the other old boy stirred, bending toward me on his seat. The bat soared again, this time alighting on my knee rather than my arm. "Before all else," he declared, "you must put the horrors behind you." Increasingly amazed, I asked, "Why should I?" "In order," he replied, "to be able to live," at which Uncle Fleischmann nodded and added, "Live freely," at which the other old boy nodded and added, "One cannot start a new life under such a burden," and I had to admit he did have a point. Except that I didn't quite understand how they could wish for something that was impossible, and indeed I made the comment that what had happened had happened, and anyway, when it came down to it, I could not give orders to my memory. I would only be able to start a new life, I ventured, if I were to be reborn or if some affliction, disease, or something of the sort were to affect my mind, which surely they didn't wish on me, I hoped. "In any case," I added, "I didn't notice any atrocities," at which, I could see, they were greatly astounded. What were they supposed to understand by that, they wished to know, by "I didn't notice"? To that, however, I asked them in turn what they had done during those "hard times." "Errm, . . . we lived," one of them deliberated. "We tried to survive," the other added. Precisely! They too had taken one step at a time, I noted. What did I mean by taking a "step," they floundered, so I related to them how it had gone in Auschwitz, by way of example. For each train—and I am not saying it was always necessarily this number, since I have no way of knowing—but at any rate in our case you have to reckon on around three thousand people. Take the men among them—a thousand, let's say. For the sake of the example, you can reckon on one or two seconds per case, more often one than two. Ignore the very first and very last, because they don't count; but in the middle, where I too was standing, you would therefore have to allow ten to twenty minutes before you reach the point where it is decided whether it will be gas immediately or a reprieve for the time being. Now, all this time the queue is constantly moving, progressing, and everyone is taking steps, bigger or smaller ones, depending on what the speed of the operation demands.

A brief hush ensued, broken only by a single sound: Aunt Fleischmann took the empty dish from in front of me and carried it away; nor did I see her return subsequently. The two old boys asked, "What has that got to do with it, and what do you mean by it?" Nothing in particular, I replied, but it was not quite true that the thing "came about"; we had gone along with it too. Only now, and thus after the event, looking back, in hindsight, does the way it all "came about" seem over, finished, unalterable, finite, so tremendously fast, and so terribly opaque. And if, in addition, one knows one's fate in advance, of course. Then indeed one can only register the passing of time. A senseless kiss, for example, is just as much a necessity as an idle day at the customs post, let's say, or the gas chambers. Except that whether one looks back or ahead, both are flawed perspectives, I suggested. After all, there are times when twenty minutes, in and of themselves, can be quite a lot of time. Each minute had started, endured, and then ended before the next one started. Now, I said, let's just consider: every one of those minutes might in fact have brought something new. In reality it didn't, naturally, but still, one must acknowledge that it might have; when it comes down to it, each and every minute something else might have happened other than what actually did happen, at Auschwitz just as much as, let's suppose, here at home, when we took leave of my father.

Those last words somehow roused old Steiner. "But what could we do?" he asked, his face part irate, part affronted. "Nothing, naturally," I said. "Or rather, anything," I added, "which would have been just as senseless as doing nothing, yet again and just as naturally." "But it's not about that," I tried to carry on, to explain it to them. "So what is it about, then?" they asked, almost losing patience, to which I replied, with growing anger on my part as well, I sensed: "It's all about the steps." Everyone took steps as long as he was able to take a step; I too took my own steps, and not just in the queue at Birkenau, but even before that, here, at home. I took steps with my father, and I took steps with my mother, I took steps with Annamarie, and I took steps—perhaps the most difficult ones of all—with the older sister. I would now be able to tell her what it means to be "Jewish": nothing, nothing to me at least, at the beginning, until those steps start to be taken. None of it is true, there is no different blood, nothing else, only . . . and I faltered, but suddenly something the journalist had said came to mind: there are only given situations and the new givens inherent in them. I too had lived through a given fate. It had not been my own fate, but I had lived through it, and I simply couldn't understand why they couldn't get it into their heads that I now needed to start doing something with that fate, needed to connect it to somewhere or something; after all, I could no longer be satisfied with the notion that it had all been a mistake, blind fortune, some kind of blunder, let alone that it had not even happened. I could see, and only too well, that they did not really understand, that my words were not much to their liking, indeed it seemed as if one thing or another was actually irritating them. I saw that every now and then Uncle Steiner was about to interrupt or elsewhere about to jump to his feet, but I saw the other old man restraining him, heard him saying, "Leave him be! Can't you see he only wants to talk? Let him talk! Just leave him be!" and talk I did, albeit possibly to no avail and even a little incoherently. Even so, I made it clear to them that we can never start a new life, only ever carry on the old one. I took the steps, no one else, and I declared that I had been true to my given fate through-out. The sole blot, or one might say fly in the ointment, the sole accident with which they might reproach me was the fact that we should be sit-ting there talking now—but then I couldn't help that. Did they want this whole honesty and all the previous steps I had taken to lose all mean-ing? Why this sudden about-face, this refusal to accept? Why did they not wish to acknowledge that if there is such a thing as fate, then free-dom is not possible? If, on the other hand—I swept on, more and more astonished myself, steadily warming to the task—if there is such a thing as freedom, then there is no fate; that is to say—and I paused, but only long enough to catch my breath—that is to say, then we ourselves are fate, I realized all at once, but with a flash of clarity I had never experienced before. I was even a little sorry I was only facing them and not some more intelligent or, if I may put it this way, worthier counterparts; but then they were the ones there right now, they are—or so it appeared at that moment at least—everywhere, and in any case they had also been there when we had said farewell to my father. They too had taken their own steps. They too had known, foreseen, everything beforehand, they too had said farewell to my father as if we had already buried him, and even later on all they had squabbled about was whether I should take the sub-urban train or the bus to Auschwitz. At this point not only Uncle Steiner but old Fleischmann as well jumped to his feet. Even now he was still striving to restrain himself, but was no longer capable of doing so: "What!" he bawled, his face red as a beetroot and beating his chest with his fist: "So it's us who're the guilty ones, is it? Us, the victims!" I tried explaining that it wasn't a crime; all that was needed was to admit it, meekly, sim-ply, merely as a matter of reason, a point of honor, if I might put it that way. It was impossible, they must try and understand, impossible to take everything away from me, impossible for me to be neither winner nor loser, for me not to be right and for me not to be mistaken that I was nei-ther the cause nor the effect of anything; they should try to see, I almost pleaded, that I could not swallow that idiotic bitterness, that I should merely be innocent. But I could see they did not wish to understand any-thing, and so, picking up my kit bag and cap, I departed in the midst of a few disjointed words and motions, one more unfinished gesture and incomplete utterance from each.

Down below I was greeted by the street. I needed to take a streetcar to my mother's place, but now it dawned on me that I had no money, of course, so I decided to walk. In order to gather my strength, I paused for a minute in the square, by the aforementioned bench. Over ahead, in the direction that I would need to take, where the street appeared to lengthen, expand, and fade away into infinity, the fleecy clouds over the indigo hills were already turning purple and the sky, a shade of claret. Around me it was as if something had changed: the traffic had dwindled, people's steps had slowed, their voices become quieter, their features grown softer, and it was as if their faces were turning toward one another. It was that peculiar hour, I recognized even now, even here—my favorite hour in the camp, and I was seized by a sharp, painful, futile longing for it: nostalgia, home-sickness. Suddenly, it sprang to life, it was all here and bubbling inside me, all its strange moods surprised me, its fragmentary memories set me trem-bling. Yes, in a certain sense, life there had been clearer and simpler. Every-thing came back to mind, and I considered everyone in turn, both those who were of no interest as well as those whose only recognition would come in this reckoning, the fact that I was here: Bandi Citrom, Pyetchka, Bohoosh, the doctor, and all the rest. Now, for the very first time, I thought about them with a touch of reproach, a kind of affectionate rancor.

But one shouldn't exaggerate, as this is precisely the crux of it: I am here, and I am well aware that I shall accept my rationale as the price for being able to live. Yes, as I looked around this placid, twilit square, this street, weather-beaten yet full of a thousand promises, I was already feel-ing a growing and accumulating readiness to continue my uncontinuable life. My mother was waiting, and would no doubt greatly rejoice over me. I recollect that she had once conceived a plan that I should be an engi-neer, a doctor, or something like that. No doubt that is how it will be, just as she wished; there is nothing impossible that we do not live through nat-urally, and keeping a watch on me on my journey, like some inescapable trap, I already know there will be happiness. For even there, next to the chimneys, in the intervals between the torments, there was something that resembled happiness. Everyone asks only about the hardships and the "atrocities," whereas for me perhaps it is that experience which will remain the most memorable. Yes, the next time I am asked, I ought to speak about that, the happiness of the concentration camps.

If indeed I am asked. And provided I myself don't forget.

FOUR

WRITING THE UNSPEAKABLE AND THE PRESSURE OF EMPTINESS

This chapter considers violence's emptying effect—the unfathomable civilian toll and voids in the landscape carved out by mass violence. Many writers express this sense of a collective societal *phantom limb syndrome* as they attempt to delineate and record the absences created by the calamities of the twentieth and twenty-first centuries. The Deportation Memorial outside the Grunewald station in Berlin, where trains deporting Jews left for Auschwitz, makes this absence concrete. Designed by the Polish artist Karol Broniatowski, this memorial consists of a long wall of concrete with the negative imprints of human bodies—their silhouettes—moving toward the station. It is the surrounding concrete that makes these nonexistent individuals visible. Nikolay Palchikoff, a Russian who grew up in Japan and served in the American army in Japan, provides another example of this phenomenon as he describes a scene in Hiroshima: "Although I had seen wartime atrocities, I wasn't prepared for what I saw: nothing . . . Outlines of human bodies burned like negatives in cement" (*New York Times*, August 6, 2001).

The Deportation Memorial "has its analogue in literature," as Ernestine Schlant writes in "The Language of Silence: West German Literature and the Holocaust," like Palchikoff's description of the legacy of wartime atrocities in Japan. Like the concrete of the Deportation Memorial or the human outlines in Hiroshima, the excerpts in this chapter demonstrate how writers attempt to frame the voids carved out by violence and to speak about events that leave us speechless.

This chapter brings together A. M. Homes, an American novelist and TV writer, reacting to September 11, 2001; the American writer Jonathan

Schell, discussing the photographic legacy of the second atomic bomb, on Nagasaki (1945); Italian Nobel laureate Eugenio Montale, writing about loss after World War I (1914–1918); African American novelist and poet Toni Morrison, addressing the victims of 9/11; Israeli writer Abba Kovner, mourning victims of the Holocaust (1939–1945) in the Jewish communities of his native Europe; and Iraqi writer Dunya Mikhail, reflecting on the cycle of violence in Iraq over the past half century. These writers explore ways to make emptiness tangible to readers, to convey how silence can become noisy, and to trace the indelible impressions that loss leaves on our visible world.

The journalist Philip Gourevitch wrote in *We Wish to Inform You That Tomorrow We Will Be Killed with Our Families* of the vital importance of "seeing emptiness" in Rwanda in the aftermath of the 1994 Hutu massacre of approximately one million Tutsis. Gourevitch interviewed Joseph, a man whose brother and sister had been killed by Hutu militia. He described Joseph making "a soft hissing click with his tongue against his teeth. 'The country is empty,' [Joseph] said. 'Empty!' . . . I, as a newcomer, could not see the emptiness that blinded Joseph to Rwanda's beauty." Gourevitch also describes a conversation with an American officer that vocalized genocide's quest to eliminate pockets of humanity. Consequently, Gourevitch became determined to appreciate and describe these absences to a wider audience. He provides a contemporary echo of the call to articulate the emptiness—the aftermath of the most extreme horrors of recent history—verbalized by Primo Levi, Alexsandr Solzhenitsyn, and Elie Wiesel, among many other prominent writers.

A. M. HOMES,
"We All Saw It, or the View from Home"—UNITED STATES

Novelist A. M. Homes was born in Washington, D.C., in 1961 and is a graduate of Sarah Lawrence College and the University of Iowa Writers Workshop. A. M. Homes's fiction and nonfiction have appeared in: the *New Yorker,* the *New York Times Magazine, Vogue,* the *Los Angeles Times,* the *Washington Post,* and numerous other magazines and newspapers. Her work has been translated into eighteen languages and is much anthologized. She has been the recipient of numerous awards, including a Guggenheim Foundation Fellowship, a National Endowment for the Arts

Fellowship, and a New York Foundation for the Arts Artists Fellowship. Additionally, she is the author of the artist's catalogs for Cecily Brown, Rachel Whiteread, and Ken Probst. A. M. Homes is currently a contributing editor to *Vanity Fair* and lives in New York City.

A. M. Homes's essay "We All Saw It, or the View from Home" (2002) describes an attempt to frame, literally—through a camera lens—the horror she witnessed in New York during 9/11. Homes watched Tower One collapse from her apartment window and reached for her camera, explaining, "When I don't know what else to do I document." Homes describes the moment Tower Two dropped "from the skyline" as "a sudden amputation." She uses the image of a missing limb to bring the incomprehensible loss down to a physical scale. Soon afterwards, Homes rushed outside. The city was mute—no cars, horns, or street sirens could be heard—yet noisy: "Everyone is talking—this is something to be shared, to be gone over, a story to be repeated, until we are empty." It is as if through retelling the story of the lost people and lost buildings, the witnesses will begin to absorb the emptiness surrounding them.

I begin the days quietly, preferring to see no one, speak to no one, to get to my desk early, before the "real world" intrudes, seeking to preserve for as long as possible that fertile creative zone which exists somewhere between sleeping and waking.

The events of September 11 ripped me from that zone, putting me on full alert. The ever-unfolding implications loom so large that for the first time my imagination remains—stilled.

It starts with a call from a friend, telling me there has been an accident, "Go to the window," she says.

I stand looking south, witness to Tower One in flames. And then I see the second plane; the instant it is in view it's clear this is not an accident.

The plane is moving towards the second tower counter-intuitively, rather than avoiding the tower, it is determinedly bearing down, picking up speed. I see the plane and I see the plane crash into the building. I see the buildings burn and I see the buildings fall down.

I see imagery that until now did not exist in reality, only in the fiction of film. Seeing it with your own eye, in real time, not on a screen, not protected by the frame of the television set, not set up and narrated by an anchor man, not in the communal darkness of a movie theater, seeing it like this is irreconcilable, like a hallucination, a psychotic break.

In the seconds after the second plane hit Tower Two, I did two things, filled the bath tub with water and pulled out my camera. When I don't know what else to do I document. I have always taken pictures as though storing what I am seeing, saving it for later when I am myself again. I take dozens of pictures, clicking faster, more frantically, as I feel myself pushing away.

When I go to re-wind my film, the camera is empty, the pictures are only in my head.

I spend the afternoon moving back and forth from the window to the television. By late in the day I have the sense that my own imagery, my memory, is all too quickly being replaced by the fresh footage, the other angle, the unrelenting loop.

I become fearful of my mind's liquidity, my ability to retain my own images and feelings rather than surrendering to what is almost instantly becoming the collective narrative. There is no place to put this experience, no folder in the mental hard drive that says, catastrophe. It is not something you want to remember, not something you want to forget.

In an act of imagination, I begin thinking about the buildings, about the people inside, the passengers on the planes. I am trying on each of the possibilities, what it might be like to be huddled in the back of a plane, to be in an office and catch a half-millisecond glimpse of the plane coming towards you, in a stairwell in one of those towers struggling to get down, to be on the ground showered with debris, to be home waiting for someone to return.

There is the sound of a plane overhead. No longer innocent, everything is suspect. The plane has become a weapon, a manned missile, a human bomb. I duck. It is a United States war plane, circling.

The phone rings, people call from around the world. Attendance is being taken and some of us are absent, missing.

I am on the phone when the first building collapses. A quarter mile high, the elevators take you up one-hundred-ten stories in fifty-eight seconds. It crumbles in less than a minute as though made of sugar cubes. The tower drops from the skyline, a sudden amputation. My eye struggles to replace the building, to paint it in, to fill in the blank.

When the second building goes, when there is just a cloud of smoke, I can no longer stand the strange isolation of being near and so incredibly far—I go outside.

The city is stilled, mute. There are no cars moving, no horns blowing, and for the most part not even any sirens. Everyone is talking—this is something to be shared, to be gone over, a story to be repeated, endlessly, until we are empty.

Coming up the West Side Highway is a post-apocalyptic exodus, men and women wandering north, walking up the center of the road, following the white lines, one foot in front of the other, mechanized. They come north gray with dust, with a coating of pulverized cement. They come in suits, clutching briefcases, walking singly or in small groups. People stand on the side lines, offering them water, cell phones, applauding them like marathon runners. They are few and far between.

Wind carries smoke uptown as if to keep the disaster fresh in people's minds, somehow begging you to breathe deeper, to be a part of it.

Those twin towers were my landscape, my navigational points, my night lights. I write staring out the window, depending on the fixedness of the landscape to give me the security to allow my thoughts to wander, my imagination to unfold. Now, I am afraid to look out the window, afraid of what I might see.

I've been sent somewhere else in time, to a different New York, a different America. Today we are all war correspondents.

ᴄᴡ JONATHAN SCHELL,
    "A View of Mountains"—UNITED STATES

> Jonathan Schell was born in 1943; he received his BA from Harvard University in 1965 and did graduate work in intensive Japanese at the International Christian University. Schell was a writer and editor at the *New Yorker* between 1967 and 1987 and the deputy editor from 1987 to 1988. He has received several awards, including the American Academy and Institute for Arts and Letters Award for Literature, the George Polk Award, and the L.A. Times Book award, and a nomination for the Pulitzer prize and the National Book Award. Schell has also been a Guggenheim Fellow and a recipient of a MacArthur Foundation grant for writing on peace and security. He has taught at Princeton University, New York University, Wesleyan University, and the New School. In addition to English, Jonathan Schell speaks French and Japanese. He is currently the *Nation's* peace and disarmament correspondent.

Like Homes's essay, Schell's essay "A View of Mountains" uses a camera lens to attempt to frame devastation, in this case in Nagasaki after it was destroyed by the second atomic bomb. Schell discusses the photographer Yosuke Yamahata's images of Nagasaki, after the second atomic bomb destroyed it in April 1945. These photos were shown for the first time in 1995, at the International Center for Photography in New York. This essay forms the epilogue to his book *The Gift of Time: The Case for Abolishing Nuclear Weapons* (1998). Schell deftly examines why Nagasaki has been largely forgotten and illuminates the exhibit's contemporary relevance; Yamahata shows what can, "in a flash, happen to any city in the world." Schell encourages his readers to focus on the emptiness created after the bomb because "that absence, even more than the wreckage, contains the heart of the matter. The true measure of the event lies not in what remains but in all that has disappeared." Schell's image of wreckage as a heart becomes literal; it exerts a pulse similar to the missing tower that Homes described as an "amputation" in the skyline.

On August 9, 1945, the day the atomic bomb was dropped on Nagasaki, Yosuke Yamahata, a photographer serving in the Japanese army, was dispatched to the destroyed city. The hundred or so pictures he took the next day constitute the fullest photographic record of nuclear destruction in existence. Hiroshima, destroyed three days earlier, had largely escaped the camera's lens in the first days after the bombing. It was therefore left to Yamahata to record, methodically—and, as it happens, with a great and simple artistry—the effects on a human population of a nuclear weapon only hours after it had been used. Some of Yamahata's pictures show corpses charred in the peculiar way in which a nuclear fireball chars its victims. They have been burned by light—technically speaking, by the "thermal pulse"—and their bodies are often branded with the patterns of their clothes, whose colors absorb light in different degrees. One photograph shows a horse twisted under the cart it had been pulling. Another shows a heap of something that once had been a human being hanging over a ledge into a ditch. A third shows a girl who has somehow survived, unwounded, standing in the open mouth of a bomb shelter and smiling an unearthly smile, shocking us with the sight of ordinary life, which otherwise seems to have been left behind for good in the scenes we are witnessing. Stretching into the distance on all sides are fields of rubble dotted with fires and, in the background, a view of mountains. We can see the mountains because the city is gone. That absence, even more than the wreckage, contains the heart of the matter. The true measure of the event lies not in what remains but in all that has disappeared.

It took a few seconds for the United States to destroy Nagasaki with the world's second atomic bomb, but it took fifty years for Yamahata's pictures of the event to make the journey back from Nagasaki to the United States. They were shown for the first time in this country in 1995, at the International Center for Photography in New York. Arriving a half-century late, they are still news. The photographs display the fate of a single city, but their meaning is universal, since, in our age of nuclear arms, what happened to Nagasaki can, in a flash, happen to any city in the world. In the photographs, Nagasaki comes into its own. Nagasaki has always been in the shadow of Hiroshima, as if the human imagination had stumbled to exhaustion in the wreckage of the first ruined city without reaching even the outskirts of the second. Yet the bombing of Nagasaki is in certain respects the fitter symbol of the nuclear danger that still hangs over us. It is proof that, having once used nuclear weapons, we can use them again. It introduces the idea of a series—the series that, with tens of thousands of nuclear weapons remaining in existence, continues to threaten everyone. (The unpredictable, open-ended character of this series is suggested by the fact that the second bomb originally was to be dropped on the city of Kokura, which was spared Nagasaki's fate only because bad weather protected it from view.) Each picture, therefore, seemed not so much an image of something that happened a half-century ago as a window cut into the wall of the photography center showing what soon could easily happen to New York. Wherever the exhibit might travel, moreover, the view of the threatened future from these "windows" would be roughly accurate, since, although every intact city is different from every other, all cities that suffer nuclear destruction will look much the same.

Yamahata's pictures afford a glimpse of the end of the world. Yet in our day, when the challenge is not just to apprehend the nuclear peril but to seize a God-given opportunity to dispel it once and for all, we seem to need, in addition, some other picture to counterpoise against Nagasaki—one showing not what we would lose through our failure but what we would gain by our success. What might that picture be, though? How do you show the opposite of the end of the world? Should it be Nagasaki, intact and alive, before the bomb was dropped—or perhaps the spared city of Kokura? Should it be a child, or a mother and child, or perhaps the Earth itself? None seems adequate, for how can we give a definite form to that which can assume infinite forms, namely, the lives of all human beings, now and in the future? Imagination, faced with either the end of the world or its continuation, must remain incomplete. Only action can satisfy.

Once, the arrival in the world of new generations took care of itself. Now, they can come into existence only if, through an act of faith and collective will, we ensure their right to exist. Performing that act is the greatest of the responsibilities of the generations now alive. The gift of time is the gift of life, forever, if we know how to receive it.

∾ EUGENIO MONTALE,
"Personae Separatae"—ITALY

Eugenio Montale was born in 1896 in Genoa, Italy. He stopped attending secondary school in order to study singing with the baritone Ernesto Sivori. Montale served as an infantry officer in World War I, which claimed Sivori's life. Consequently, Montale turned toward literature, focusing on poetry and literary criticism. In 1925, he published his first collection of poems, *Ossi di sepia* (Bones of the Cuttlefish), which quickly became a classic. In 1928, Montale moved to Florence, where he became director of a major library, remaining politically nonconformist. In 1938, he was dismissed from his directorship because he refused to join the Fascist Party. Montale withdrew from public life and spent his time translating such writers as William Shakespeare, T. S. Eliot, and Eugene O'Neill into Italian. After the war he moved to Milan, where he wrote the literary page for *Corriere Della Sera*, the most influential Italian daily newspaper. In 1961, Montale was awarded an honorary degree at the University of Rome and, shortly afterwards, degrees from the universities of Milan, Cambridge, and Basel. In 1967, the Italian president appointed him a member-for-life of the Italian Senate "in recognition of his distinguished achievements in the literary and artistic fields." In 1975, he was awarded the Nobel Prize for Literature. Eugenio Montale died in Milan on September 12, 1981.

Montale uses several images in his poem *Personae Separatae* (1985), here translated by Jonathan Galassi, to convey the desire to circumscribe the palpable absence of a loved one: a parallel

silhouette outline of the absent person, sunlight *framing* the
clearing of fresh-cut trunks, and hollow stumps. The parallel
figures or shadows with which the poem's speaker yearns to print
the ground recall the chalked body outlines at crime scenes. A
silhouette aptly conveys the conflicting desire to see the absence
and the futility of the quest; the shadowy silhouette gives the
shape but does not fill it in.

Like the scale of gold that lifts off from
the black backdrop and liquefied runs down
the corridor of carobs turned to bones,
are we too separate persons
in another's eyes? The word's
a little thing, space is little
in these raw,
misted new moons: what's missing,
what torments our hearts and holds me here
waiting for you in the trees, is a lost sense,
or, if you will, the fire that brands the earth
with parallel figures, shadows in agreement,
shafts of a sun that orders the new
trunks in the clearing and even fills
the hollow stumps, ant-nets.
The human forest is too flayed,
that voice of always too unlistened to,
the rent unclouding over the Lunigiana's
snowy passes too uncertain.
Your form passed this way,
stayed by the ditch among the grounded eel-nets,
then faded like a sigh, around—
and there was no gushing horror then; in you
the light could still find light, but not longer:
now at daybreak it's already night.

~ TONI MORRISON,
　　"The Dead of September 11"—UNITED STATES

Born Chloe Anthony Wofford in Lorain, Ohio, in 1931, Toni
Morrison displayed an early interest in literature. Morrison, the

second of four children, immersed herself in the close-knit community spirit and the folklore, myth, and supernatural beliefs of her culture. Storytelling was a common practice in her family. She subsequently attended Howard and Cornell universities and then worked as an editor at Random House. Morrison began her novelistic career in 1970 and was admitted to the American Academy of Arts and Letter in 1981. She has taught writing or literature at Texas Southern University, Howard University, Yale, and Princeton, where she became the chair of Creative Writing in 1989. In 1988 she won a Pulitzer Prize, and in 1993 she received the Nobel Prize for Literature.

Like Montale's poem about paradoxical silhouettes, Toni Morrison's poem "The Dead of September 11" both articulates the absence—the victims have been turned into atoms—and casts a poetic mold to preserve them through literature. She writes, "I have nothing to say—no words / stronger than the steel that pressed you into itself; no scripture / older or more elegant than the ancient atoms you / have become." Morrison first read this poem at a memorial service at Princeton University in September 2001, and it appeared in *Vanity Fair* in October 2001. The only italicized line in the poem, *"I want to hold you in my arms,"* grabs the reader's attention. On the printed page, Morrison's words connect her to the victims she seeks to embrace, as if poetry becomes a place where something impossible in the physical world becomes possible. Yet because Morrison has "no words" stronger than the reality of loss, her arms will ultimately remain empty. Both this specific image of empty arms and the poem in general, *reaching* toward absence, echo Morrison's 1993 Nobel speech, in which she said, "Language can never 'pin down' slavery, genocide, war. Nor should it yearn for the arrogance to be able to do so. Its force, its felicity is in its *reach toward the ineffable.*"

Some have God's words; others have songs of comfort
for the bereaved. If I can pluck courage here, I would
like to speak directly to the dead—the September dead.
Those children of ancestors born in every continent
on the planet: Asia, Europe, Africa, the Americas . . . ;
born of ancestors who wore kilts, obis, saris, geles,
wide straw hats, yarmulkes, goatskin, wooden shoes,

feathers and cloths to cover their hair. But I would not say
a word until I could set aside all I know or believe about
nations, wars, leaders, the governed and ungovernable;
all I suspect about armor and entrails. First I would freshen
my tongue, abandon sentences crafted to know evil—wanton
or studied; explosive or quietly sinister; whether born of
a sated appetite or hunger; of vengeance or the simple
compulsion to stand up before falling down. I would purge
my language of hyperbole; of its eagerness to analyze
the levels of wickedness; ranking them; calculating their
higher or lower status among others of its kind.
Speaking to the broken and the dead is too difficult for
a mouth full of blood. Too holy an act for impure thoughts.
Because the dead are free, absolute; they cannot be seduced by blitz.
To speak to you, the dead of September 11, I must not claim
false intimacy or summon an overheated heart glazed
just in time for a camera. I must be steady and I must be clear,
knowing all the time that I have nothing to say—no words
stronger than the steel that pressed you into itself; no scripture
older or more elegant than the ancient atoms you have become.
And I have nothing to give either—except this gesture,
this thread thrown between your humanity and mine:
I want to hold you in my arms and as your soul got shot of its box of
        flesh to
understand, as you have done, the wit
of eternity: its gift of unhinged release tearing through
the darkness of its knell.

❧ ABBA KOVNER,
    "What's Not in the Heart"—ISRAEL

Abba Kovner was born in Sebastopol, Russia, and grew up in
Vilnius, where he joined the Zionist Socialist youth movement.
Kovner was part up of the armed Jewish resistance movement in
Lithuania during the Second World War and in 1946 helped found
the underground organization Brehia, which smuggled Jews out
of Europe. Kovner also joined a Kibbutz in Israel and was active
in Israel's independence war of 1948. His poetry and prose touch

on both the Holocaust and Israeli-Palestinian conflicts. In 1970, Kovner received the Israel Prize for literature. He was also director of the Israel Society of Writers, designer of the Diaspora House at Tel Aviv University, and a founder of Moreshet, a center for collecting the testimonies of concentration camp survivors and resistance fighters from the ghettos.

   The speaker in Kovner's poem "What's Not in the Heart," translated by Shirley Kaufman, also strives to articulate unspeakable human loss. He ends his poem with the following lines: "I try now to define who you were— / word shadow! Only your returning shadow / exists. My hands will never / touch you. Your coffin / never leaves my shoulders." Kovner conjures up the image of the speaker's hands reaching out to touch a shadow of a lost loved one even though they will never actually be able to do so. Yet the weight of this person's absence never leaves the speaker's shoulders.

I

I do not hold a mirage in my hand—
my shirt's in my hand. The plain filled
with my wheat. All of it. Soaked by dew
flat at my feet. Its beauty
turns each image pale. The returning heron
and the apple garden. Sun
plucks at my shoulders like my daughter's fingers.
And this day
recalling soon
the smell of the harvest:
this morning (I say to myself)
even in the burned forest the bird
has come back to sing.

II

Useless. I try now to understand what happened.
We declared two minutes of silence
so silence would not grow in the windows
of our homes. And no way out, my brother.
The world does not stand on a cry

at night. On a man
with something in his heart, because
what's in the heart is nothing. Because
the living live by the will of those who go
where they were not willing to go.

Useless: I try now to define who you were—
word shadows! Only your returning shadow
exists. My hands will never
touch you. Your coffin
never leaves my shoulders.

꩜ DUNYA MIKHAIL,
   "O"—IRAQ

Born in 1965 in Baghdad, Dunya Mikhail received a degree in
English literature at Baghdad University and has worked as the
literary editor for the *Baghdad Observer*. She frequently writes
about the pressure of absence that she felt daily, living through
the violence of the 1980–1988 Iraq-Iran War and the first Persian
Gulf War in 1991. Her fiancé was absent for twelve years while she
was building her career in Iraq, and she kept encountering women
whose husbands and sons had left the country or had been killed.
"Absence was the number one presence in the lives of these people,"
said Mikhail in an April 2005 interview with the Legacy Project.
Facing increasing threats from Iraqi authorities for her writing,
she fled to Jordan and then the United States. She did graduate
work in Near East Studies at Wayne State University and she now
teaches Arabic. In 2001, she was awarded the United Nations
Human Rights Award for Freedom of Writing. She has published
four collections of poetry in Arabic, and her first collection
published in English, *The War Works Hard*, was translated by
Elizabeth Winslow in 2005 with a PEN Translation Fund Grant.
    Mikhail's poem "O" literally circumscribes the absence she
witnessed. The poem spirals inward and the visual discomfort of
reading while spinning the page seems to mimic the disorientation
of large-scale violence and death generally. "The circle is my
favorite shape," she said in an interview with the Legacy Project

in April 2005, because on the daily television she always watched soldiers moving in military lines, squares, and rectangles. "We never had the shapes of circles in our lives. I missed it and loved it. There is more freedom in the movement of a circle."

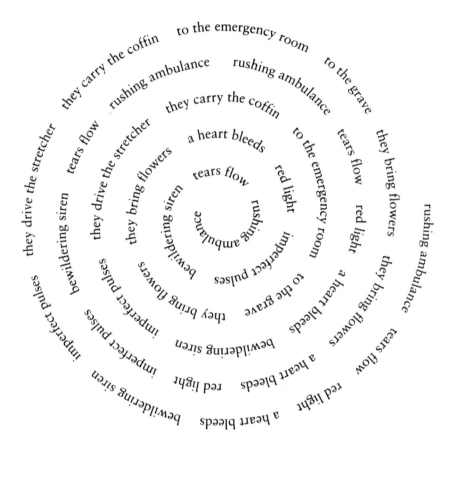

PART II

COMMANDING OBLIVION

FIVE

SURVIVING SURVIVAL

In three different locations ravaged by violence in the past century a similar, gutting scene played out. In Armenia, following the slaughter of Armenians by the Turks in 1918; in Germany, following the bombing of Hamburg after World War II; and in Iraq, following a government attack on a Kurdish town, women who had survived the immediate danger walked or rode away from the site of devastation carting dead children with them.

In his book *Double Vision*, Ben Bagdikian writes about scores of Armenian mothers in the town of Mararash who trudged along, blindly carrying small children on their backs, dazed and unaware that the children had died.

William Sebald writes, in a *New Yorker* article, of survivors of the bombings of Hamburg and quotes Friedrich Reck, who describes a train station in upper Bavaria where a cardboard suitcase "falls open on the platform, burst open and spills its contents. Toys, a manicure case, singed underwear. And last of all, the roasted corpse of a child, shrunk like a mummy, which its half-deranged mother has been carrying about with her, the relic of a past that was still intact a few days ago."

Finally, the Iraqi filmmaker Maysoon Pachachi describes the journey of a Kurdish woman named Yada, whose situation resonates with the women in Turkish Armenia and Germany that Bagdikian and Sebald described elsewhere. Yada was from the town of Halabsha in the north of Iraq. She survived a chemical attack by the Iraqi government. As she fled, Yada picked up a two-year-old child whose parents had been killed and held him as she sat on a cart trundling to the Iranian border. Within half an hour of beginning the journey, the child died, but Yada was unable to put him down even though she could feel his chemical-ridden body burning her arm. When they crossed the border, she was finally able to release him. Her arm remains scarred to this day.

Pachachi's following comments on Yada's situation also apply to the ongoing struggles of survival for many trauma victims: "This is an image of what happens when people are the victims of traumatic incidents, they have a dead burden which burns them which they nevertheless have to carry around with them as they make their way around."

The writers in this chapter address the ongoing struggles of survival. Most bystanders assume survival has been achieved once someone escapes the immediate situation of duress, be it a repressive dictatorial society or the reach of genocidal violence. But survival after a large-scale atrocity is an ongoing process that continues uncertainly from one moment to the next. Ben Bagdikian writes of his family, who survived the Armenian Genocide of 1915–1918; Philip Gourevitch discusses the survivors he came across in Rwanda after the Rwandan Genocide of 1994; Kenzaburo Oe describes the courageous doctors who worked in the aftermath of Hiroshima in 1945; Charlotte Delbo describes how she copes with the memory of life in a concentration camp during the Holocaust; and Alexander Molot describes life after September 11, 2001.

ᕬ BEN BAGDIKIAN,
Excerpt from *Double Vision: Reflections on My Heritage, Life, and Profession*—UNITED STATES

Ben Bagdikian was born in 1920 in Maras in the Ottoman Empire, now Turkey. His family moved to the United States, and he graduated from Clark University in 1941 and became a reporter at the *Springfield Morning Union*. From 1942 until 1944 he was an aerial navigator with the U.S. Air Force. From 1947 to 1970, he worked at the *Providence (R.I.) Journal-Bulletin* as a reporter, foreign correspondent, and, finally, chief of the Washington Bureau. In 1970 he started as the assistant managing editor for national news at the *Washington Post* and in 1973 became the national correspondent for the *Columbia Journalism Review*. From 1976 until 1990 he taught at the Graduate School of Journalism at the University of California at Berkeley, where in 1985 he became dean. He retired in 1991.

Bagdikian's book *Double Vision: Reflections on My Heritage, Life, and Profession* (1995) is part autobiography and part media-critique. The selected excerpt details his family's escape from Armenia in the years after the massacres of 1915–1918 and illuminates the nearly all-consuming need to survive excruciating violence.

Somewhere, ahead of the refugees, on a lower rutted road, the French soldiers and the American missionaries were not much better off. Even Dr. Elliott was walking, though she, like all the Americans, had been given permission to ride on wagons with the Army baggage train.

Mabel Elliott had been medical director of the hospital, and the old Marash photographs show a sturdy Boston face with steady gaze, hair pulled back in a bun, rimless glasses, firm jaw and mouth, classical WASP nose.

Most of her patients were women. In Marash, after the genocide, there were always more women than men. As a massacre came to each community, the men were marched to the outskirts of their cities and shot in masses. Soldiers returned for the women, who were marched with the children to the distant desert, most to be raped, kidnapped or killed. In the end more children survived. Marash became "the City of Orphans."

The battle for Marash had brought out her anger. When she saw the mounting piles of butchered Armenian bodies and was told to prepare for the French retreat, she wrote in her diary:

"They had relied on us, on the great, powerful Allies. They had come back to Marash, to their wrecked homes and lived under protection. . . ." Once more, she wrote bitterly, they faced Turkish rapes and death.

"I think that all the rest of my days I shall suddenly hear from time to time that sentence quietly said . . . 'What shall we do now, doctor?'"

Later, she found that one of her favorite patients, a young tubercular woman too weak to escape over the mountains, took off her clothes and sat by an open window, to freeze quietly to death in the night rather than wait for the Turks to enter the hospital for the sick and wounded left behind.

In the blizzard, the doctor dared not ride any longer. She walked on the trail to stay alive by moving.

"In time, I, too, was a blind machine . . . I thought of nothing, cared for nothing, simply struggled to keep my balance . . . The temptation of it! Just to lie down and let the snow cover us."

She saw Armenian mothers carrying small children on their backs. Typically the child's arms crossed over the mother's shoulder, the struggling mother clutching both hands of the child onto her own breast.

"I do not know how many hours we had been walking when I found the first dead child on its mother's back. I walked beside her, examining it; she trudged on, bent under the weight . . . The child was certainly dead, and she did not know it . . . I spoke to her, touched her, finally shook her arm violently to arouse her. When she looked up, I pointed to the child and said, 'Finished.' The mother . . . let go the child's hands. The body fell. . . . There were perhaps fifty more after that, always the same."

Lydia, angry at Tirzah, for the first time pushed ahead of her sister. A sudden, fierce, saving anger carried them both rapidly up the line until they saw Mozart. Lydia began to run to her mother, crying about Tirzah, but when she saw her mother, she stopped. Her mother looked sick and was swaying. Elmas, holding the baby, looked more dejected than ever.

My father rushed to my mother's side.

"Are you all right? Maybe you should ride a little."

He helped my mother into the saddle and they all moved faster to Mozart's pace.

Lydia soon fell back again. She stopped, exhausted. She looked down at the trail and cried out. Her shoes had burst. Her stiff, stockinged toes were in the snow. She stood still in the trail, staring at the open shoes and the strange bloated look of her toes.

Up ahead, the scene at the horse was even more depressed. It had stopped snowing and the wind had died down. But Elmas had been unable to get a reaction from the baby. My father, walking behind the horse, took the bundle and tried arousing the baby. Out of sight of my mother and Cynthia, my father uncovered the baby and examined it. He decided that this was not the time to tell the others that I was dead. He put the covers back over the bundle and walked rapidly to catch up. As he approached the horse, my mother fainted and began slipping off the horse. My father dropped the bundle in the snow and grasped my mother's falling body. When the bundle hit the snow there was an infant cry. Elmas picked up the crying bundle and kept it moving in her arms.

At the next turn of the trail they found themselves in another abandoned village. Fires had already been lit. When Lydia and Tirzah came within sight, they saw the family group around the fire. But that was the last Lydia remembered before she fainted. She did not wake up until sometime later when someone was holding her up and urging her to drink something warm.

My father said, "Don't worry. Tomorrow we will reach the railroad."

In the morning, when Lydia opened her eyes, she was dazzled. The sight was startling. Skies were clear and deep blue. The sun created a brilliant glaze over what seemed like endless stretches of new snow on the downward slope of a vast plain.

They were soon on the trail again. There were more bodies in the snow, most of them naked. Lydia looked sidelong at naked bodies of children, but only long enough to make sure the missing Nora was not among them.

In the far distance, across the blinding field of white snow, there was a black smudge. The sound of a distant locomotive whistle carried through the open fields.

Instantly, the long mass of huddled figures stopped. Something like a massive whisper rose in the air.

"Islahiye!"

The black streak was the railroad.

Hundreds of the motionless figures suddenly came to life. They began to run, stumbling through snow two feet high, seduced by an illusion of closeness, optical treachery induced by desperate yearning, by the transparent air, by the unbroken white plain made smooth by a setting sun, all of it foreshortening the unseen miles.

The next summer, after the snows had melted, missionaries located the final trail by the hundreds of skeletons of those who fell frozen and exhausted on the last fatal rush within sight of salvation.

By that next summer, missionaries already had calculated what had happened to those who had gone before: of the 3,400 Armenians who, like the Bagdikian family, left immediately behind the retreating French, 1,000 had died in the mountains. Another 2,000 left Marash two hours later, 1,800 of them killed within sight of the city in an ambush by waiting Turks; of the surviving 200 of the second wave, only 20 were known to have reached Islahiye. In their own account of the retreat, the French military records show that of the 3,000 young and healthy French troops who left Marash, 1,200 died in the mountains, 630 of them never accounted for. At least 150 of the soldiers required emergency amputations of frozen limbs.

Armenians remaining in Marash were not luckier. In the following months, missionaries counted 10,000 Armenians who died slowly of starvation, disease, or murder because the Turks permitted no one to sell or give food to an Armenian. Those who survived could thank bribes paid to Turkish officials by the American missionaries.

Lydia hurried ahead until she saw my mother, father, Cynthia, and Elmas around a fire. A neighbor from Marash stopped to ask why the family was not going on to Islahiye.

My father told him one of his daughters was missing. They would wait here. There were cows they could milk and good huts to sleep in. The family would wait for the missing ones to catch up.

That night in the mountain, Lydia was settled by my father next to the fire. He made sure everyone had milk, checked the sleeping baby, and returned to the trail to look for Bedros and Nora. The family members around the fire said their family service, praying Nora and Bedros were safe.

When Lydia woke the next morning, Nora and Elmas and my father were not there. My mother looked sick with what looked like a bad cold. Lydia felt hot and took off her scarf. My mother said, "Don't do that, Lydia. Even if you feel hot, don't take off any clothes. You will need protection from the cold. We will soon be in Islahiye."

"Where is Papa?"

"He's looking for Nora and Bedros. They may have missed us in the night and gone on to Islahiye. We will probably see them there."

My father returned empty-handed. They started the movement downward to the railroad, plodding through the packed snow.

Suddenly, in a daze, Lydia realized they were outside a train station. A French officer approached. He had often dined with them in Marash and had always brought favors for Nora.

"This is the only train today. It will take only Army people. But my commandant said that if you will take this train, you may board with your family. You are in great danger if you wait here."

My mother said, "I cannot go without my daughter."

"Madam, you are ill. The rest of your family is exhausted and not well. There may not be another chance."

"I cannot go without Nora."

A group of women refugees had gathered around the family. One of the women cried out:

"You should be grateful! I have lost two in the mountains. You still have most of your family. I will take your place right now!"

My mother wept. She said to the woman that she was sorry for her loss, but she could not go without her daughter.

The woman was bitter.

"You had servants to help you. You have a servant now. You want everything."

My mother wept and shook her head.

"I am sorry. May God comfort you. But I cannot leave my daughter behind."

The train whistle blew.

"Madam, you must decide. I urge you to get aboard. We must leave in a few minutes."

While the officer had spoken and the crowd of women murmured, Lydia could hear her father somewhere shouting over and over, "Bedros! Nora!" Suddenly he stopped and stared toward the edge of the station.

"Bedros!"

The boy was alone.

"Where is Nora?"

"I don't know. When we started this morning she said she didn't want to be carried anymore."

My father lost his temper.

"Why didn't you hold her hand? What kind of a person are you? You gave me your word of honor! How far back did this happen?"

"I don't know. She just jumped off my back and ran."

The officer pleaded with my father.

"Sir, your wife is sick and you have your other children to think about."

My mother shook her head again.

The Armenian woman said, "Look. She still wants everything."

Another Armenian woman said, "I don't blame her. I would not leave one of mine behind, either."

Somewhere in the growing circle of people around the family, someone shouted:

"Take the train! Take the train!"

My mother, weeping, raised her head as though to answer. She stared suddenly at a woman in the crowd and gasped, "Nora's scarf!" then fainted.

My father brought her to consciousness, told Elmas and Tirzah to tend her, and ran to the woman.

"That is my daughter's scarf. Where did you get it?"

"It's mine."

By now my mother was standing again and went quietly to the woman.

"No. That is my daughter's. There is no other like it in Marash. We bought it in Aleppo. We do not care for the scarf. You may have it. But you must tell us where you found it. Was it today? How far back?"

The train whistle blew again. The officer held up his hand toward the front of the train and turned:

"'Madam, we cannot wait longer.'"

Lydia's heart sank. My father could be seen looking wildly among the stragglers still coming to the station. Suddenly, he began to run.

My mother cried out:

"Nora! Nora! Thank God! Nora!"

Nora was running toward them, crying. She was naked.

The officer said they must now get on.

My father told the officer he needed only two minutes.

"Elmas, please come with us to America."

Elmas shook her head. She had always said she would stay. She repeated it. My father reached into Mozart's saddlebag and tied a large amount of gold in a piece of cloth and gave it to her. My mother kissed Elmas. Both women were weeping.

My father gave a remaining packet of gold to Bedros.

"Bedros, you may have the horse, too. Take care of it. It is valuable."

In the confusion of the crowded railroad car, Lydia felt dizzy. It was hot and steamy. Soldiers were drinking from flasks. Somewhere one of the soldiers began singing in French. Then she lost consciousness again.

 PHILIP GOUREVITCH,
   Excerpt from *We Wish to Inform You That Tomorrow We Will Be Killed with Our Families: Stories from Rwanda*—UNITED STATES

   Born in Philadelphia in 1961, Philip Gourevitch grew up in
   Middletown, Connecticut. He earned a bachelor's degree from
   Cornell University in 1986, followed by a master of fine arts from
   Columbia University in 1992. Gourevitch has reported from
   Africa, Asia, and Europe for a number of magazines, including
   Granta, Harper's, and the *New York Review of Books.* In 1997,
   Gourevitch became a staff writer for the *New Yorker.* His first
   book, *We Wish to Inform You That Tomorrow We Will Be Killed
   with Our Families: Stories from Rwanda* (1998) won numerous
   awards, including the National Book Critics' Circle Award
   for Nonfiction and the George Pope Book Award for Foreign
   Reporting, among others. Gourevitch is now the chair of the
   International Committee of PEN American Center, a senior

fellow at the World Policy Institute, and the editor-in-chief of the *Paris Review*.

In *We Wish to Inform You*, Gourevitch writes of the struggles of Rwandan survivors after the 1994 genocide of Tutsis by Hutus: "All across the ghostly countryside, survivors sought each other out, assembling surrogate families and squatting together in abandoned shacks, in schoolyard shanties and burned-out shops, hoping for safety and comfort. A hastily assembled household. A shadow world of the severely traumatized and achingly bereft established itself in the ruins." The plight of survivors in Rwanda is complicated by the fact that victims and killers live side by side. Gourevitch urges the outside world to be patient since "it takes us time to overcome the loss of a family member who dies of cancer. Imagine what it's like for a society where virtually every family either contains killers or victims of those killers from a period of a hundred days."

Bonaventure Nyibizi and his family were evacuated to the RPF zone from the Sainte Famille church in mid-June of 1994. Looking out from the convoy, he saw Kigali as a necropolis: "Just blood and"—he made a shivering sound, like a tire deflating—"pffthhh-h-hh."

In the RPF collection camps for survivors, Bonaventure sought news of his family and friends. It didn't take him long to conclude that "it was unrealistic to hope that somebody had survived." A sister of his was found alive, but three of her five children had been killed, as were his mother and everyone who lived with her. Most of his wife's family and friends had also been wiped out. "Sometimes," he said, "you met someone who you thought had been killed, and you learned that somehow they had managed to stay alive." But the euphoria of such reunions, which punctuated the survivors' gloom for months after the genocide, was tempered by the constant tallying of losses. "Mostly," Bonaventure said, "you didn't even want to hope."

Around July 20, Bonaventure returned home, and sank into despair. "Kigali was difficult to believe," he told me. "The place smelled of death. There were very few people whom you knew from before, and no water or electricity, but the problem for most people was that their houses were destroyed. Most of my house was destroyed. People were finding their furniture and belongings in the homes of neighbors who'd run away, or taking the neighbors' things. But to me that was not important at all. I was not really interested in doing anything."

Bonaventure believed that survival was meaningless until one found "a reason to survive again, a reason to look to tomorrow." This was a widely held view in Rwanda, where depression was epidemic. The so-called survival instinct is often described as an animal urge to preserve oneself. But once the threat of bodily annihilation is relieved, the soul still requires preservation, and a wounded soul becomes the source of its own affliction; it cannot nurse itself directly. So survival can seem a curse, for one of the dominant needs of the needy soul is to be needed. As I came to know survivors, I found that, when it comes to soul preservation, the urge to look after others is often greater than the urge to look after oneself. All across the ghostly countryside, survivors sought each other out, assembling surrogate families and squatting together in abandoned shacks, in schoolyard shanties and burned out shops, hoping for safety and comfort in hastily assembled households. A shadow world of the severely traumatized and achingly bereft established itself in the ruins. The extent of orphanhood was especially staggering: two years after the genocide, more than a hundred thousand children were looking after one another in homes that lacked any adult presence.

Bonaventure still had his wife and his children, and he began adopting more children. He recovered his car and what remained of his home, and he was receiving back pay from his foreign employer. But even he needed more to live for—a future, as he said. One day, in August, he learned that USAID was sending someone to reestablish its mission in Kigali. Bonaventure picked the man up at the airport and returned to work with a vengeance. "Every day, fourteen hours," he told me. "I was very tired, but it helped a lot." Bonaventure came to dread the idleness and disengagement that he associated with his recent victimization. "In most cases," he said, "with a person who lost his family and friends, when you look— what's he doing?—actually he's doing nothing. So there is no hope for him. To keep busy is very, very important."

Everything needed doing—at once. Bonaventure couldn't imagine how Rwanda would be restored to anything resembling working order, and the international disaster experts who began teeming through on assessment missions agreed that they had never seen a country so laid to waste. When the new government was sworn in, there wasn't a dollar or a Rwandan franc left in the treasury; not a clean pad of paper, or a staple, much less a working stapler, left in most government offices. Where doors remained, nobody had keys to the locks; if a vehicle had been left behind, the odds were it wouldn't run. Go to the latrine, it was likely to be stuffed with dead people, and the same went for the well. Electric, phone, and water lines—forget it. All day long in Kigali, there were explosions because somebody had stepped on a land mine or jarred a bit of unexploded ordnance. Hospitals lay in ruins, and the demand for their services was overwhelming. Many of the churches, schools, and other public facilities that hadn't been used as slaughterhouses had been sacked, and most of the people who had been in charge of them either were dead or had fled. A year's tea and coffee harvests had been lost, and vandals had left all the tea factories and about seventy percent of the country's coffee-depulping machines inoperable.

Under the circumstances, one might suppose that the dream of return would have lost some of its allure for the Tutsis of the Rwandan diaspora; that people who had sat in safe homes abroad, receiving the news of the wholesale slaughter of their parents and siblings, their cousins and in-laws, would reckon their prospects for a natural death in exile and stay there. One might suppose that a simple desire not to go mad would inspire such people to renounce forever any hope of again calling Rwanda "home." Instead, the exiles began rushing back to Rwanda even before the blood had dried. Tens of thousands returned immediately on the heels of the RPF, and hundreds of thousands soon followed. The Tutsi returnees and throngs of fleeing Hutus jockeyed past one another at the frontiers.

The returning Rwandans came from all over Africa and from further afield—from Zurich and Brussels, Milan, Toronto, Los Angeles, and La Paz. Nine months after the RPF liberated Kigali, more than seven hundred and fifty thousand former Tutsi exiles (and almost a million cows) had moved back to Rwanda—nearly a one-to-one replacement of the dead. When Bonaventure remarked that he found few familiar faces on returning to Kigali, he was speaking not only of the missing but also of all the people he'd never seen there before. When Rwandans asked me how long I'd been in Rwanda, I often asked the same of them, and after I'd spent a few months in the country it was not unusual to find that I'd been there longer than the Rwandan I was talking to. When I asked people why they had come, I usually got casual answers—to have a look, to see who was alive, to see what they could do to help out—and almost always I'd be told, "It's good to be home."

Once again, strange little Rwanda presented the world with a historically unprecedented, epic phenomenon. Even the RPF leaders, who had been working the refugee diaspora networks for years—consciousness-raising, fund-raising, and recruiting—were astonished by the scale of this return.

What possessed these people, a great many of whom had never before set foot in Rwanda, to abandon relatively established and secure lives in order to settle in a graveyard? The legacy of exclusion, the pressures of exile, and the memory of, or longing for, a homeland all played a part. So did a widespread determination to defy the genocide, to stand and be counted in a place where one was meant to have been wiped out. And for many, the sense of belonging was mingled with a straightforward profit motive.

Drawn by empty housing free for the taking and by a demand for goods and services vastly greater than the supply, the returnees rolled into the country hauling loads of dry goods, hardware, medicines, groceries, you name it. If you came with a car, you could immediately claim standing in the transportation industry; if you had a truck, you could become a freight handler; if you had a few thousand dollars you could pretty much pick your niche in a small trade, and with a hundred thousand you might become a captain of industry. There were stories of people who pooled a little cash, hired a vehicle, packed it with cigarettes, candles, beer, fuel, or triple-A batteries, drove to Rwanda, unloaded for a profit of two hundred or three hundred percent, then repeated the process ten or fifteen times, and made themselves rich in the course of a few weeks.

You or I might have done nearly as well if we'd put our enterprising minds to it, and a few foreign carpetbaggers did make out in the Rwandan aftermath. But if fast money was the objective, there was no need for mid-career Rwandan professionals, living in exile with little children whose heads had never been at risk of being chopped off by a neighbor, to move their entire families into the country. The profit motive only explains how return was a viable option and how in the course of a few months minibus taxis were again plying the main routes in Kigali; stores were open for business, public utilities were mostly revived, and new banknotes issued, invalidating the old currency that had been carted off by the fleeing genocidaires. The Rwandan franc had suffered a devaluation of at least two hundred fifty percent between the beginning and end of 1994, but with money flowing across the borders, a nightclub had only to switch on the generator and turn up the music to maintain a packed dance floor. The old dictum that it's much easier to destroy than to create remained true, but the speed with which much of Rwanda's basic physical plant was restored to working order was nearly as baffling as the speed with which it had been demolished.

It was impossible not to be moved by the mass return of the "fifty-niners," and it was impossible not to be troubled by it as well. In 1996 more than seventy percent of the people in Kigali and Butare, and in some rural areas of eastern Rwanda, were said to be newcomers. People who had never left the country—Tutsi and Hutu—often felt displaced in their own homes. Their complaints always came with the caveat "Don't quote me by name." Such requests for anonymity can have many meanings. They suggest an atmosphere of intrigue and fear; and a desire to speak truthfully in circumstances where the truth is dangerous. But they can also bracket secretive moments in a longer conversation, moments in which the speaker seems to doubt what he's saying, or is getting personal, even petty, or is exaggerating wildly, perhaps lying outright, to make a point he knows he cannot fully defend. The recipient of such confidences must try to discern the calculation behind the request. With Rwandans, whose experience had taught them not to underestimate any fear, this could get very tricky. I was especially wary of anonymous remarks that attributed one or another quality to an entire group of people, including the speaker's own. So when people who were speaking openly suddenly asked not to be quoted and then said terrible things about the Tutsi "fifty-niners," as if the whole crowd were one person, I was skeptical. But I heard the same stories and attitudes hundreds of times.

A Tutsi survivor said, "They come here, they see us, and they say, 'How did you survive? Did you collaborate with the *interahamwe?*" They think we were fools to have stayed in the country—and maybe we were—so they disdain us. They don't want to be reminded. It shocks us to the bones."

An anti-Habyarimana Hutu said, "The Tutsis were in trouble in last year's massacres, and the army is now dominated by Tutsis. So we thought the survivors would be taken care of, that it would be the first task of the new government. But only those returning from outside are getting homes. And meanwhile, if these people from outside have a problem with a Hutu, they accuse him of committing the genocide they weren't even here for."

A Tutsi said, "We survivors find it very difficult to integrate into the present society and—I hate to say it—into the government, too. They have their own style from outside, and they don't have much trust in us either. When they came they took the country as in a conquest. They thought it was theirs to look after. They said of us Tutsis who were here, 'The smart ones are dead and those who survived are traumatized.' The young RPF fighters all had their parents coming from outside the country and they were tired of the austerity of fighting, so they took homes and goods for their families and they didn't like the survivors getting in the way. And they would say, 'If they killed everyone and you survived, maybe you collaborated.' To a woman who was raped twenty times a day, day after day, and now has a baby from that, they would say this. To a Tutsi who was intermarried or a child who was orphaned they would say this. Can you imagine? For us, it was too hard at first, finding that everyone was dead, that we didn't know anyone. It didn't occur to us to grab better houses, and now it's we who are taking care of most of the orphans."

A Hutu said, "They don't know the country. They trust only each other. They weren't here, and they can't understand. Some of the influence is good. We needed change, fresh ideas. But there are many extremists among them. And many Hutus who were in trouble during last year's killings are in trouble again under this regime. People who were targeted then for being RPF followers are now accused of being *genocidaires*. Some are in prison. Some run to another country. Some are killed. It's the army that controls the government, and inside the army there is not enough control. Truly, if I could afford not to live under plastic sheeting in a camp with *genocidaires*, I would become a refugee."

A Tutsi said, "Our women used to do collections to send Tampax to the women with the RPF when they were up in the mountains, and now when we are with our old Hutu friends, some of the people we're closest to in the world, these people look at us like 'Why are you always with this Hutu?' And we say to ourselves, 'We've lived together with Hutus all our lives, and we speak almost the same language, and we saw our families killed by Hutus, but you're more racist than we are.' It's an enemy in their subconscious. Their idea of cohabitation is really very theoretical. For Hutus now, it's like for us before the RPF came. Even if you live quietly, you can't say many things, you can't criticize a politician, you must live in fear. Of course, all the Hutus now have someone in the camps or in prison, and you can't abandon your brother even if he killed people. So it's a real problem, whom to trust. But the returnees don't even want to discuss it."

Even among the returnees there was a good deal of grumbling about other returnees. They had imagined they were one people engaged in a homecoming, only to discover that they were all kinds of people from all kinds of places. Those who had spent the past three decades in Uganda being called Rwandans were, in fact, deeply Ugandan, and people called Rwandans who had lived in Burundi seemed alien to them. They had no better reason to regard each other as kin than a child of Sicilians born in Argentina would have to feel related to a Milanese who had lived his entire adult life as an immigrant in Sweden. Adapting to life in Zaire under the capricious dictatorship of Mobutu Sese Seko and in Tanzania under the authoritarian socialism of Julius Nyerere had not been comparable experiences. Some of the returnees had lived in Francophone countries, others in Anglophone countries, and although most still spoke at least some Kinyarwanda, many were more at home in Swahili or some other foreign African language which other returnees didn't speak.

Hutu Power created a world in which there was just us and them, and Rwanda was still generally regarded from within and without as a bipolar world of Hutus and Tutsis. But an elaborate grid of subcategories lay just beneath the surface. There were Hutus with good records, and suspect Hutus, Hutus in exile and displaced Hutus, Hutus who wanted to work with the RPF, and anti-Power Hutus who were also anti-RPF, and of course all the old frictions between Hutus of the north and those of the south remained. As for Tutsis, there were all the exiled backgrounds and languages, and survivors and returnees regarding each other with mutual suspicion; there were RPF Tutsis, non-RPF Tutsis, and anti-RPF Tutsis; there were urbanites and cattle keepers, whose concerns as survivors or returnees had almost nothing in common. And, of course, there were many more subcategories, which cut across the others and might, at any given moment, be more important. There were clans and families, rich and poor, Catholics, Muslims, Protestants of various stripes, and a host of more private animists, as well as all the normal social cliques and affiliations, including male and female, who were marrying each other at a fantastic clip, now that the war was over and it was allowed in the RPF, and now that so many had lost any other form of family.

It made one's head spin. Even Rwandans didn't claim to have it all mapped. For the most part, they stuck with the people they knew from before, and didn't care so much if they made no new friends so long as they didn't acquire new enemies. In the long view, it seemed to my American mind that there was some hope in the fact that a country which had been destroyed by a mad wish for every citizen to have exactly the same identity as every other—the identity of a mass murderer, no less—contained more diversity than ever. But that was taking a very long view. Intermarriage rates were at an all-time low, scoring another point for the *genocidaires* in the new, officially ethnicity-free Rwanda; and not a day went by without a new story going around on *radio trottoir* of an imminent Hutu Power invasion from Zaire.

"They say the war was won but for us too much was lost," Odette Nyiramilimo told me. After the genocide, she and Jean-Baptiste had adopted ten children, and took it upon themselves to treat child survivors for free at their clinic. "We feel it's a moral obligation," she said, "but the children are so traumatized that we hardly know how to help them."

After the family was evacuated from the Hotel des Milles Collines, Jean-Baptiste had gone to work with an RPF medical unit helping survivors, and Odette had taken their three children to Nairobi, vowing never to return to Rwanda. Then she received news that some of her nephews and nieces had survived. "As soon as I heard that, I knew I had to come back," she said. "We began to find them and to take them in, but it's very difficult to satisfy all their needs. One of them—a four-year-old—weighed just seventeen pounds when he was found." Once she told me, "We were in the car, Jean-Baptiste and I, and our three children, and one of the kids said, 'I'm so happy just to be all five of us together again.' We said, 'Aren't you happy to live with your cousins?' But they didn't say anything."

Odette looked over at her children in the pool of the Cercle Sportif. When she turned back to me, she said, "This life after a genocide is really a terrible life." The fluidity and urgency with which she had told the story of her earlier ordeals had given way to a hopscotch, free-associating rhythm as she described life in the aftermath. "When I was still in Nairobi, saying I'd never come back, there was a group of young Rwandan fifty-niners who'd gone to visit Rwanda for the first time," she said. "They got back to Nairobi and said how beautiful and wonderful it all was, and the only problem in Rwanda was the survivors who want to tell you all their stories forever. That really got to me."

She said, "The trauma comes back much more as time passes—this year more than last. So how can I look forward to next year? We take refuge a bit in our work, but many people become very depressed. I'm afraid it gets worse. I dream more of my sisters and cry through my dreams."

Odette had one nephew who survived the genocide in Kinunu, on the hill where she was born in Gisenyi. She had visited him only once, to help bury the dead, who were numerous, and she did not want to go back. "All the Hutus there watched us come, and some wanted to hug me," she said. "I cried out, 'Don't touch me. Where did you put everyone?' One was married to a cousin of mine. I said, 'Where's Therese?' He said, 'I couldn't do anything.' I said, 'What do you mean?' He said, 'It wasn't me who did it.' I said, 'I don't want to see you. I don't want to know you.' Now whenever the Hutus there see a car coming to my nephew's, they all hide. People will say I'm an extremist because I can't accept or tolerate the people who killed my family. So if they're afraid once in their lives—I was afraid since I was three years old—let them know how it feels."

She said it was hard to make new friends among the returnees. "They came with all their things. They can laugh, have a party. Among us it's always tales of genocide, and they don't like to hear about it. If they see I'm married to a Hutu, that I have some old Hutu friends, they don't understand. Really, everyone lives for himself now."

She said, "I was talking to my youngest, Patrick. I said, 'What are you thinking about?' He said, 'Those two guys who came with machetes. It comes back all the time.' The children don't go out—you have to push them—they like to stay home. They think about it a lot. My little Patrick, he goes alone into a room, and he looks under the bed for *interahamwe*. My daughter Arriane was in a very good boarding school in Nairobi, and one night she sat up reliving everything, and she cried. At midnight the dorm monitor came by and they spent nearly the whole night together. Arriane told her what had happened, and the monitor was amazed."

∾ KENZABURO OE,
　　Excerpt from *Hiroshima Notes*—JAPAN

Kenzaburo Oe was born in 1935 in a remote village on the island of Shikoku in Japan. He was six when the Second World War broke out. He received his BA in French literature from the University of Tokyo in 1959. Oe's first novel, *Memushiri Kouchi* (Nip the Buds, Shoot the Kids), appeared in 1958 and won the Akutagawa Prize given to young fiction writers. In 1960 Oe married Yakari Itami, and in 1963 he became the father of a baby boy, Hikari, who was born with a congenital abnormality of the skull. When the doctors advised Oe and his wife to let Hikari die, he rejected their advice. The birth of Hikari was a turning point in Oe's life and in his literary career. Oe has written many essays and short stories in addition to his novels and has traveled globally to lecture. Oe considers himself a "writer of the periphery." He has said, "Literature must be written from the periphery towards the center, and we can criticize the center. Our credo, our theme, or our imagination is that of the peripheral human being. The man who is in the center does not have anything to write."

Hiroshima Notes (1965) describes the techniques doctors used to survive when working in the aftermath of the atomic bomb blast: "Only the person with duller vision, who sees crisis as part of ongoing life, can possibly cope with it. It is precisely the 'dullness,' the restricted vision that permits one to act with reckless human courage in the face of crisis, without succumbing to despair."

Twentieth-century literature has dealt with a variety of extreme situations, most of which are concerned with the evil found in man or in the universe. If the word "evil" sounds too moralistic, it may be replaced with "absurdity." But in the various extreme situations—wars, storms, floods, pestilence—there is usually some sign of hope and recovery. These signs are found not in the fearful crisis dimensions of extremity but, rather, in the human goodwill and in the order and meaning that appear implicitly in the faint light of everyday life. A plague that ravages a city in North Africa, for example, appears as an abnormal phenomenon; but the doctors and citizens who struggle against it rely on their normal everyday human traits such as mechanical repetition, routine habits, and even patient endurance of tedium.

If a person is so clear-eyed as to see a crisis in its totality, he cannot avoid falling into a despair. Only the person with duller vision, who sees a crisis as part of ongoing life, can possibly cope with it. It is precisely the 'dullness,' the restricted vision, that permits one to act with reckless human courage in the face of crisis, without succumbing to despair. The lesser vision is backed by patience and, in fact, is capable of penetrating insight into the nature of a crisis.

Immediately after the atomic bombing in Hiroshima, it is recorded, a certain prophetic voice said that no grass would grow in Hiroshima's soil for seventy-five years. Was it the voice of a foolish prophet who made a hasty mistake? Hardly. It was the voice of one making a forthright observation of a crisis situation. The prophecy soon proved false when late summer rains washed the wasted land and urged it to new growth. But was not the true damage done at a deeper level? I remember the strong, physical nausea I felt when, through a microscope, I saw the magnified leaf cells of a specimen of *Veronica persica Poir*, the cells were slightly crooked in an unspeakably ugly way. I wonder whether all plants that now grow green in Hiroshima may not have received the same fatal damage.

There is no way of keeping one's balance in daily life and not be overwhelmed by crises except to believe in the green grass if it sprouts from the scorched earth before our very eyes, and thus not indulge in desperate imaginings so long as nothing abnormal happens. This is the only truly human way of living in Hiroshima. No one would continue indefinitely to make one effort after another if there were absolutely no hope for several decades that the grass would grow green again; but human beings cannot help hoping, at least for a while, that the grass will grow.

It takes a person of great care and insight to watch for any abnormality in the green grass even while it grows abundantly and healthily. A person, that is, who is humanistic in the truest sense—neither too wildly desperate nor too vainly hopeful. Such genuine humanists were definitely needed in Hiroshima in the summer of 1945. Fortunately, there were such people in Hiroshima at the time; and they were the first cause for hope of survival in the midst of the most desolate wasteland of human experience. When the young dentist agonized, "Why must the Hiroshima people suffer even after the war's end?" (and thereby marked the onset of another cruel battle) the older doctor remained silent. Even if the young man had shouted his question loud enough to be heard around the world, none of us could have answered him. His query merely voiced an absurdity for which no one has the answer. So, the old doctor kept quiet. He was busy with relief work and, naturally, overworked. Thirty minutes later the young man hanged himself, perhaps because he realized that the doctor's silence was not just that of one individual, but of all human beings. No one could have prevented so desperate a man, with so absurd a question, from committing suicide. Hence, he hanged himself. The old doctor survived and continued his relief work, and he became known as the doctor with dull but daring eyes, a man who never succumbed to despair.

That is not to say that the old doctor never uttered a word of despair in his heart. He may well have been seized with a sense of despair heavier than the young man's; but he did not surrender to it. Indeed, he had neither the freedom to surrender nor the time for suicide. With what a bitter, grief-stricken heart he took down the lifeless body of the young dentist from the broken wall—the corpse of his young co-worker whose fatal affliction was mental, not physical, despite his fractured hands and half-burned body. Each evening the bodies of the dead were piled up in the hospital yard and burned. Perhaps the old man himself had to put the young man's body on the great heap of corpses. Surely an absurd question still lingered in his bitter, heavy heart: 'Why did the Hiroshima people still suffer so, even after the war had ended?' Yet, for twenty years he never surrendered; he simply could not.

The old doctor, Fumio Shigeto, could have been overwhelmed by a despair far heavier than that of the young dentist, for he came to know concretely and increasingly what the young man had felt and vaguely feared.

Dr. Shigeto had arrived at the Hiroshima Red Cross Hospital just a week before the atomic disaster occurred. But that unprecedented event linked him to Hiroshima for life and made him a genuine Hiroshima man. Following the explosion, the first thing the doctor did, after getting back on his feet with a bloody head at the east entrance of Hiroshima Railroad Station, was to run through the utterly destroyed and still flaming streets to the Red Cross Hospital, closer than the railroad station to the central bombed area. At first, complete silence hovered over everything there. Then, suddenly, fierce cries filled the city, and these cries never ceased during the rescue activity of the doctor and his colleagues at the Red Cross Hospital. Soon the dead bodies piled up in the hospital yard began to emit a relentless foul odor.

Give Me Water

Give me water!
Oh! Give me water to drink!
Let me have some!
I want rather to die—
To die!
Oh!
Help me, oh, help me!
Water!
A bit of water!
I beg you!
Won't anyone?
Oh— Oh— Oh— Oh!
Oh— Oh— Oh— Oh!
The heaven split;
The streets are gone;
The river
The river flowing on!
Oh— Oh— Oh— Oh!
Oh— Oh— Oh— Oh!
Night!
Night coming on
To these eyes parched and sore
To these lips inflamed.

Ah! The moaning of a man,
Of a man
Reeling,
Whose face is
Scorched, smarting;
The ruined face of man!

—Tamaki Hara

While persevering in rescue work, Dr Shigeto approached the moment of awesome reality when the nature of the overwhelming, grotesque explosion would be revealed to him. Many others in Hiroshima were on the threshold of the same critical moment. A medical scholar who from his days as an unpaid junior assistant in Kyushu Imperial University's department of internal medicine had been interested in radiology, he discovered that hermetically sealed X-ray film stored in the Red Cross Hospital had been exposed [by radiation] and that camera film with which he had tried to photograph the A-bomb victims' injuries had likewise been rendered useless. When investigating the city streets, he picked up tiles on which the outline of a shepherd's purse [herb] had been imprinted. In his mind, the horrifying truth about the bomb's radioactivity began to take shape clearly. Three weeks later atomic scientists from Tokyo confirmed the nature of the bomb—an atomic bomb made with uranium (U-235).

Confirmation of the bomb's nature, however, by no means resolved the immense difficulty facing the doctors: how to treat the various radiation injuries. The atomic scientists merely confirmed for Dr Shigeto and others that the "enemy" they struggled with was the worst and strongest ever encountered. And all they had to treat the massive, complex injuries with were surgical instruments and injections of camphor and vitamins. How did the doctors cope with what they increasingly recognized as acute radiation symptoms? Dr Tsurayuki Asakawa, chief of internal medicine in Hiroshima Red Cross Hospital at the time, speaks very frankly about this predicament, as recorded in the "Hiroshima A-bomb Medical Care History":

People with no discernible injuries came and said that they felt listless, though they did not know why. In time, they developed nosebleeds, bloody stools, and subcutaneous hemorrhages; then they would die. At first, we did not know the cause of death. As it was common sense when an illness is not clearly diagnosed to check the patient's blood, I went to the hospital basement to fetch blood analysis equipment; and when I examined the blood cells, I was astonished. It was, I realized, only natural that the patients had died, for their white cell counts were extremely low. They could not possibly have lived.

I am impressed by this physician's "common sense," by his perseverance in a crisis situation. There was, however, no medicine available to treat what he discovered. For a nosebleed, he could only insert a pressure tampon into the nose; the doctor did not know clearly the cause of the nosebleed. By the time the bleeding began, the A-bomb victims were already on the verge of death.

By the winter following the atomic bombing, most of the patients with acute radiation symptoms had died; and, at least outwardly, the critical stage of radiation illness had passed. In the struggle against the worst-ever attack on human life, mankind was defeated before the battle had hardly begun. The doctors faced such severe handicaps that they were in a losing position from the outset. Even so, Dr Shigeto and his colleagues never surrendered. They simply could not, for leukemia—the most dreadful aspect of the enemy—was beginning to rear its ugly head.

Although the enemy's overwhelming power became unmistakably clearer, the doctors did not surrender. More precisely, they simply refused to surrender. There was nothing whatsoever in the situation that encouraged them not to give up; they simply refused to do so.

If they had surrendered, the "Hiroshima A-bomb Medical Care History" would have concluded with an account of defeat after the first few pages. Neither did the occupation forces that came into Hiroshima soon after the bombing know how to cope with the enormous monster they themselves had released. They sought clues by setting up the Atomic Bomb Casualty Commission atop Hijiyama hill and by undertaking medical examinations. But treatment of the stricken people depended entirely upon the human efforts of the surviving doctors in the A-bomb-assaulted city. And the doctors never surrendered, even though enveloped by darkness more real and urgent than that which drove the young dentist to suicide. For two decades they could not, simply would not, give up. The atomic monster increasingly exhibited its painful, ominous powers—always superior to the strength of the doctors. But Dr Shigeto and his colleagues stood fast.

꩜ CHARLOTTE DELBO,
Excerpt from *Days and Memory*—FRANCE

Charlotte Delbo was born in Vigneux sur Seine, France, in 1913.
In 1941, Delbo stopped her work for a French theater director in
order to join the Resistance, fighting the Nazis. In March 1942,
both Delbo and her husband were arrested. Her husband was shot
two months later, while she was moved to Auschwitz and later to
Ravensbruck. After the war Delbo returned to writing. She also
worked for the United Nations and the philosopher Henri Lefevre
in the 1960s. Charlotte Delbo died in Paris in March 1985.

In *Days and Memory* (first published in 1985 in French as
La Mémoire et Les Jours), Delbo writes of the way she has
compartmentalized the memories of the Holocaust, the absolute
splitting of "before" and "after" as an ongoing technique of
survival. Yet those memories also go with her wherever she goes.
Delbo writes, "Auschwitz is so deeply etched in my memory that
I cannot forget one moment of it. So you are living with it?—
No, I live next to it. Auschwitz is there, unalterable, precise
but enveloped in the skin of memory, an impermeable skin
that isolates it from my present self."

Explaining the inexplicable. There comes to mind the image of a snake
shedding its old skin, emerging from beneath it in a fresh, glistening one.
In Auschwitz I took leave of my skin—it had a bad smell, that skin—worn
from all the blows it had received, and found myself in another, beautiful and clean, although with me the molting was not as rapid as the snake's.
Along with the old skin went the visible traces of Auschwitz: the leaden
stare out of sunken eyes, the tottering gait, the frightened gestures. With
the new skin returned the gestures belonging to an earlier life; the using
of a toothbrush, of toilet paper, of a handkerchief, of a knife and fork,
eating food calmly, saying hello to people upon entering a room, closing
the door, standing up straight, speaking, later on smiling with my lips and,
still later, smiling both at once with my lips and my eyes. Rediscovering
odors, flavors, the smell of rain. In Birkenau, rain heightened the odor
of diarrhea. It is the most fetid odor I know. In Birkenau, the rain came
down upon the camp, upon us, laden with soot from the crematoriums,
and with the odor of burning flesh. We were steeped in it.

It took a few years for the new skin to fully form, to consolidate.

Rid of its old skin, it's still the same snake. I'm the same too, apparently. However . . .

How does one rid oneself of something buried far within: memory and the skin of memory. It clings to me yet. Memory's skin has hardened, it allows nothing to filter out of what it retains, and I have no control over it. I don't feel it anymore.

In the camp one could never pretend, never take refuge in the imagination. I remember Yvonne Picart, a morning when we were carrying bricks from a wrecker's depot. We carried two bricks at a time, from one pile to another pile. We were walking side by side, our bricks hugged to our chests, bricks we had pried from a pile covered with ice, scraping our hands. Those bricks were heavy, and got heavier as the day wore on. Our hands were blue from cold, our lips cracked. Yvonne said to me: "Why can't I imagine I'm on the Boulevard Saint-Michel, walking to class with an armful of books?" and she propped the two bricks inside her forearm, holding them as students do books. "It's impossible. One can't imagine either being somebody else or being somewhere else."

I too, I often tried to imagine I was somewhere else. I tried to visualize myself as someone else, as when in a theatrical role you become another person. It didn't work.

In Auschwitz reality was so overwhelming, the suffering, the fatigue, the cold so extreme, that we had no energy left for this type of pretending. When I would recite a poem, when I would tell the comrades beside me what a novel or a play was about while we went on digging in the muck of the swamp, it was to keep myself alive, to preserve my memory, to remain me, to make sure of it. Never did that succeed in nullifying the moment I was living through, not for an instant. To think, to remember was a great victory over the horror, but it never lessened it. Reality was right there, killing. There was no possible getting away from it.

How did I manage to extricate myself from it when I returned? What did I do so as to be alive today? People often ask me that question, to which I continue to look for an answer, and still find none.

Auschwitz is so deeply etched in my memory that I cannot forget one moment of it.—So you are living with Auschwitz?—No, I live next to it. Auschwitz is there, unalterable, precise, but enveloped in the skin of memory, an impermeable skin that isolates it from my present self. Unlike the snake's skin, the skin of memory does not renew itself. Oh, it may harden further . . . Alas, I often fear lest it grow thin, crack, and the camp get hold of me again. Thinking about it makes me tremble with apprehension. They claim the dying see their whole life pass before their eyes . . .

In this underlying memory sensations remain intact. No doubt, I am very fortunate in not recognizing myself in the self that was in Auschwitz. To return from there was so improbable that it seems to me I was never there at all. Unlike those whose life came to a halt as they crossed the threshold of return, who since that time survive as ghosts, I feel that the one who was in the camp is not me, is not the person who is here, facing you. No, it is all too incredible. And everything that happened to that other, the Auschwitz one, now has no bearing upon me, does not concern me, so separate from one another are this deep-lying memory and ordinary memory. I live within a twofold being. The Auschwitz double doesn't bother me, doesn't interfere with my life. As though it weren't I at all. Without this split I would not have been able to revive.

The skin enfolding the memory of Auschwitz is tough. Even so it gives way at times, revealing all it contains. Over dreams the conscious will has no power. And in those dreams I see myself, yes, my own self such as I know I was: hardly able to stand on my feet, my throat tight, my heart beating wildly, frozen to the marrow, filthy, skin and bones; the suffering I feel is so unbearable, so identical to the pain endured there, that I feel it physically, I feel it throughout my whole body which becomes a mass of suffering; and I feel death fasten on me, I feel that I am dying. Luckily, in my agony I cry out. My cry wakes me and I emerge from the nightmare, drained. It takes days for everything to get back to normal, for everything to get shoved back inside memory, and for the skin of memory to mend again. I become myself again, the person you know, who can talk to you about Auschwitz without exhibiting or registering any anxiety or emotion.

Because when I talk to you about Auschwitz, it is not from deep memory my words issue. They come from external memory, if I may put it that way, from intellectual memory, the memory connected with thinking processes. Deep memory preserves sensations, physical imprints. It is the memory of the senses. For it isn't words that are swollen with emotional charge. Otherwise, someone who has been tortured by thirst for weeks on end could never again say "I'm thirsty. How about a cup of tea." This word has also split in two. *Thirst* has turned back into a word for commonplace use. But if I dream of the thirst I suffered in Birkenau, I once again see the person I was, haggard, halfway crazed, near to collapse; I physically feel that real thirst and it is an atrocious nightmare. If, however, you'd like me to talk to you about it . . .

This is why I say today that while knowing perfectly well that it corresponds to the facts, I no longer know if it is real.

🖎 ALEXANDER MOLOT,
    "Earlier Winter"—CANADA

> The Canadian writer Alex Molot obliquely addresses the fear that lingers after surviving the attacks of 9/11. Even though he never mentions September 11, 2001 directly, his essay "Earlier Winter" was written for a specially commissioned collection: *110 Stories: New York Writes after September 11*. In Molot's essay, the looming threat in the story lurks almost entirely beneath the surface. Molot writes, "So tightly have I packed down my memories that they almost crunch under the telling. . . . How we must hide and shelter our true selves beneath icy overlays. That we trap or are ourselves trapped by this art of remembrance." Molot suggests that we freeze part of our selves in an effort to perpetuate survival.

When I say Canada, people always ask about the winter. How cold does it get up there? Very cold. Much colder than here. So cold that you can feel your cheekbones beneath your skin.

How much snow do you get? So much that you can still see it come May or even June, at least in some places. But when it snows, I continue voluntarily, the streets are always cleared overnight. Only once, maybe, did I miss school. And everyone is used to the cold. So tightly have I packed down my memories that they almost crunch under the telling.

But it's only a typical winter scene. I am clearing the snow from our driveway. This business of clearing snow can be strangely satisfying. Splitting the snowy seas one sweep after another, I liberate the driveway. A gradual stretch of pavement rises, growing longer and longer. But a layer of ice remains overtop, the ice of snow melted and re-frozen. It is ugly ice, dark and rough. The thin sections give way quickly, the thicker after several hard pounds, and the thickest not at all.

By now I do not feel the cold; I am warmed by my exertions. I look up and see my father approaching. Perhaps he is returning from work. Or maybe just out for a walk. As he nears, I wave. When he reaches the driveway, he looks down and says, "That's good enough. Remember, the ice protects the pavement."

Words burdened by so much. Of the wisdom that passes from fathers to sons. How we must hide and shelter our true selves beneath icy over-lays. That we trap or are ourselves trapped by this art of remembrance. What strikes me hard, though, is how simple the telling is and that I can-not. It forces on me all that has since happened. Loss and disillusion. Sad-ness and regret. The gap between what I feel and what I know.

The ice protects the pavement. How well the pavement controls its fear. For pavement, that is. And what of the boy clinging to the firm and faith-ful feel of his shovel? Often sleepless with fear, I wonder.

LANDSCAPE AND MEMORY

In the suburban Argentine town of Morón, the community has embraced the excavation of a former torture site. The Argentine military had taken over the Mansión Seré, originally a private home, as a clandestine detention center between 1976 and 1978. It was then abandoned, and by 1986 the building had been razed, and the land was incorporated into a sports complex and park built by the municipality. In 2000, a local human rights organization launched the reclamation project, in cooperation with city officials. A team from the University of Buenos Aires, many of whose students from the 1970s are counted among the *desaparecidos*, began the painstaking process of excavation. Now one of the park buildings incorporates an informal exhibition giving the history of the site and the background of human rights abuses in Argentina. The physical recovery of long-buried places in order to transform them into such public sites of reflection and memory is especially important when the site is actually a resting place for the irretrievable remains of the fallen: Lincoln's "hallowed ground" at Gettysburg, the extermination camp sites in Eastern Europe, or the World Trade Center site, "Ground Zero."

The graphic artist Art Spiegelman depicted the traumatized New York landscape in his cover for the collection *110 Stories: New York Writes after September 11*. A black funeral shroud seemingly covers the Two Towers, hovering a little above the New York skyline. Funeral shrouds usually encase bodies rather than buildings, but in this case the image is appropriate since the buildings and the surrounding area became a de facto graveyard for many victims, as casualties merged with the earth itself. When the remains of the fallen cannot be retrieved because they have become too numerous to attend to properly, or because they have been pulverized beyond retrieval, landscape becomes a receptacle for mass killing. In effect, the dead become the landscape. As time passes, landscapes and nature can also begin the healing and renewal process. As Mel Gussow of the *New York Times* wrote, reflecting on the literary responses to 9/11 in America, "But on an apparently barren tree, there were small hidden buds of life."

This chapter brings together writers who explore the links between landscape, violence, and memory from a variety of angles. The Haitian writer Edwidge Danticat touches on the Duvalier dictatorships in Haiti in the 1960s, '70s and '80s; the South African journalist Bloke Modisane laments the demise of his home, Sophiatown, during Apartheid; British poet Robert Graves reflects on how the passing of time binds his memories of World War I increasingly tightly with the landscape; Saadat Hasan Manto touches on the blurring of identity as a result of the India-Pakistan Partition in 1947; and the American poet John Hoppenthaler addresses the way the violence of 9/11 affects our connection to the landscape after September 11, 2001.

∾ EDWIDGE DANTICAT,
  "Nineteen Thirty Seven"—HAITI

Edwidge Danticat was born in Port-au-Prince, Haiti in 1969. Her father immigrated to the United States in 1971, and her mother followed him in 1973. Danticat remained in Haiti eight more years, raised by her aunt through several years of the repressive, corrupt, and violent regime of President Francois Duvalier, "Papa Doc Duvaliver." In 1981 at age twelve, she reunited with her parents in a predominantly Haitian–American neighborhood in Brooklyn, New York City. Danticat received a degree in French literature from Barnard College and a MFA from Brown University. Her short stories have appeared in many periodicals and have been anthologized, and she won a 1995 Pushcart Short Story Prize. *Breath, Eyes, Memory* was an Oprah Book Club selection and *The Farming of Bones* won an American Book Award. Her work has been translated into Korean, Italian, German, French, Spanish, and Swedish.

The young female narrator in Danticat's short story "Nineteen

Thirty Seven" visits her mother, who has been imprisoned for accusations of being a witch. As they sit together, memories of shared landscapes float into the narrator's mind. She remembers visiting Massacre River, a river between Haiti and the Dominican Republic, where her mother thrust her hand into the river. The narrator writes, "When we dipped our hands, I thought that the dead would reach out and haul us in, but only our own faces stared back at us, one indistinguishable from the other." Her mother made yearly pilgrimages to the river because it connected her to her past: it was the site of an indiscriminate butchery by the Dominican army of an estimated fifteen to twenty thousand Haitians, including Danticat's grandmother. But the river is also the site of renewal. The narrator writes, "We came from the bottom of the river where the blood never stops flowing, where my mother's dive toward life—her swim among all those bodies slaughtered in flight—gave her those wings of flames. The river was the place where it had all begun."

Now, Maman sat with the Madonna pressed against her chest, her eyes staring ahead, as though she was looking into the future. She had never talked very much about the future. She had always believed more in the past.

When I was five years old, we went on a pilgrimage to the Massacre River, which I had expected to be still crimson with blood, but which was as clear as any water that I had ever seen. Maman had taken my hand and pushed it into the river, no farther than my wrist. When we dipped our hands, I thought the dead would reach out and haul us in, but only our own faces stared back at us, one indistinguishable from the other.

With our hands in the water, Maman spoke to the sun. "Here is my child, Josephine. We were saved from the tomb of this river when she was still in my womb. You spared us both, her and me, from this river where I lost my mother."

My mother had escaped El Generalissimo's soldiers, leaving her own mother behind. From the Haitian side of the river, she could still see the soldiers chopping up *her* mother's body and throwing it into the river along with many others.

We went to the river many times as I was growing up. Every year my mother would invite a few more women who had also lost their mothers there.

Until we moved to the city, we went to river every year on the first of November. The women would all dress in white. My mother would hold my hand tightly as we walked toward the water. We were all daughters of that river, which had taken our mothers from us. Our mothers were the ashes and we were the light. Our mothers were the embers and we were the sparks. Our mothers were the flames and we were the blaze. We came from the bottom of that river where the blood never stops flowing, where my mother's dive toward life—her swim among all those bodies slaughtered in flight—gave her those wings of flames. The river was the place where it had all begun.

"At least I gave birth to my daughter on the night that my mother was taken from me," she would say. "At least you came out at the right moment to take my mother's place."

ᦁ Bloke Modisane,
Excerpt from *Blame Me on History*—south africa

Bloke William Modisane was born in Sophiatown, in Johannesburg, in 1923. While in South Africa, he worked for the publication *Drum.* He used his position as a newspaper columnist to lobby to make theater and concerts available to black audiences and to promote the free dissemination of culture between the black and white races. Yet as a black South African writer, Bloke Modisane did not have the power to publish his scathing observations about the hypocrisy of life under Apartheid. Encountering countless legislative difficulties in making culture accessible to black audiences, Modisane was exiled in 1954 to London, where he continued to write. Modisane took to the stage himself in 1958 in *No Good Friday,* one of Athol Fugard's first plays. He first published his autobiography in the United States in 1963, as an exile. Bloke Modisane died in Germany in 1986.

Modisane also writes of a victimized landscape, or a landscape which has absorbed the harms done to the humans within it, in his autobiography, *Blame Me on History* (1963). He writes of his hometown: "Sophiatown was like one of its own many victims; a man gored by the knives of Sophiatown, lying in the open gutters, a raisin in the smelling drains, dying of multiple stab wounds, gaping wells gushing forth blood." Yet his return to the town of

Sophiatown is also very nostalgic, and he lovingly explores both its beautiful and horrible sides. He concludes, "Whatever else Sophiatown was, it was home; we made the dessert bloom. . . . We took the ugliness of life in a slum and wove a kind of beauty."

Something in me died, a piece of me died, with the dying of Sophiatown; it was in the winter of 1958, the sky was a cold blue veil which had been immersed in a bleaching solution and then spread out against a concave, the blue filtering through, and tinted by, a powder screen of grey; the sun, like the moon of the day, gave off more light than heat, mocking me with its promise of warmth—a fixture against the grey-blue sky—a mirror deflecting the heat and concentrating upon me in my Sophiatown only a reflection.

It was Monday morning, the first working day away from work; exactly seven days ago I had resigned my job as a working journalist on *Golden City Post*, the Johannesburg weekly tabloid for the locations. I was a free man, but the salt of the bitterness was still in my mouth; the quarrel with Hank Margolies, the assistant editor, the whiteman-boss confrontation, the letter of resignation, these things became interposed with the horror of the destruction of Sophiatown. I was a stranger walking through the streets of blitzed Sophiatown, and although the Western Areas removal scheme had been a reality dating back to some two years, I had not become fully conscious of it.

In the name of slum clearance they had brought the bulldozers and gored into her body, and for a brief moment, looking down Good Street, Sophiatown was like one of its own many victims; a man gored by the knives of Sophiatown, lying in the open gutters, a raisin in the smelling drains, dying of multiple stab wounds, gaping wells gushing forth blood; the look of shock and bewilderment, of horror and incredulity, on the face of the dying man.

My Sophiatown was a blitzed area which had suffered the vengeance of political conquest, a living memorial to the vandalism of Dr. Hendrik Frensch Verwoerd; my world was falling away, Martha Maduma's shebeen was gone, she had moved her business to Meyer Street, but the new shebeen lacked the colour and the smell of the long passage, the stench from the puddles of urine. I walked through the passage, the puddles were dried up and the smells were gone; and at the end of it was the door into Martha's shebeen, but she was not there.

Across the door over the corrugated iron fence was destruction, the tenement houses were razed to the ground; and somewhere among the ruins was the room of Nene, a boyhood friend, who had grown up to be a murderer doing a seven-year term of imprisonment; he would never see his room again or the woman he lived with. I hurried away from the scene, through the long passage and back to Good Street, past Aly's fish and chip shop which always smelt of old dripping. I stopped at the Odin Cinema to look at the stills; the films were always the same blood and thunder tuppeny horrors with memorable titles like *Two Guns West, The Fastest Gun Alive, Guns over the Prairie.*

Over the street facing the cinema was one of those enormous communal yards accommodating thirty-two families in thirty-two rooms; the people had been removed and the four blocks of eight rooms had not been demolished yet, but the roofs, doors and window-frames had been removed. Only the walls remained, the walls with the gaping wounds. On the walls of two of the rooms were slogans painted, perhaps hurriedly, and the pain bled down from the letters: "WE WON'T MOVE," "ONS POLA HIER," "HANDS OFF SOPHIATOWN." Against the background of the demolition the slogans were only a dusty mockery of the boast.

The building structures, the naked walls, seemed unprotected and helpless against the bulldozers, like trees, their leaves blown off by autumn winds, standing bare and numb to the winter cold; as I had stood on Christmas day three years ago in front of the cinema with the muzzle of a .38 revolver pointing at my stomach.

"Just open your mouth, Bloke," Lelinka had said, "open your mouth and I'll shoot you."

I stood there numb with fear, I was helpless, unarmed, I did not want to die.

"You bloody shit house," he said.

Gilbert "Kwembu" Moloi, former non-European heavyweight boxing champion, employed as the bouncer doorman, pleaded for my life, persuading Lelinka to put away the gun; and ten minutes later, during which my life had hung in the balance, ten minutes of obscenities thrown at me, Lelinka had put his gun away. I had won yet another reprieve.

I was working as an emergency usher in the Odin Cinema, and it was during the Christmas day matinée; suddenly a woman screamed in the one-and-tenpenny stalls.

"You'd better see what that's all about," said Mr. Berman, the manager.

"That's where the Americans are sitting," I replied. "You're a white man, they won't start anything with you."

"You're not afraid, are you?" he joked. "Don't worry, they'll touch you over your dead body."

I walked up the aisle to Row R and there was this girl crying, I flicked on the torch.

"Fock off," a voice said.

I flashed the torch in the face of the speaker; it was Lelinka, the knife-happy rough-house brother of Selenki and Boykie, the foundation members of the Americans, Sophiatown's best-dressed boys, whose fashions came right out of the pages of *Esquire*.

"Lelinka, that girl's making noise," I said.

"What do you want to see, Bloke?" Lelinka said, rising from his seat and removing his hand from under the girl's dress. "I said, fock off, shit house."

We exchanged words, insults and vulgarities, down the aisle out into the foyer, and it was only out in the light that I became aware of the revolver; I became silent immediately when I looked into his eyes.

The gaping scars of the bare walls began to frighten me, I hurried down the street, past Dr. Bayever's surgery and Dr. Wolfson's, stopping opposite the petrol-filling station; the "Thirty-Nine Steps," Fatty's famous shebeen, was demolished. I reconstructed in my mind the rickety steps—thirteen in all—which led up into the shebeen with neon lighting and contemporary furniture, and the seductive Fatty. It was perhaps the only shebeen which served ice cold beers; and definitely a famous Sophiatown landmark. It was gone.

Gone too were the stories which grew out of the "Thirty-Nine Steps," stories of excitement and terror; like the night The Spoilers, the gang from Alexandra Township, came to Fatty's and taunted the Durango Kid; word had gone out that the Durango Kid had gone straight, that he was no longer carrying guns. The Spoilers had come to Sophiatown in their De Soto and inside the "Thirty-Nine Steps" they taunted the Durango Kid, baiting him into a fight; but the Durango Kid was patient, refusing to be provoked, and in the end when the threats were becoming more explicit, he got up.

"Wait for me," he said, "I'll be right back."

A quarter of an hour later he was walking down Good Street with two guns, like his namesake, and at that particular moment The Spoilers were leaving the shebeen in the De Soto; the Durango Kid started shooting, from both hands, and the De Soto jerked away like a jet, with the Durango Kid shooting until it went out of range.

All that was gone.

Walking down Good Street and up Gerty Street was like walking through a ghost town of deserted houses and demolished homes, of faded dreams and broken lives, surrounded by rousing memories, some exciting others terrifying; for Sophiatown was like our nice-time parties or the sound of the penny whistle, a mounting compulsion to joyousness, but always with the hint of pain. Sophiatown was also like our week-ends, it was the reason, or rather the excuse we used to stop the progress of time, to celebrate a kind of wish fulfillment; we cherished Sophiatown because it brought together such a great concentration of people, we did not live in it, we were Sophiatown. It was a complex paradox which attracted opposites; the ring of joy, the sound of laughter, was interposed with the growl and the smell of insult; we sang our sad happy songs, were carried away by our erotic dances, we whistled and shouted, got drunk and killed each other.

I stopped opposite 21 Gerty Street, there was only the debris of the house in which Emily lived; the memory of happy nights spent there rushed back to tease and irritate me, and it was then that loneliness penetrated. The people I had known, and loved, were gone; the relative, the friend, the childhood sweetheart, last year's beauty queen, the nice-time girls, the shebeen queens, the beggars, the thieves, the frauds, the gangsters, the killers; they were all gone, and with them had gone the only world I knew. The music had gone, the colour, the violence, only the desolation remained.

I drifted aimlessly into yards reconstructing the hovels, the shacks, the slum dwellings, from out of the debris and the dust; avoiding the open gutters, walking round the garbage cans, the lavatories, knowing that these were the things I hated most in Sophiatown and because they were no longer mine to complain about I loved them. And there in the rubble was a piece of me.

The pride of having grown up in Sophiatown shrivelled inside me; I had failed my children as my father and my forefathers and the ancestral gods of my fathers had failed me; they had lost a country, a continent, but I had failed to secure a patch of weeds for my children, a Sophiatown which essentially was a slum. I stood over the ruins of the house where I was born on Bertha Street, and knew that I would never say to my children: this is the house where I was born, that when I was a boy Sophiatown was a bare veld; that there once was a tree here, perhaps the only one in the location, round and about and into which we played, dreamt a little and built a fairy location with parks and gardens beautiful with flowers; a location with playgrounds like the ones white children played in; that the dreams we weaved were bold. But not for them even the pleasant reminiscences, only the interminable tragedy of dispossession; all that I can bequeath to them is the debris and the humiliation of defeat, the pain of watching Sophiatown dying all around me, dying by the hand of man.

The house in which I had been born was now grounded into the dust and it seemed especially appropriate that I should be standing there, as if to witness the closing of the cycle of my life in its destruction; my friends were leaving the country, Ezekiel Mphahlele had taken a job in Nigeria, the Millners were gone to Ireland, Arthur Maimane was in Ghana, and soon Elly and Lionel Rogosin and the crew of "Come Back Africa" would be leaving. Then Mr. De Wet Nel, Minister of Bantu Administration and Development, under Section 9 (7) (f) of the Natives (Urban Areas) Act No. 25 of 1945, threatened that "the Minister of Bantu Administration and Development may, unless the local authority objects, by notice in the *Gazette*, prohibit a social gathering in a private home in a town, at which an African is present, if, in his opinion, such gathering is undesirable having regard to the locality in which the house is situated. Any African attending such a gathering is guilty of an offence and liable to a fine not exceeding ten pounds or to imprisonment not exceeding two months or to both such fine and such imprisonment."

The Minister then proceeded to publish the names of thirteen white South Africans, prohibiting them from having parties or, in the words of the Minister, he barred the thirteen citizens of Johannesburg from "attending, holding or organising, directly or indirectly, any gathering at which an African is present." These mixed gatherings are being held by "irresponsible persons, and which are un–South African and subversive in nature, in direct contravention to well-known South African custom," and the Minister concluded, inferring dark and strange events, that "lately, liquor has flowed freely at such parties, and the results can be left to the imagination."

It was a tactical move on the part of the Minister, the announcement was sufficient in itself, it was not necessary to solicit the consent of the local authority; the liberals buckled, they had been intimidated, and became careful not to be listed with "the thirteen," most of whom had been banned under the Suppression of Communism Act and were treason trialists.

White friends who had usually invited me to their homes for that "illegal drink" became appropriately careful, and when they did invite me the rendezvous was my room in Sophiatown. I was incensed by this; it was objectionable enough for the Government to regulate our private lives, but this intrusion upon private freedom made me recalcitrant. I invited more white friends to my home as a registration of protest, hoping to inspire in them a physical objection to this intrusion; but the Minister had put the fear of the tyrant in them, and when I fully realised this, that they were afraid and were accommodating this intolerable situation, the country began to die for me.

I began to suffocate, and with Sophiatown dying my whole world was falling apart; my marriage had been festering away and my wife, Fiki, had taken my daughter and "gone to mother." The quarrel with Hank Margolies closed the ring; I did not have to resign my job, I could have swallowed my pride and allowed the assistant editor the privilege of being white. There was an unwritten law that on "Drum" publications we were equal, black and white, if in nothing else but in that as human beings we were equal, but apparently this had not been brought to the attention of the assistant editor.

"Mr. Margolies," I said, "If it's possible I wish to be excused from working this afternoon."

"Why should you be excused?" Hank Margolies said, all forthright and American.

"Monday afternoon is our day off, and I made alternative arrangements," I said. "If we had been told on Saturday, I wouldn't have committed myself."

"What's so important it can't wait?"

"I'm helping Lionel Rogosin with the shooting of his film."

Hank Margolies smiled benignly and adjusted his cigar in his mouth; he clanged his teeth into it.

"I don't understand you," he said, "what's more important to you? Your job or Rogosin's film?"

"Hank, the notice came out this morning," I emphasised. "I've made promises."

"Modisane, your first loyalty is to your paper," he said, smiling in that superior way he had. "It's your life. What kind of a journalist are you?"

"Opening envelopes couldn't be that important," I said, "one more or less won't make any difference."

"Look, Modisane," he said, jabbing a finger at me, "I don't want to argue with you. You either do the job or take your hat and go—I don't want to argue."

"But, Mr. Margolies . . ."

"I'm not arguing with you, Modisane," his voice boomed, turning his back and walking to his desk.

It was a terrible confrontation; my colleagues were embarrassed and sympathetic, half hoping I would precipitate a showdown which would finally resolve the dichotomous relationship between the black journalists and the white staff; the cub reporters were surprised that a senior member had been confronted like a cub. They were all staring at me, anticipating, silently urging on a dramatic situation. I sank into my chair, formulating my decision, and some minutes later I lifted the receiver and dialled Lionel Rogosin's number.

"Lionel? Bloke," I said. "Look, Lionel, something important has come up at the office, I can't meet you this afternoon. Meet you tonight? Your flat, about eight, okay. Sorry, Lionel."

Conversation through the lunch hour was halting, Simon Mogapi, the sports editor, was mumbling something like, "he'll never talk to me like that," mostly we ate in silence; too many things wanted to be said, and I did not intend to discuss my decision which had been an arbitrary one since I did not have a wife at home to discuss it with. We returned to the office by way of the shebeen which was on the roof of the office building, and right through the afternoon we opened envelopes, checking entries sent in by readers. It was the weekend following the July Handicap, South Africa's Derby, and *Golden City Post* awarded annual prizes for the correct forecast of the first four horses; there were thousands of entries and the opening of envelopes, sorting and checking took us through to seven o'clock that evening.

Lloyd, the copy boy, came round collecting signatures of the journalists who had sacrificed their afternoon off; a compensation of fifteen shillings would be paid against the signatures. I refused to sign.

"Look, Bra-Bloke, this is money," Lloyd said.

"Yes, I know," I said, "but I didn't do the work for money, it was out of loyalty. I donate mine to 'Drum' publications."

The work was done, the winning entries locked in the safe, the rubbish cleared, I sat behind my desk and typed out my letter of resignation; I was obliged to give a month's notice, but the company owed me three weeks' holiday which I submitted as part of my obligation, to be deducted from the four weeks. I worked one week and walked out of the office a free man. The editor, Cecil Eprile, who was a personal friend, was disturbed by the remarks I made in my letter concerning the white attitudes on the paper. I was disappointed that Mr. Margolies seemingly failed to realise the significance of what I had done.

Perhaps the concentrated impact had not crystallized in my mind; at the time it had seemed the heroic thing to do, but standing there on the ruins of the house in which I was born I seemed to be looking at my whole life, the body which contained that life reduced to dust; I kept remembering a line of Omar Khayyám: "I came like water, and like wind I go." Sophiatown and I were reduced to the basic elements, both of us for the same reason: we were black spots.

Sophiatown died, not because it was a social embarrassment, but because it was a political corn inside the Apartheid boot. The then Minister of Bantu Administration and Development, Mr. Verwoerd, condemned Sophiatown because it was a slum; true there were no parks, playgrounds, civic halls, libraries; true that a large number of people lived in what was described as "appalling conditions," in corrugated iron shanties, subdivided by cardboard walls; true that on 50 by 100 feet areas, up to eighty people were huddled in back-yard shacks; but it is also true that Moroka was an approved shanty started in 1946 as an emergency camp where every family was housed in hessian shacks.

If the Government was concerned with alleviating the living conditions of the Africans, the shanties of Moroka, Edenvale, Eastern Township, deserved this consideration far more than did Sophiatown, where the real problem was overcrowding; the shanties of Sophiatown were erected behind solid houses; but the politicians saw political gains and the sociologists and the race relationists saw only textbook solutions—new townships, with recreation centres, parks, schools, libraries, playgrounds; poverty it seems is less disturbing to the public conscience if it is suffocated in model housing estates.

Sophiatown belonged to me; when we were not shaking hands or chasing the same girl or sharing a bottle of brandy, we were sticking knives into each other's backs. The land was bought with the sweat, the scrounging, the doing without, and it not only was mine, but a piece of me; the house was mine even if the rain leaked through the roof and the cold seemed to creep through the cracks in the ceiling, and crawled through the rattling window-frames and under the door.

It was widely conceded that Sophiatown was a slum, and slum clearance was a programme the principles of which were generally accepted; but it was Sophiatown the "black spot" which had to be ravaged, and as Can

Themba said: "I have long stopped arguing the injustice, the vindictiveness, the strong arm authority of which prostrate Sophiatown is a loud symbol."

. . .

Whatever else Sophiatown was, it was home; we made the desert bloom; made alterations, converted half-verandas into kitchens, decorated the houses and filled them with music. We were house-proud. We took the ugliness of life in a slum and wove a kind of beauty; we established bonds of human relationships, which set a pattern of communal living, far richer and more satisfying—materially and spiritually—than any model housing could substitute. The dying of a slum is a community tragedy, anywhere.

ᕦ Robert Graves,
"Recalling War"—ENGLAND

Poet, novelist, and critic Robert Graves was born in 1895 in Wimbledon, England. Graves enlisted in August 1914, fought in the Battle of Loos, and was injured in 1916 in the Battle of the Somme. Over the next two years, he wrote three volumes of poetry and spent a year in the trenches on the front, where he was again severely wounded.

After the war, Graves taught at Oxford, and in 1929 he published *Goodbye to All That*, an autobiography that explored the residual horror of his war experiences that lingered with him years later. In the following decade, he moved to Majorca and continued writing verse and criticism and co-founded Seizin Press in 1928 and *Epilogue,* a semiannual magazine, in 1935. At the onset of the Spanish Civil War in 1936, Graves fled Majorca, settling in America but returning to Majorca after the Second World War. During his lifetime he published more than 140 books, including fifty-five collections of poetry (he reworked his *Collected Poems* repeatedly during his career), fifteen novels, ten translations, and forty works of nonfiction, autobiography, and literary essays. Robert Graves died in Majorca in 1985, at the age of ninety.

In Graves's poem "Recalling War" (1938), landscape and violence blur together with the passing of time. The speaker reflects on World War I, fought twenty years ago, which "now assumes the nature-look of time. . . . What, then, was war? No mere discord of flags / But an infection of the common sky . . . War was return of earth to ugly earth." Graves's words highlight a particularly gruesome preoccupation of these depictions of traumatized landscapes: the reduction of a once-living person to a simple mass of organic matter, returning earth to the earth. Though this is the fate of all living things, the accelerated pace and overwhelming scale of this return of "dust to dust" is the distinct product of massive violence.

Entrance and exit wounds are silvered clean,
The track aches only when the rain reminds.
The one-legged man forgets his leg of wood,
The one-armed man his jointed wooden arm.
The blinded man sees with his ears and hands
As much or more than once with both his eyes.
Their war was fought these twenty years ago
And now assumes the nature-look of time,
As when the morning traveler turns and views
His wild night-stumbling carved into a hill.

What, then, was war? No mere discord of flags
But an infection of the common sky
That sagged ominously upon the earth
Even when the season was the airiest May.
Down pressed the sky, and we, oppressed, thrust out
Boastful tongue, clenched fist and valiant yard.
Natural infirmities were out of mode,
For Death was young again; patron alone
Of healthy dying, premature fate-spasm.

Fear made fine bed-fellows. Sick with delight
At life's discovered transitoriness,
Our youth became all-flesh and waived the mind.
Never was such antiqueness of romance,
Such tasty honey oozing from the heart.
And old importances came swimming back—
Wine, meat, log-fired, a roof over the head,
A weapon at the thigh, surgeons at call.
Even there was a use again for God—

A word of rage in lack of meat, wine, fire,
In ache of wounds beyond all surgeoning.

War was return of earth to ugly earth,
War was foundering of sublimities,
Extinction of each happy art and faith
By which the world has still kept head in air,
Protesting logic or protesting love,
Until the unendurable moment struck—
The inward scream, the duty to run mad.

And we recall the merry ways of guns—
Nibbling the walls of factory and church
Like a child, piecrust; felling groves of trees
Like a child, dandelions with a switch.
Machine-guns rattle toy-like from a hill,
Down in a row the brave tin-soldiers fall:
A sight to be recalled in elder days
When learnedly the future we devote
To yet more boastful visions of despair.

∽ SAADAT HASAN MANTO,
Excerpt from *Toba Tek Singh*—PAKISTAN

Saadat Hasan Manto was born in 1912 in Punjab's Ludhiana
district. Manto worked for All India Radio during World War II
and was a successful screenwriter in Bombay before moving to
Pakistan during Partition. He wrote over a dozen films and the
last one was shot after Manto moved to Pakistan in January 1948.
Manto was tried for obscenity three times before and thrice after
independence. Manto's *Toba Tek Singh,* considered his greatest
work by many, was produced in the last seven years of his life.
His controversial career in literature, journalism, radio scripting,
and film writing spread over more than two decades in which he
published twenty-two collections of stories, seven collections of
radio plays, three collections of essays, and a novel. He died in
January 1955 in Lahore.

The characters in Manto's tale *Toba Tek Singh* (1948) have

become disconnected from their roots and identities because they are unhinged from their landscape. The story takes place a year after the India-Pakistan Partition and centers on the government's exchange of lunatics in the same way they had exchanged civilian prisoners. The story ends with the poignant image of a Sikh man, nicknamed Toba Tek Singh after a plot of land he once owned that he discussed endlessly while in the asylum. After the night of the exchange, the guards hear a scream and find Toba Tek Singh "lying face down on the ground. India was on one side, behind a barbed wire fence. Pakistan was on the other side, behind another fence. Toba Tek Singh lay in the middle, on a piece of land that had no name." Ironically, Toba Tek Singh, named after a plot of land, dies on a nameless piece of land.

Two or three years after Partition, the governments of Pakistan and India decided to exchange lunatics in the same way that they had exchanged civilian prisoners. In other words, Muslim lunatics in Indian madhouses would be sent to Pakistan, while Hindu and Sikh lunatics in Pakistani madhouses would be handed over to India.

I can't say whether this decision made sense or not. In any event, a date for the lunatic exchange was fixed after high level conferences on both sides of the border. All the details were carefully worked out. On the Indian side, Muslim lunatics with relatives in India would be allowed to stay. The remainder would be sent to the frontier. Here in Pakistan nearly all the Hindus and Sikhs were gone, so the question of retaining non-Muslim lunatics did not arise. All the Hindu and Sikh lunatics would be sent to the frontier in police custody.

I don't know what happened over there. When news of the lunatic exchange reached the madhouse here in Lahore, however, it became an absorbing topic of discussion among the inmates. There was one Muslim lunatic who had read the newspaper *Zamindar* [Landowner] every day for twelve years. One of his friends asked him: "Maulvi Sahib! What is Pakistan?" After careful thought he replied: "It's a place in India where they make razors."

Hearing this, his friend was content.

One Sikh lunatic asked another Sikh: "Sardar ji, why are they sending us to India? We don't even speak the language."

"I understand the Indian language," the other replied, smiling. "Indians are devilish people who strut around haughtily," he added.

While bathing, a Muslim lunatic shouted "Long live Pakistan!" with such vigor that he slipped on the floor and knocked himself out.

There were also some lunatics who weren't really crazy. Most of these inmates were murderers whose families had bribed the madhouse officials to have them committed in order to save them from the hangman's noose. These inmates understood something of why India had been divided, and they had heard of Pakistan. But they weren't all that well informed. The newspapers didn't tell them a great deal, and the illiterate guards who looked after them weren't much help either. All they knew was that there was a man named Mohammed Ali Jinnah, whom people called the Qaid-e-Azem. He had made a separate country for the Muslims, called Pakistan. They had no idea where it was, or what its boundaries might be. This is why all the lunatics who hadn't entirely lost their senses were perplexed as to whether they were in Pakistan or India. If they were in India, then where was Pakistan? If they were in Pakistan, then how was it that the place where they lived had until recently been known as India?

One lunatic got so involved in this India/Pakistan question that he became even crazier. One day he climbed a tree and sat on one of its branches for two hours, lecturing without pause on the complex issues of Partition. When the guards told him to come down, he climbed higher. When they tried to frighten him with threats, he replied: "I will live neither in India nor in Pakistan. I'll live in this tree right here!" With much difficulty, they eventually coaxed him down. When he reached the ground he wept and embraced his Hindu and Sikh friends, distraught at the idea that they would leave him and go to India.

One man held an M.S. degree and had been a radio engineer. He kept apart from the other inmates, and spent all his time walking silently up and down a particular footpath in the garden. After hearing about the exchange, however, he turned in his clothes and ran naked all over the grounds.

There was one fat Muslim lunatic from Chiniot who had been an enthusiastic Muslim League activist. He used to wash fifteen or sixteen times a day, but abandoned the habit overnight. His name was Mohammed Ali. One day he announced that he was the Qaid-e-Azem, Mohammed Ali Jinnah. Seeing this, a Sikh lunatic declared himself to be Master Tara Singh. Blood would have flowed, except that both were reclassified as dangerous lunatics and confined to separate quarters.

There was also a young Hindu lawyer from Lahore who had gone mad over an unhappy love affair. He was distressed to hear that Amritsar was now in India, because his beloved was a Hindu girl from that city. Although she had rejected him, he had not forgotten her after losing his mind. For this reason he cursed the Muslim leaders who had split India into two parts, so that his beloved remained Indian while he became Pakistani.

When news of the exchange reached the madhouse, several lunatics tried to comfort the lawyer by telling him that he would be sent to India, where his beloved lived. But he didn't want to leave Lahore, fearing that his practice would not thrive in Amritsar.

In the European Ward there were two Anglo-Indian lunatics. They were very worried to hear that the English had left after granting independence to India. In hushed tones, they spent hours discussing how this would affect their situation in the madhouse. Would the European Ward remain, or would it disappear? Would they be served English breakfasts? What, would they be forced to eat poisonous bloody Indian chapattis instead of bread?

One Sikh had been an inmate for fifteen years. He spoke a strange language of his own, constantly repeating this nonsensical phrase: "Upri gur gur di annexe di be-dhiyan o mung di daal of di lalteen." [Literally, "The lack of contemplation and lentils of the annex of the above raw sugar of the lantern."] He never slept. According to the guards, he hadn't slept a wink in fifteen years. Occasionally, however, he would rest by propping himself against a wall.

His feet and ankles had become swollen from standing all the time, but in spite of these physical problems he refused to lie down and rest. He would listen with great concentration whenever there was discussion of India, Pakistan and the forthcoming lunatic exchange. Asked for his opinion, he would reply with great seriousness: "Upri gur gur di annexe di be-dhiyana di mung di daal of di Pakistan gornament." ["Gornament" is Punjabi pronunciation of the English word "government."]

Later he replaced "of di Pakistan gornament" with "of di Toba Tek Singh gornament." He also started asking the other inmates where Toba Tek Singh was, and to which country it belonged. But nobody knew whether it was in Pakistan or India. When they argued the question they only became more confused. After all, Sialkot had once been in India, but was apparently now in Pakistan. Who knew whether Lahore, which was now in Pakistan, might not go over to India tomorrow? Or whether all of India might become Pakistan? And was there any guarantee that both Pakistan and India would not one day vanish altogether?

This Sikh lunatic's hair was unkempt and thin. Because he washed so rarely, his hair and beard had matted together, giving him a frightening appearance. But he was a harmless fellow. In fifteen years, he had never fought with anyone.

The attendants knew only that he owned land in Toba Tek Singh district. Having been a prosperous landlord, he suddenly lost his mind. So his relatives bound him with heavy chains and sent him off to the madhouse.

His family used to visit him once a month. After making sure that he was in good health, they would go away again. These family visits continued for many years, but they stopped when the India/Pakistan troubles began.

This lunatic's name was Bashan Singh, but everyone called him Toba Tek Singh. Although he had very little sense of time, he seemed to know when his relatives were coming to visit. He would tell the officer in charge that his visit was impending. On the day itself he would wash his body thoroughly and comb and oil his hair. Then he would put on his best clothes and go to meet his relatives.

If they asked him any question he would either remain silent or say: "Upri gur gur di annexe di be-dhiyana di mung di daal of di laaltein."

Bashan Singh had a fifteen-year-old daughter who grew by a finger's height every month. He didn't recognize her when she came to visit him. As a small child, she used to cry whenever she saw her father. She continued to cry now that she was older.

When the Partition problems began, Bashan Singh started asking the other lunatics about Toba Tek Singh. Since he never got a satisfactory answer, his concern deepened day by day.

Then his relatives stopped visiting him. Formerly he could predict their arrival, but now it was as though the voice inside him had been silenced. He very much wanted to see those people, who spoke to him sympathetically and brought gifts of flowers, sweets and clothing. Surely they could tell him whether Toba Tek Singh was in Pakistan or India. After all, he was under the impression that they came from Toba Tek Singh, where his land was.

There was another lunatic in that madhouse who thought he was God. One day, Bashan Singh asked him whether Toba Tek Singh was in Pakistan or India. Guffawing, he replied: "Neither, because I haven't yet decided where to put it!"

Bashan Singh begged this "God" to resolve the status of Toba Tek Singh and thus end his perplexity. But "God" was far too busy to deal with this matter because of all the other orders that he had to give. One day Bashan Singh lost his temper and shouted: "Upri gur gur di annexe di be-dhiyana di mung di daal of wahay Guru ji wa Khalsa and wahay Guru ji ki fatah. Jo bolay so nahal sat akal!"

By this he might have meant: "You are the God of the Muslims. If you were a Sikh God then you would certainly help me."

A few days before the day of the exchange, one of Bashan Singh's Muslim friends came to visit from Toba Tek Singh. This man had never visited the madhouse before. Seeing him, Bashan Singh turned abruptly and started walking away. But the guard stopped him.

"He's come to visit you. It's your friend Fazluddin," the guard said.

Glancing at Fazluddin, Bashan Singh muttered a bit. Fazluddin advanced and took him by the elbow. "I've been planning to visit you for ages, but I haven't had the time until now," he said. "All your relatives have gone safely to India. I helped them as much as I could. Your daughter Rup Kur . . ."

Bashan Singh seemed to remember something. "Daughter Rup Kur," he said.

Fazluddin hesitated, and then replied: "Yes, she's . . . she's also fine. She left with them."

Bashan Singh said nothing. Fazluddin continued: "They asked me to make sure you were all right. Now I hear that you're going to India. Give my salaams to brother Balbir Singh and brother Wadhada Singh. And to sister Imrat Kur also . . . Tell brother Balbir Singh that I'm doing fine. One of the two brown cows that he left has calved. The other one calved also, but it died after six days. And . . . and say that if there's anything else I can do for them, I'm always ready. And I've brought you some sweets."

Bashan Singh handed the package over to the guard. "Where is Toba Tek Singh?" he asked.

Fazluddin was taken aback. "Toba Tek Singh? Where is it? It's where it's always been," he replied.

"In Pakistan or in India?" Bashan Singh persisted.

Fazluddin became flustered. "It's in India. No no, Pakistan."

Bashan Singh walked away, muttering: "Upar di gur gur di annexe di dhiyana di mung di daal of di Pakistan and Hindustan of di dar fatay mun!"

Finally all the preparations for the exchange were complete. The lists of all the lunatics to be transferred were finalized, and the date for the exchange itself was fixed.

The weather was very cold. The Hindu and Sikh lunatics from the Lahore madhouse were loaded into trucks under police supervision. At the Wahga border post, the Pakistani and Indian officials met each other and completed the necessary formalities. Then the exchange began. It continued all through the night.

It was not easy to unload the lunatics and send them across the border. Some of them didn't even want to leave the trucks. Those who did get out were hard to control because they started wandering all over the place. When the guards tried to clothe those lunatics who were naked, they immediately ripped the garments off their bodies. Some cursed, some sang, and others fought. They were crying and talking, but nothing could be understood. The madwomen were creating an uproar of their own. And it was cold enough to make your teeth chatter.

Most of the lunatics were opposed to the exchange. They didn't understand why they should be uprooted and sent to some unknown place. Some, only half-mad, started shouting "Long live Pakistan!" Two or three brawls erupted between Sikh and Muslim lunatics who became enraged when they heard the slogans.

When Bashan Singh's turn came to be entered in the register, he spoke to the official in charge. "Where is Toba Tek Singh?" he asked. "Is it in Pakistan or India?"

The official laughed. "It's in Pakistan," he replied.

Hearing this, Bashan Singh leapt back and ran to where his remaining companions stood waiting. The Pakistani guards caught him and tried to bring him back to the crossing point, but he refused to go.

"Toba Tek Singh is here!" he cried. Then he started raving at top volume: "Upar di gur gur di annexe di be-dhiyana mang di daal of di Toba Tek Singh and Pakistan!"

The officials tried to convince him that Toba Tek Singh was now in India. If by some chance it wasn't they would send it there directly, they said. But he wouldn't listen.

Because he was harmless, the guards let him stand right where he was while they got on with their work. He was quiet all night, but just before sunrise he screamed. Officials came running from all sides. After fifteen years on his feet, he was lying face down on the ground. India was on one side, behind a barbed wire fence. Pakistan was on the other side, behind another fence. Toba Tek Singh lay in the middle, on a piece of land that had no name.

∾ JOHN HOPPENTHALER,
   "A Jar of Rain"—UNITED STATES

John Hoppenthaler was born in 1960 and received his MFA
in creative writing from Virginia Commonwealth University in
1988. His poetry appears in such journals and anthologies as
*Ploughshares, Virginia Quarterly Review, Southern Review,
McSweeney's, September 11, 2001: American Writers Respond,
Chance of a Ghost,* and *Wild, Sweet Notes II: More Poetry from
West Virginia.* His first book of poetry is *Lives of Water* (2003),
and his second collection was published in 2007. He is currently
teaching English at West Virginia University at Parkersburg.

    Hoppenthaler's poem "A Jar of Rain" examines the restorative
value of nature, a common thread in many of this section's
selections, how nature inevitably begins to heal itself. The
protagonist travels to New York to wash away any remaining
ashes of her brother—who perished in 9/11—with rain water
from his cherished home in Ohio. The poem ends as the
characters near New York: "She saw / the brimming hole in a
sky- / line she'd never seen / before begin to unfold."

Wrapped in threadbare & faded
cotton towels, snuggled
between the hub & Beth Ann's
sneakered feet, the faint
sloshing of jarred rainwater
too muffled to hear
above road whine & Rolling
Stones on the tape deck.
But like some rare & fragile
egg, she nestled it
there all four hundred long miles
east to Manhattan.
When her brother left Wheeling,
it had been springtime.
He allowed how he'd miss it—
yearning green mountains,
misty Ohio river,
& mostly the rain

how it sluiced off mom's rooftop
to collect & brim
in an old metal oil drum,
how when he would thwack
its steel side with his finger
rings would shiver toward
dark water's chilly center.
He would miss the rain,
& they would miss him,
gone to the city, dream job
among skyscrapers
the "big break" of his young life.
They'd sung the theme from
the *Mary Tyler Moore Show*
together that night
he first heard he'd been hired
& flung cloth napkins
high at the kitchen ceiling,
"You're gonna make it
after all" deflecting off
walls & rising like
hymnal passages till dawn.
Alvin hit a bump.
Careful, she hissed, her left leg
swiveling on raised
toes, hard up against the jar.
It was what she could
still do, the only thing more:
to wash what ashes were left yet of his—gutter
to river to sea—
with West Virginia rainfall
dipped up from a drum
whose surface October had started to freeze over.
Mick Jagger was belting out
"Paint It Black." She saw
the brimming hole in a skyline she'd never seen
before begin to unfold.

SEVEN

FADING MEMORY
AND THE ROLE OF ART

A rt and literature are unique lenses through which to explore memory because they can both permanently capture an ephemeral memory and simultaneously chart its inevitable decay. The writers in this chapter wrestle with this dilemma, illustrated in a visual manner by the Chinese artist Zhang Xiaogang. He created an evocative series of paintings in the 1990s called the *Bloodline* series, inspired by Chinese family photos of the 1920s. Each painting draws on the formality of the staged family photo and features a different family constellation of parents, children, and siblings, who stare ahead with blank, fixed gazes. Through these paintings Zhang illuminates the strain exacted on family relations during China's Cultural Revolution when, among other things, children were encouraged to denounce their parents for a lack of political orthodoxy. Yet unlike most portraits where the subjects are in focus, in Zhang's paintings the family members' faces are in detailed focus, but their hair, bodies and outlines of their bodies become fuzzy, and the background is blurred and drained of color. This effect reflects the effects of time on memory, and the inevitable loss of focus that comes, no matter how much we wish to hold onto the past.

In his poem "September 12, 2001," South African writer Breyten Breytenbach ends with the question, "Will any poem some day ever carry sufficient weight / to leave the script of scraps recalling fall and forgetting / will death remain quivering in the paper?" Breytenbach alludes to the scene many in New York—including Breytenbach—witnessed firsthand after the towers fell, when clouds of dust and paper scraps filled the air. After the initial chaotic hours, it became clear that those clouds of debris also likely contained the pulverized remains of many who perished in the towers. Breytenbach raises the crucial question of how poetry or any record of that day can adequately convey to those who did not witness the attack the visceral reality of the hours and days that followed. Breytenbach's lyrically phrased questions could also apply to any number of twentieth-century calamities and epitomize the concerns of successor communities around the world. How will these events be remembered by subsequent generations? What role can literature play in the process?

Memory does not stand still. It moves away, elusive, from those who would hold it too close. Yet, memory's movement—through shifts of proximity and distance—preserves traces of vitality in relationships that would otherwise wither. In memory and through writing, losses can be restored. Not fully, but loved ones can be revived in some manner. The excerpts in this chapter demonstrate a variety of creative strategies for holding onto what is missing and for acknowledging what will never return. The Russian writer Varlam Shalamov writes of the eternal quality of graphite used to mark the bodies of the dead in the Siberian labor camps of Stalin's Gulag in the 1930s; Breyten Breytenbach touches on the transformational quality of art in processing memories of 9/11; the American British poet Hilda Doolittle, otherwise known as H. D., writes from within the London blitz about World War II; and the French poet Guillaume Apollinaire writes about World War I.

ᏐᎥ Varlam Shalamov,
"Graphite"—Russia

Varlam Tikhonovich Shalamov was born in Vologda, Russia, on June 18, 1907. He entered Moscow University in 1926 in order to study law. Shalamov was first arrested in 1929 and sentenced to hard labor in Solovki, a Soviet labor camp. He was arrested again in 1934 during the purges and sent to Kolyma, the northeastern area of Siberia, known as "the land of white death." He was charged both times with "counter-revolutionary Trotskyite activities." After seventeen years in Kolyma, Shalamov was released in 1951. While he had been writing since 1932, his stories were first published in the West in 1966. Solzhenitsyn asked Shalamov to coauthor *The Gulag Archipelago,* but Shalamov declined for health reasons. John Glad, a preeminent Shalamov translator, describes how Shalamov's stories are a testament to his "determination to turn those lost years somehow into art." Varlam Shalamov died in 1982.

In this essay "Graphite," an excerpt from *Dying* (1966), Shalamov writes of the mineral graphite, "carbon that has been subject to enormous pressure for millions of years and that might have become coal or diamonds. Instead, however, it has been transformed into something more precious than diamond; it has become a pencil that can record all that it has seen." In the camps of Kolyma, graphite is used to write on the plywood tags that must be attached to the left shin of every dead body, a type of very flimsy grave marker. Graphite in the environment of the labor camps is double-edged. It ensures that the deaths of these individuals will be recorded for eternity: "a trace left in the taiga by a graphite pencil is eternal." Yet it also underscores the fact that the dead are reduced simply to a number.

Which ink is used to sign death sentences—chemical ink, the India ink used in passports, the ink of fountain pens, alizarin? No death sentence has ever been signed simply in pencil.

In the taiga we had no use for ink. Any ink will dissolve in rain, tears, and blood. Chemical pens cannot be sent to prisoners and are confiscated if discovered. Such pens are treated like printer's ink and used to draw the homemade playing cards owned by the criminal element and therefore. . . . Only the simple, black graphite pencil is permitted. In Kolyma, graphite carries enormous responsibility.

The cartographers discussed the matter with the heavens, peered into the starry sky, measured the height of the sun, and established a point of reference on our earth. Above this point a marble tablet was set into the stone of the mountaintop, and a tripod, a log signal, was affixed to the spot. This tripod indicates the precise location on the map, and an invisible network of meridians and parallels extends from this point across valleys, clearings, and marshes. When a road is cut through the taiga, each landmark is sighted through the crosshairs of the level and the theodolite. The land has been measured, the taiga has been measured, and we come upon the bench mark of the cartographer, the topographer, the measurer of the earth—recorded in simple black graphite.

The topographers have crossed and crisscrossed the Kolyma taiga with roads, but even so these roads exist only in areas surrounding settlements and mines. The clearings and naked hills are crossed only by ethereal, imaginary lines for which there are no reliable bench marks, no tagged trees. Bench marks are established on cliffs, riverbeds, and bare mountaintops. The measurement of the taiga, the measurement of Kolyma, the measurement of a prison is based on these reliable points of reference, whose authority is biblical. A network of clearings is indicated by bench marks on the trees, bench marks which can be seen in the crosshairs of the theodolite and which are used to survey the taiga.

Only a simple black pencil will do for making a notation of a bench mark. Ink will run, be dissolved by the tree sap, be washed away by rain, dew, fog, and snow. Nothing as artificial as ink will do for recording eternity and immortality. Graphite is carbon that has been subject to enormous pressure for millions of years and that might have become coal or diamonds. Instead, however, it has been transformed into something more precious than a diamond; it has become a pencil record all that it has seen. . . . A pencil is a greater miracle than a diamond, although the chemical makeup of graphite and diamond is identical.

It is not only on bench marks that topographers may not use pens. Any map legend or draft of a legend resulting from a visual survey demands graphite for immortality. Graphite is nature. It participates in the spinning of the planet and resists time better than stone. Limestone mountains are washed away by rains, winds, and waves, but a 200-year-old larch tree is still young, and it will live and preserve on its bench mark the code that links today's world with the biblical secret. Even as the tree's fresh wound still bleeds and the sap falls like tears, a number—an arbitrary mark—is written upon the trunk.

In the taiga, only graphite can be used for writing. A topographer always keeps pencil stubs, fragments of pencils in the pockets of his vest, jacket, pants, overcoat. Paper, a notebook, a carrying case—and a tree with a bench mark—are the medium of his art.

Paper is one of the faces, one of the transformations of a tree into diamond or graphite. Graphite is eternity, the highest standard of hardness, which has become the highest standard of softness. A trace left in the taiga by a graphite pencil is eternal.

The bench mark is carefully hewn. Two horizontal cuts are made at waist level on the trunk of a larch tree, and the edge of the ax is used to break off the still living wood. A miniature house is formed, a clean board sheltered from the rain. This shelter preserves the recorded bench mark almost forever—till the end of the larch's six-hundred-year life.

The wounded larch is like a prophetic icon—like the Chukotsk Mother of God or the Virgin Mary of Kolyma who awaits and foretells a miracle. The subtle, delicate smell of tree sap, the larch's blood spilled by a man's ax, is like a distant memory of childhood or the incense of dew.

A number has been recorded, and the wounded larch, burned by wind and sun, preserves this "tag" which points the way from the forsaken spot in the taiga to the outside world.

The way leads through the clearings to the mountaintop with the nearest tripod, the cartographic tripod, under which is a pit filled with rocks. Under the rocks is a marble tablet indicating the actual latitude and longitude—a recording not made with a graphite pencil. And we return to our world along the thousands of threads that lead from this tripod, along the thousands of lines that lead from one ax mark to another so that we may remember life. Those who work in the topographic service work in the service of life.

In Kolyma, however, not only the topographer must use a graphite pencil. The pen is forbidden not only in the service of life, but also in the service of death. "Archive NO. 3" is the name of the office in camp that records convict deaths. Its instructions read that a plywood tag must be attached to the left shin of every dead body. The tag records the prisoner's "case number." The case number must be written with a simple graphite pencil—not a pen. Even here an artificial writing tool would interfere with eternity.

The practice strikes one as odd. Can there really be plans for exhumation? For immortality? For resurrection? For reburial? There are more than enough mass graves in Kolyma, into which untagged bodies have been dumped. But instructions are instructions. Theoretically speaking, all guests of the permafrost enjoy life eternal and are ready to return to us that we might remove the tags from their left shins and find their friends and relatives.

All that is required is that the tag bear the required number written in simple black pencil. The case number cannot be washed away by rains or underground springs which appear every time the ice yields to the heat of summer and surrenders some of its subterranean secrets—only some.

The convict's file with its front- and side-view photographs, fingerprints, and description of unusual marks is his passport. An employee of "Archive NO. 3" is supposed to make up a report in five copies of the convict's death and to note if any gold teeth have been removed. There is a special form for gold teeth. It had always been that way in Kolyma, and the reports in Germany of teeth removed from the dead bodies of prisoners surprised no one in Kolyma.

Certain countries do not wish to lose the gold of dead men. There have always been reports of extraction of gold teeth in prisons and labor camps. The year 1937 brought many people with gold teeth to the investigators and the camps. Many of those who died in the mines of Kolyma, where they could not survive for long, produced gold for the state only in the form of their own teeth, which were knocked out after they died. There was more gold in their fillings than these people were able to extract with pick and shovel during their brief lives in the mines.

The dead man's fingers were supposed to be dipped in printer's ink, of which employees of "Archive NO. 3" had an enormous supply. This is why the hands of killed escapees were cut off—it was easier to put two human palms in a military pouch than transport an entire body, a corpse for identification.

A tag attached to a leg is a sign of cultural advance. The body of Andrei Bogoliubsky, the murdered twelfth-century Russian prince, had no such tag, and it had to be identified by the bones, using Bertillon's calculation method.

We put our trust in fingerprinting. It has never failed us, no matter how the criminals might have disfigured their fingertips, burning them with fire and acid, and slashing them with knives. No criminal could ever bring himself to burn off all ten.

We don't have any confidence in Bertillon, the chief of the French Criminal Investigation Department and the father of the anthropological principle of criminology which makes identifications by a series of measurements establishing the relative proportions of the parts of the body. Bertillon's discoveries are of use to artists; the distance from the tip of the nose to the earlobe tells us nothing.

We believe in fingerprinting, and everyone knows how to give his prints or "play the piano." In '37, when they were scooping up everyone who had been marked earlier for doom, each man placed his accustomed fingers into the accustomed hands of a prison employee in an accustomed movement.

These prints are preserved forever in the case histories. The tag with the case number preserves not only the name of the place of death but also the secret cause of that death. This number is written on the tag with graphite.

The cartographer who lays out new paths on the earth, new roads for people, and the gravedigger, who must observe the laws of death, must both use the same instrument—a black graphite pencil.

∾ BREYTEN BREYTENBACH,
  "New York, 12 September 2001"—SOUTH AFRICA

Breyten Breytenbach was born in September 1939 in Bonnievale, South Africa. Breytenbach moved to Paris when Apartheid policies invaded the University of Cape Town, where he was studying. When Breytenbach applied for a visa in 1965 to return to South Africa to receive a literary prize, he was warned that he could be arrested under the Immorality Act for his interracial marriage to Yolande Ngo Thi Hoang Lien, who was of Vietnamese origin. Breytenbach subsequently became more deeply involved in anti-Apartheid activities and co-founded Okehela (the "Spark" in Zulu), whose ultimate goal was to build anti-Apartheid infrastructures in white South African communities. Back in South Africa on a false passport to set up contacts for his organization, Breytenbach was imprisoned in 1975 for seven years, spending two of those in solitary confinement. Breytenbach now teaches part of the year at New York University as a Distinguished Global Professor and is also the executive director of the Gorée Institute in the Bay of Dakar. Breytenbach has written a prison memoir and multiple volumes of poetry and prose and has held art exhibitions in a number of countries, including France, the Netherlands, Sweden, and Germany.

Breytenbach was working on a balcony one block south of Washington Square Park in New York during the attacks of 9/11 and watched the planes screaming down the length of Manhattan. He wrote the poem "New York, 12 September 2001" in response. Breytenbach found the experience of writing in response to violence and loss in New York similar in a number of ways to writing about Apartheid. "I remember when I was in prison writing poems about those taken down a corridor to be executed, singing and praying as they went. In a similar way, 9/11 involved instinctively reaching out to a diction that might be adequate to carry the emotion," he said in an interview with the Legacy Project. "When one is faced by absolute horror and the

inexplicability of it, one instinctively reaches into areas of the
self that probably only really find, at that particular moment,
adequate expression in certain rhythms and in certain images."

will the hand endure moving over the paper
   will any poem have enough weight
   to leave a flightline over a desolate landscape
   ever enough face to lift against death's dark silence
   who will tell today?

   the huge anthill of people remains quiet
   somber and shrill, bright and obscure
   as if brown effluvium of sputtering towers
   still sweeps the skyline with a filthy flag
   who will tell today?

   today images wail for voice behind the eyes
   planes as bombs stuffed with shrapnel of soft bodies
   then the fire inferno flame-flowers from skyscrapers
   human flares like falling angels from the highest floor
   down, down all along shimmering buildings of glass and
   steel
   weightless and willowy and flame-winged streamlined
   reflections fleeting in the fugitive language of forgetting
   the hellhound of destruction has a red tongue of laughter
   who will tell?
   gouged eyes do not understand that the sky is blue
   through the dismal and chilly nuclear winter
   people stumble people shuffle
   stumble-people shuffle-people worm-white-people
   where are the faces
   old before their ending or their wedding
   greyed in ashes from head to toe
   as if clothed in the coast of the snowing knowing of ages

   beneath rummage and debris rosy corpses move and
   mumble
   and in the East River confidential files and folders float
   with shreds and feathers lacerated human meat
   scorched confetti for the dog's feast

who will tell tomorrow tomorrow
where are the faces
will the tongue still think
still pulse its dark lair
with the flaming memory of bliss
will any poem some day ever carry sufficient weight
to leave the script of scraps recalling fall and forgetting
will death remain quivering in the paper

∾ H. D.,
Excerpt from "The Walls Do Not Fall"
—UNITED STATES AND UNITED KINGDOM

H. D., Hilda Doolittle, was born in 1886, in Bethlehem,
Pennsylvania. She attended Bryn Mawr and later the University
of Pennsylvania, where she befriended William Carlos Williams
and Ezra Pound. She traveled to Europe in 1911 and remained
abroad for the rest of her life. In London literary circles,
H. D. also became close friends with T. S. Eliot and D. H. Lawrence.
In 1933, H. D. underwent analysis with Freud, and she subsequently
used certain techniques of psychoanalysis (e.g., free association)
to model her poetics. She was very involved in the production of
the magazine *Close-Up*, the first magazine to be dedicated solely to
the discussion of film as a serious artistic medium. H. D. suffered
from World War II–induced post-traumatic stress disorder for
most of her adult life. Her poetry debunks the myth that women
didn't write war poetry, and in many ways H. D. survived the war
by writing her way through it. In addition to her poetry from the
war years, which was first published in *Life and Letters Today,* she
also wrote several book reviews for the magazine using the nom
de plume Sylvania Penn. H. D. died in 1961.
   "The Walls Do Not Fall," the first poem in *Trilogy,* was
published in the midst of the "fifty thousand incidents" of the
London Blitz of World War II. H. D. did not leave London
during the German bombing of the city. Using the technique of
palimpsest, H. D. layers the memories of World War II's shattering
impact with historical, cultural, scientific, and religious echoes
from different time periods in an effort to synthesize religion, art,

and medicine that had become, in H. D.'s opinion, increasingly
fragmented during this era. In the first section of the excerpt
below, H. D. addresses the bombing in London, likening it to
the opening of a dead and static tomb. After the critical "Yet,"
in the first line of the final stanza of section 1, the poem moves
decidedly from shock to survival. Section 6 of the excerpt
explores the task of the writer when writing about calamity.
H. D believed the poet had an ethical responsibility to find
inspiration in devastation. And thus through personification,
she likens the poet's task to that of a silkworm, which consumes
detritus and decay in order to spin silk. Section 9 addresses the
Nazi book burnings and the wasteful consumption of paper by
both the Nazis and the Allies. Finally, section 10 addresses
H. D.'s overarching theme—the struggle between the *Word* and
the *Sword* or the power of literature to effect such change that it
can triumph over violence in certain situations.

For Karnak 1923
From London 1942

[1]

An incident here and there,
And rails gone (for guns)
From your (and my) old town square:

mist and mist-grey, no colour,
still the Luxor bee, chick and hare
pursue unalterable purpose

in green, rose-red, lapis;
they continue to prophesy
from the stone papyrus:

there, as here, ruin opens
the tomb, the temple; enter,
there as here, there are no doors;

the shrine lies open to the sky,
the rain falls, here, there
sand drifts; eternity endures:

ruin everywhere, yet as the fallen roof
leaves the sealed room
open to the air,

so, through our desolation,
thoughts stir, inspiration stalks us
through gloom.

unaware, Spirit announces the Presence;
shivering overtakes us,
as of old, Samuel:

trembling at a known street-corner,
we know not nor are known;
the Pythian pronounces—we pass on

to another celler, to another sliced wall
where poor utensils show
like rare objects in a museum;

Pompeii has nothing to teach us,
we know crack of a volcanic fissure,
slow flow of terrible lava,

pressure on heart, lungs, the brain
about to burst its brittle case
(what the skull can endure!):

over us, Apocryphal fire,
under us, the earth sway, dip of a floor,
slope of a pavement

where men roll, drunk
with a new bewilderment,
sorcery, bedevilment:

the bone-frame was made for
no such shock knit within terror,
yet the skeleton stood up to it:

the flesh? it was melted away,
the heart burnt out, dead ember,
tendons, muscles shattered, outer husk dismembered,

yet the frame held:
we passed the flame: we wonder
what saved us? what for?

[6]

In me (the worm) clearly
Is no righteousness, but this—

Persistence; I escaped spider-snare,
bird-claw, scavenger bird-beak,

clung to grass-blade,
the back of a leaf

when the storm-wind
tore it from its stem;

I escaped, I explored
rose-thorn forest,

was rain-swept
down in the valley of a leaf;

was deposited on grass,
where mast by jeweled mast

bore separate ravellings
of encrusted gem-stuff

of the mist
from each banner-staff:

unintimidated by multiplicity
of magnified beauty,

such as your gorgon-great
dull eye can not focus

nor compass, I profit
by every calamity;

I eat my way out of it;
gorged on vine-leaf and mulberry,

parasite, I find nourishment:
when you cry in disgust,

a worm on the leaf,
a worm in the dust,

a worm on the ear-of-wheat,
I am yet unrepentant,

for I know how the Lord God
is about to manifest, when I,

the industrious worm,
spin my own shroud.

[9]

Thoth, Hermes, the stylus,
the palette, the pen, the quill endure,

though our books are a floor
of smouldering ash under our feet;

though the burning of the books remains
the most perverse gesture

and the meanest
of man's mean nature,

yet give us, they still cry,
give us books,

folio, manuscript, old parchment
will do for cartridge cases;

irony is bitter truth
wrapped up in a little joke,

and Hatshepsut's name is still circled
with what they call the cartouche.

[10]

But we fight for life,
we fight, they say, for breath,

so what good are your scribblings?
this—we take them with us

beyond death; Mercury, Hermes, Thoth
invented the script, letters, palette;

the indicated flute or lyre-notes
on papyrus or parchment

are magic, indelibly stamped
on the atmosphere somewhere,

forever; remember, O Sword,
you are the younger brother, the latter-born,

your Triumph, however exultant,
must one day be over,

in the beginning
was the Word.

◞ GUILLAUME APOLLINAIRE, "Shadow"—FRANCE

Guillaume Apollinaire, the son of a Polish noblewoman and an Italian aristocrat, was born in 1880 in Rome and raised in Monaco, Paris, and the French Riviera. During his education in Cannes, Nice, and Monaco, he assumed the identity of a Russian prince. At the age of twenty, Apollinaire settled in Paris, where he worked briefly for a bank. In Paris, he established himself as a leading avant-garde poet and defender of progressive art. Apollinaire is credited with having coined the term "surrealism." Having become a French citizen in order to enlist for service in World War I, he was seriously wounded in March 1916. Guillaume Apollinaire died in the influenza epidemic of 1918.

Apollinaire's poem "Shadow" (1916), translated by Anne Greet, explores the memories of the speaker's comrades in battle, memories that cling to him and leave an indelible mark, an invisible "Shadow solar ink / Handwriting of my light." Even though he can no longer see his comrades, he wraps the memory of them around himself: "Memories composing now a single memory, / As a hundred furs make only one coat." He calls his memories his "Destinies" and suggests his past is in some manner connected to his future.

Here you are near me once more
Memories of my comrades in battle
Olive of time
Memories composing now a single memory
As a hundred furs make only one coat
As those thousands of wounds make only one newspaper article
Impalpable dark appearance you have assumed
The changing form of my shadow
An Indian hiding in wait throughout eternity
Shadow you creep near me
But you no longer hear me
You will no longer know the divine poems I sing
But I hear you I see you still
Destinies
Multiple shadow may the sun watch over you
You who love me so much you will never leave me
You who dance in the sun without stirring the dust
Shadow solar ink
Handwriting of my light
Caisson of regrets
A god humbling himself

EIGHT

BEATING BACK
THE GHOSTS OF THE PAST

T he American writer Robert Polito addresses the missing people in
New York after 9/11 in his essay "Last Seen." Polito describes D. H.
Lawrence's reflection on absence from earlier in the twentieth cen-
tury; it resonates with the scene in Manhattan:

> *There are terrible spirits, ghosts, in the air of America*, D. H. Lawrence wrote
> in 1923.
>
> I thought of Lawrence's ghosts often those early days after the towers
> came down, particularly when the flyers of the missing—always "the miss-
> ing"—started to cover Lower Manhattan, most spectacularly throughout
> Union Square, but also on nearly every wall, store front, telephone booth,
> lamp pole, and tree south of Fourteenth Street. . . . You needed to imagine
> a legion of the missing—5,000 those first weeks—wandering New York, lost,
> amnesiac, waiting for someone to recognize them from their photo and
> life story, and send them home. (*110 Stories: New York Writes after Septem-
> ber 11*, edited by Ulrich Baer [New York: New York University Press, 2002])

The missing posters, ephemeral paper tombstones, visually reinforced the
arresting absence of the "legion of the missing," as Polito describes the
victims of the attacks on the World Trade Center Towers.

Remembering the missing becomes increasingly important as generations pass and direct witnesses become more and more rare. In this subsequent stage, writers often focus on the complicated struggle to integrate
memory and remembrance into contemporary life, an act of what might
be called imaginative restoration. Or, to put this in other terms, there is

a need to acknowledge the ways in which the voids still exert pressure, without allowing remembrance to breed an all-consuming obsession with the past. As writers address the theme of integrating memory, they focus on the chasm that exists between direct victims and bystanders, a gap that only widens with the passing of time and generations. In order to convey the complex aftermath of these events to their audience, writers often destabilize the notion of survival. Traumatic memories can unexpectedly interrupt survivors' lives many years later, eliciting the same psychosomatic responses. Carol Edgarian's narrator, Seta Loon—in the excerpt in this section—comments on this phenomenon in relation to her grandmother, an Armenian Genocide survivor: "It was a mystery to me that an event so far in the past could still hold power over our lives now. How could it hurt Grandma just to have it mentioned? Of course, I did not realize that to talk about the genocide was to make it happen all over again, right there on her Persian carpet. She turned her head and piles of skulls appeared, and, in the corner by the fairy lamp, the butcher Turks." Survival, therefore, begins when a person escapes such a calamity, but also constitutes a constant, ongoing struggle to live with memories of violence.

The writers in this chapter, including Edgarian, use one common storytelling technique to convey the ongoing struggle to survive, when memories return unexpectedly, thwarting efforts to build a new life. These writers disorient the reader through their use of a mysterious ghostly character, a technique particularly suited to the written world, where all characters are, in fact, ghostly literary creations, inky shadows on a white page. The readers are left guessing how real these ghost characters are— often they seem as "real" as the other characters within the text. Similarly for trauma victims, like the grandmother in Edgarian's tale, memories can feel very "real" because they elicit the same psychosomatic responses produced by terror and extreme grief.

This chapter brings together Carol Edgarian, writing about third-generation encounters with the Armenian Genocide in *Rise the Euphrates* (1994); Cynthia Ozick, writing about the Holocaust in *The Shawl* (1980); Can Xue, addressing the Chinese Cultural Revolution in "Hut on a Mountain" (1989); Vladimir Nabokov, reflecting on violence in Russian and European history of the first half of the twentieth century in *Pnin* (1957); and Toni Morrison, writing of traumatic memories of slavery in the U.S. in the nineteenth century. *Beloved.* In all the selections in this chapter, time collapses and the past is not simply a rosy memory but a present that demands attention. Ghostly and yet somehow present, figments of memory convey this unexpected return of a past that threatens trauma victims and illuminates the balance between remembering the past and being over-whelmed by it.

～ CAROL EDGARIAN,
   Excerpt from *Rise the Euphrates*—UNITED STATES

American writer and journalist Carol Edgarian is of Armenian descent and attended Stanford University. She is now an editor of *Narrative* magazine in San Francisco. She is co-editor (with Tom Jenks) of *The Writer's Life: Intimate Thoughts on Work, Love, Inspiration, and Fame from the Diaries of the World's Great Writers* (1997).
      Edgarian's novel *Rise the Euphrates* (1994) is written from the perspective of a third-generation Armenian genocide survivor, Seta, who struggles to understand her grandmother's traumatic past. The excerpt centers on Martyr's Day, held every year throughout the world on April 24, to mark the first day of the 1915 genocide of Armenians. The grandmother, Casard, does not want to speak with her grandchildren about the "Indignities," the torture and rape many Armenian girls suffered. She does not even want to attend the memorial services. Her family convinces her to go, and she finds the pressure of past memories so overwhelming that it feels as if it is literally pressing down on her chest and she suffers a heart attack. Through this character, Edgarian illuminates the fact, mentioned earlier, that traumatic memories can produce psychosomatic symptoms from the original moment of catastrophe.

The first chance I had, I asked Casard about Martyrs' Day, and just as Theresa predicted, I learned that my grandmother hated it worse than filth.
   "Grandma, why won't you talk about it?"
   Casard snapped the newspaper and stared at me with fish eyes. "Why aren't you outside with your brother?"
   "Because I want to talk."
   Casard fumed—"I said *Out*. Go on, take your sister." She pointed at Melanie, who was seated across the room. "You know better than to traipse Indignities in my house."
   Casard shook the paper, raising it like a wall in front of her, so there

was nothing more to argue with—just the hem of her housedress, her Bad Leg resting on the hassock, her gray tie shoes and a wall of print. I knew she was on the other side of that wall, fish eyes blinking.

It was a mystery to me that an event so far in the past could still hold power over our lives now. How could it hurt Grandma just to have it mentioned? Of course, I did not realize that to talk about the genocide was to make it happen all over again, right there on her Persian carpet. She turned her head and piles of skulls appeared, and, in the corner by the fairy lamp, the butcher Turks.

Since my afternoon with Theresa, I had learned on my own about Martyrs' Day. Every year on April 24, throughout the world, Armenians held a service to mark the first day of the 1915 genocide. But each year Casard refused to participate in a public display that she perceived as toxic, worse than public toilets and public buses, worse than money tainted by "people's" hands, worse than dirty feet on the bed.

"Out"—she panted, shaking the newspaper.

Melanie and I marched to the foyer. "Wait here," I told my sister, and ran upstairs to Casard's room and brought down a book. We slipped out the front door, to where Van had propped a ladder against the trunk of the oak. Melanie and I climbed up and onto the garage roof. Over the peak, on the far side, Van was lying on his back. We stretched out on either side of him, our feet braced in the gutter, the sun's rays prickly on our faces, the heat from the tar shingled roof radiating beneath our clothes.

"Check this out," I said and flashed the book I had removed from its hiding place in Casard's room, high up on a shelf above Grandpa Vrej's desk. It was a book about the genocide; I had discovered it the week before when taking a nap on Casard's bed. We rolled over on our bellies to have a look.

On the back cover, there was a photograph of eight Armenian women, naked and crucified, their long black hair hanging to their waists. Inside, a photograph showed men's heads impaled on sticks, and another, a pyramid of thousands of skulls collected in the desert of Der el Zor. The caption read that at least one million Armenians had been buried in shallow graves in the desert of Der el Zor.

There were photographs of the survivors: emaciated children with bloated bellies and deep-set eyes gazing vaguely into the camera. The caption read: "Armenian orphans in Syria."

We leaned in close, our noses just inches from the page and turned to a photograph of a beautiful dark-haired Armenian girl standing against a wall, her shirt open to her navel. The tattoos on her forehead, throat and breasts were the names of the Turks who had bought and sold her as a slave.

"Jesus Christ—" Van stammered.

And then I said what we were all thinking, "Grandma."

Melanie began to cry, and Van and I each put an arm around her. We glanced from the orphaned children to the slave girl, and back again, silently imagining our grandmother with bloated belly and round saucer eyes, with tattoos hidden beneath the bodice of her housedress.

We had been there awhile, a half hour maybe, when Casard began looking for us.

"Van-Seta-Melanie," she called, summoning us as one person.

"Quiet," Van whispered. "Maybe she's just fishing."

"Van-Seta-Melanie, I see you-on the roof. Show your faces.'

I peered over the peak. Casard was hanging out one of the upstairs windows.

"Get down, you. I said Immediately—Now. You too, Mister Grown."

We all stood at the same time and stared at her. What we had just seen must have been on our faces, for she looked us over and said nothing. After a few moments she tucked her head back into the house and brought the window gliding slowly down onto the sill.

That evening, Casard came over to our house and sat at the kitchen table, waiting for Momma to bring her a cup of tea.

"Araxie. Honey," Casard began. "Those children. They have no business at Martyrs' Day."

Momma stared grimly at the old woman's face and sighed. Momma's face revealed the inner conversation she was having, which went, Will we have to have another fight? Yes, of course. Do I have the strength? Does it matter? Can we get it over quick? With her, is there any such thing as quick?

Momma began patiently, her voice soothing, as though she were speaking to a child. "Mayrig, I understand how you feel. I do. But the children—Seta, especially, wants to go. They have brought this request to us out of their own need. They want to know what happened. I think it's time—this not talking about it doesn't help anyone. Before Pop died, he took me to Martyrs' Day. Don't look at me that like that, Mayrig! It was my right to know. You, even you, can't wish away the genocide. It made you, it made me. And Mayrig, it's made these kids, too. Seta wants to go—now, why shouldn't she?"

"Araxie!" Casard boomed, stabbing her finger in the air. "What is this ridiculous I am hearing? They're interested. You let them play with guns, they're interested?"

Momma said firmly, pointing her own finger. "What I'm saying is they have a right. That's all. Mayrig, every kid in that Sunday school of yours knows what happened in 1915. Why shouldn't ours? Here they are: their own Grandma a survivor."

"That's right, that's right, Araxie. Now you've made a good point. Their own Medz-mayrig lived through it and she is the one to judge. I say, Stay out. Don't give me interested! You let them take drugs, they're interested? You let them read dirty books? I say children have no business poking in filthy Indignities."

Momma, abandoning patience, began to shriek. "Mayrig, listen to me! How many times do we have to go 'round and 'round? George and I have discussed this. That's all. You hear me? Final."

"Ho-ho!" Casard bellowed. "So now it's the odar inviting me to my own Indignities. You tell that Mister: Look out."

Tipping forward in her chair, Casard squinted her eyes at Momma. "Araxie. I'm looking right into you."

Momma nodded. "Mayrig, I know."

"I'm looking right into you," Casard said.

Momma tucked in her lips and chin, as if suppressing a burp.

She nodded solemnly.

"So-so-so," Casard said.

"So, I already told you," Momma said.

In the end it was decided that we would all attend Martyrs' Day. Casard said she would meet us at the church.

Each of us tried to imagine the event. Van said that the priest would re-create the Massacre on the altar, using fake blood. Momma said she remembered people coming forth from the pews to tell their stories. The pain of the survivors, she said, made her weep. Dad said what he always said, "We'll see."

I told Melanie there was nothing to be frightened of; the service would be theatrical: we would put ashes on our hands and faces and dance the shourchbar, the circle dance, in honor of the martyrs. I wondered if Theresa would insist on leading, the way she did every year at Sunday school, but I decided that it was unlikely.

At one o'clock in the afternoon we piled into the Buick. Halfway to church Momma looked into the visor mirror and touched up her lipstick.

"Seta," she said, "I'm counting on you, especially. Watch after Grandma. Take her hand nice, sit beside her."

I flicked the metal lid on the ashtray open and shut, open and shut. Pressing my finger inside, I studied the soot on my skin. All that week I had tried to imagine a million and a half dead. I had tried to picture a million trees and saw only a forest. It was a strange and eerie lesson that, beyond a certain number, everything diminishes to the eye. Everything becomes one.

I could not stop thinking about the girl with the tattoos. Her lonely, melancholy face captured the essence of the feeling in my belly, the feeling awakened by the duduk. I closed my eyes and saw the slave girl's tattooed breasts and her black soul-dead eyes. And then I thought about Casard and felt frightened, convinced that I was about to learn something that would irrevocably change the way I saw her.

Dad pulled the car up in front of the church. As we opened the doors of the car, Momma swiveled in her seat. "Now I'm counting on you," she said. "All of you—best behavior."

We entered the church basement and were immediately confronted by Hitler's famous words sewn on an enormous felt banner: WHO AFTER ALL SPEAKS TODAY OF THE ANNIHILATION OF THE ARMENIANS?

The banner hung from the ceiling. Beneath Hitler's pronouncement, as if in defiance of the doom therein, the basement teemed with living breathing Armenians, everyone talking all at once.

The women were dressed in navy or gray, the walls draped in black crepe. Bulletin boards with newspaper accounts and photographs of the atrocities were set up on easels along the four walls.

In the center of the room, below Hitler's quote, two aged men were engaged in a passionate discourse, poking each other's chest. The two men looked old enough to be survivors of the Turks' genocide, which Hitler had studied and augmented to suit his own plans. The sight of these two cronies fighting below a banner that proclaimed them wiped out like the buffalo terrified me, and I grabbed hold of Van's arm. Perhaps he was scared too, for he put his hand over mine and held on.

Momma touched her palm to the nape of my neck. Her touch sent shivers through me. "Stay close," she said. "We'll wait for Dad before heading upstairs to the church." Then Momma took Melanie by the hand and steered us through the crowd.

I glanced around the room trying to find Theresa, but she was nowhere in sight. With Momma in the lead, we pushed through the crowd toward the coffee bar in the back of the room. We wound along the side wall, stopping to gaze at photographs of the genocide, the dead captured in postures of sleep, their knees bent to one side, as if the covers had just been removed. I accidentally bumped into an easel, nearly toppling it, and when I saw pinned to it the photograph of the slave girl from Casard's book, I cried out. The caption read, "Armenian Girls Tattooed by Turks Sold as Slaves."

Momma must have heard me, for she touched me on the arm and studied my face, to see if I was all right. She was about to say something when Ani Baboostian, the oldest member of the church, called to her, "Araxie! Araxie, where have you been hiding! We've been looking all over for you."

Momma turned to the old woman and kissed her cheeks. But Ani pursed her lips and frowned.

"Ani, something the matter?" Momma said. Although Casard was the leader of the church, Ani Baboostian, eighty-nine years old, was its soul. Stout, with lively green eyes, long white hair and a handsome face creased like a good, soft glove, Ani was adored. Her vanity showed in the gold and ruby rings she wore on every finger including her thumbs, and the vibrant scarves she wrapped around her neck, this one orange with crimson tulips. Ani fingered her scarf, straightening it at her throat. Frowning, she shook her head, as if to say the matter was impossible to put in words. "Your mother, in the kitchen" was all she could manage.

Momma dispatched Van to go find Dad, while Melanie and I pushed behind her through the crowd. People cleared a path, eyeing the kitchen door.

We found Casard stretched out on a stainless-steel worktable the center of the kitchen, a blanket folded under her head. Above her, hanging from the ceiling, was a huge rack of shiny pots. The old women of the church were gathered around Casard, talking Armenian, trying to decide what should be done.

"Ah." Poppee clapped her hands. "Finally, Araxie."

The women nodded in our direction, their hands clasped together as though they were praying.

Poppee whispered something to Momma. As she spoke, Poppee put her hand over her heart and thumped a quick rhythm. Momma listened with her brow knit tight, the way she looked when one of us was telling her a fib.

Momma turned to Casard, and cupping her palms gently on Casard's cheeks, she whispered softly, "Mayrig," followed by something in Armenian that I could not hear.

Casard nodded weakly. "Scared me awful," she croaked. "My heart: Boom. Boom. Boom. Boom."

Momma placed her hand over her own heart. The women watched her and some shook their heads, while others rubbed their lips together, as though fighting the urge to speak.

Then Dad came into the kitchen, escorted by one of the deacons. He looked at Momma and they each read the other's mind.

Frowning, Dad asked, "Can she sit up?"

Momma spoke to Casard in Armenian. "She says the palpitations are less now."

The old women looked to Dad to see what he would do.

He studied the situation and then he said to Momma, "Come on. Let's take her home."

The old women nodded approval and helped Dad as he lifted Casard to her feet. With Momma holding her on one side and Dad on the other, Casard shuffled like an aged queen out the kitchen door and up the steps into the churchyard.

At the car, Dad tucked Casard in the front seat and held the back door open for the rest of us. Melanie hopped in, followed by Momma.

"No," I said, backing away from the car.

Van stood with me. "Go on, Dad," he said, "we'll save your seats till you get back."

Dad grimly shook his head. "Seta, Van, I'm sorry, but the show's over. You might as well get into the car."

"But you promised," I said.

"I know," Dad agreed, holding up a hand. "But it's over now. Surely you can see that. Let's take Grandma home and we'll see about next year."

"Next year," I repeated bitterly, as if he had said, Not ever. "No way. I'm going inside."

Dad shook his head. "Now, Seta, I can't allow that."

I hated him then, I hated them all—and Dad knew it. He looked away, studying the road. "I suppose you two can walk back to Grandma's on your own, if you want." He swung the back door closed and then got in behind the wheel.

Casard gazed straight ahead as if we were not there, as if the car were already en route.

"Grandma," I snapped, lunging toward Dad's open window. "Give me one good reason why we all can't go inside."

She would not look at me and I began to shriek, "You're a fake, Grandma.

That's what you are: a fake. You're fine enough to sit in the car, but you can't sit in the church."

"Start the car," she said, her gaze never leaving the hood.

Dad glanced at us one last time, and was about to start up the engine when Momma reached over the seat and squeezed his shoulder. "We're not going anywhere," she said, "until Mayrig says something to these kids."

"Enough talk"—Casard sniffed.

"What was that?" I yelled.

Casard lifted her chin.

"Aw Jees," Van said, and took off down the street. He went a ways, then turned back and bellowed, "Just forget it, Seta. Forget her. It's our massacre just as much as hers. She doesn't own fucking anything!"

I followed Van down the road. We were careful not to look back until the car had passed us and disappeared around the corner. Then Van and I turned on our heels and headed back to the church.

The bells tolled. The Der Hyre bowed his head, making the cross. One by one, the old people rose to speak on behalf of martyrs. Among the seated congregation they rose like pillars from an ancient ruin:

I am Arshag and I speak for my father, who was taken by the soldiers. I lost my mother and four brothers on the road to Aleppo.

I am Sarah and I stand in honor of my mother, who I remember baking the bread. The night the Turketa came, they violated her in front of me and my sister. All night they went at it and all night she suffered without a word. In the morning they stabbed my mother in the throat.

I am Kevork and I speak for our people. I speak for my family. My mother hid my sister and me in a cupboard in two woven sacks. She told us not to move. When the Turks came and took my mother and father away, we were safe. We stayed in that cupboard until it was very dark, the smell inside the sack making me sick all over myself.

I am Yerchanig. You Christian scum, they called us. They corralled our people like cattle into the church. I was a small boy. I ran from the group and hid behind a bush, no bigger than this. My mother and father, and my two brothers, I saw them being shoved into the church. I saw my mother at the last minute turn and look for me. The Turks pushed her into the church with their bayonets. They sealed the doors and threw burning hay into the windows and set fire to the roof. I will not describe the smell and the moaning. I will not tell you what I heard, hiding under that bush. To this day every time I close my eyes I see my mother's eyes searching for me.

I am Khentir. I stand in memory of my brother, Alexan, who also hid under a bush. Only he was not so lucky.

I am Ani. I was with my mother on the death road when the peasant women came down from the hills. First we heard their cry, "Aayyyeee! Aayyyeee!" and we thought: At last, they've come to save us. But we were very mistaken. You see, they carried knives for killing Christians and securing themselves a place in Paradise. I watched them put a knife through my mother, but they spared us young ones. I was then in my twenties and still a virgin. Now I am an old, sick woman, who has made her peace with God. But perhaps you have wondered why all these years Ani Baboostian wears a scarf. Now you will know.

Ani untied her orange and crimson scarf and raised her chin so the whole congregation could see the letters that covered her from neck to sternum. The tattoos were in the shape of a cross.

"You young ones can't read Turkish," Ani said, her green eyes opened wide. "Look here, young ones. Look at Ani Baboostian, slave girl. These letters are the names of her owners. These are the ones who violated her. Look now and remember what you see."

At first Van and I could not believe our eyes, but Ani lifted her chin and gave us time. Later, when the Der Hyre gently guided Ani to her seat, I could still see her in front of the altar, the writing on her throat irrevocably linked to the brass candelabras and the velvet curtain and the Cross. Suddenly, it made sense to me why the ancient songs were written in a minor key, why they seemed most true when paired with the sorrowful lament of the duduk. The duduk was the keening voice of the slave girl, and the martyred men and children. It was the voice of Casard, the part that could not speak. At last I understood that the trouble in my belly was my grandmother calling out to me, and I was miserable and brokenhearted, listening to Casard.

෴ CYNTHIA OZICK,
Excerpt from *The Shawl*—UNITED STATES

Cynthia Ozick was born in 1928 in New York City, the daughter of Russian émigrés. She received her BA from New York University in 1949 and her MA from Ohio State University in 1950. Ozick received a National Endowment for the Arts fellowship in 1968, an American Academy of Arts Award for Literature in 1973 and a Guggenheim fellowship in 1982. Most recently, Ozick received the National Book Critics Circle Award in 2000 for *Quarrel and Quandry.*

In Ozick's two-part novella, *The Shawl* (1980), Rosa Lublin struggles with the traumatic memory of her daughter's murder. Years later, after immigrating to Miami, Rosa writes long letters to Magda, a Holocaust victim, using Magda's old shawl to conjure up her "phantom" daughter, with "ghostly strains." Yet Ozick's narrator also describes Rosa as a "madwoman" in the first line of the novella, and Ozick embodies the perspective of a distant, doubtful reader through the character of Stella, Rosa's relative and a fellow Holocaust survivor. Stella encourages Rosa to forget the past completely and discard the shawl, Rosa's only memento of her dead daughter, Magda. Stella's character highlights both the danger of completely wiping out the past and the spectrum of trauma victims' coping mechanisms.

In a May 1997 article for the *Atlantic,* Ozick recounted how when *The Shawl* was first published in the *New Yorker* in May 1980, she received two letters, unsettling in different ways. The first was from a psychiatrist who said he dealt with many Holocaust survivors. "He said he was certain that I was such a survivor because only a survivor could write such a story," wrote Ozick. "I was shocked by the utter confidence of his assumption; he knew nothing about imagination." The second letter was from a Holocaust survivor who found Ozick's story both "emotionally and morally disruptive." Ozick concluded, "I sided with the survivor and thought the psychiatrist foolish. I finally assuaged the survivor by convincing her that I was not an enemy of her unreplicable experience."

"Maaaa—"

It was the first noise Magda had ever sent out from her throat since the drying up of Rosa's nipples.

"Maaaa . . . aaa!"

Again! Magda was wavering in the perilous sunlight of the arena, scribbling on such pitiful little bent shins. Rosa saw. She saw that Magda was grieving for the loss of her shawl, she saw that Magda was going to die. A tide of commands hammered in Rosa's nipples: Fetch, get, bring! But she did not know which to go after first, Magda or the shawl. If she jumped

out into the arena to snatch Magda up, the howling would not stop, because Magda would still not have the shawl; but if she ran back into the
barracks to find the shawl, and if she found it, and if she came after Magda
holding and shaking it, then she would get Magda back, Magda would
put the shawl in her mouth and turn dumb again.

Rosa entered the dark. It was easy to discover the shawl. Stella was
heaped under it, asleep in her thin bones. Rosa tore the shawl free and
flew—she could fly, she was only air—into the arena. The sunheat murmured of another life, of butterflies in summer. The light was placid,
mellow. On the other side of the steel fence, far away, there were green
meadows speckled with dandelions and deep-colored violets beyond them,
even farther, innocent tiger lilies, tall, lifting their orange bonnets. In the
barracks they spoke of "flowers," of "rain": excrement, thick turd-braids,
and the slow stinking maroon waterfall that slunk down from the upper
bunks, the stink mixed with a bitter fatty floating smoke that greased
Rosa's skin. She stood for an instant at the margin of the arena. Sometimes the electricity inside the fence would seem to hum; even Stella said
it was only an imagining, but Rosa heard real sounds in the wire: grainy
sad voices. The farther she was from the fence, the more clearly the voices
crowded at her. The lamenting voices strummed so convincingly, so pas-
sionately, it was impossible to suspect them of being phantoms. The voices
told her to hold up the shawl, high; the voices told her to shake it, to whip
with it, to unfurl it like a flag. Rosa lifted, shook, whipped, unfurled. Far
off, very far, Magda leaned across her air-fed belly, reaching out with the
rods of her arms. She was high up, elevated, riding someone's shoulder.
But the shoulder that carried Magda was not coming toward Rosa and
the shawl, it was drifting away, the speck of Magda was moving more and
more into the smoky distance. Above the shoulder a helmet glinted. The
light tapped the helmet and sparkled it into a goblet. Below the helmet
a black body like a domino and a pair of black boots hurled themselves
in the direction of the electrified fence. "Maamaa, maaamaaa," they all
hummed together. How far Magda was from Rosa now, across the whole
square, past a dozen barracks, all the way on the other side! She was no
bigger than a moth.

All at once Magda was swimming through the air. The whole of Magda
traveled through loftiness. She looked like a butterfly touching a silver
vine. And the moment Magda's feathered round head and her pencil legs
and balloonish belly and zigzag arms splashed against the fence, the steel
voices went mad in their growling, urging Rosa to run and run to the spot

where Magda had fallen from her flight against the electrified fence; but of course Rosa did not obey them. She only stood, because if she ran they would shoot, and if she tried to pick up the sticks of Magda's body they would shoot, and if she let the wolf's screech ascending now through the ladder of her skeleton break out, they would shoot; so she took Magda's shawl and filled her own mouth with it, stuffed it in and stuffed it in, until she was swallowing up the wolf's screech and tasting the cinnamon and almond depth of Magda's saliva; and Rosa drank Magda's shawl until it dried.

∾ CAN XUE,
"Hut on a Mountain"—CHINA

Can Xue (whose real name is Deng Xiaohua) was born in the Hunan Province in 1953. Can Xue's parents were condemned as ultra-rightists in 1957. Can Xue was forced to leave school at the age of thirteen. Through the Cultural Revolution period, she was raised by her grandmother and worked as an iron worker for ten years, often on the brink of starvation. She later taught herself to sew, and she and her husband became self-employed tailors. She first began writing in 1983, adopting the pen name Can Xue, which means "the dirty snow that refuses to melt." Her stories have appeared in various literary magazines in mainland China, Hong Kong, and Taiwan. Can Xue is an honorary member of the International Writing Program at the University of Iowa and lives in the People's Republic of China.

The narrator in Can Xue's "Hut on a Mountain" (1989) presents a microcosmic perspective of life during the repressive Chinese Cultural Revolution. Can Xue's tale reflects an acutely psychological trauma, particularly subtle in the case of China, where the government's repression, or "vague accusation," as Princeton professor Perry Link has coined it, caused (and still causes) citizens to preemptively self-censor themselves. Since this process occurs in the "recesses of private minds," it is more lethal, because with the "passage of time, threats and prohibitions come to seem normal, even natural," wrote Link in his April 2002 *New York Review of Books* essay, "China: The Anaconda in the Chandelier."

Can Xue's ghostly hut dweller seems as real as any of the other
characters in her nightmare tale and embodies the imagined "Big
Brother" threat posed by the government; he exists solely in the
characters' minds yet, like the "vague accusation," still causes them
to curtail their behavior. Can Xue's tale, however, could not
practically be so direct for fear of governmental reprimand (Deng
Xiaohua already distances herself from the tale through her pen
name, Can Xue), nor would it be as effective stylistically if it
didn't make a reader's skin crawl with so many loose ends and
unanswered questions.

On the bleak and barren mountain behind our house stood a wooden
hut. Day after day I busied myself by tidying up my desk drawers. When
I wasn't doing that I would sit in the armchair, my hands on my knees,
listening to the tumultuous sounds of the north wind whipping against
the fir-bark roof of the hut, and the howling of the wolves echoing in the
valleys.

"Huh, you'll never get done with those drawers," said Mother, forcing
a smile. "Not in your lifetime."

"There's something wrong with everyone's ears," I said with suppressed
annoyance. "There are so many thieves wandering about our house in
the moonlight, when I turn on the light I can see countless tiny holes
poked by fingers in the window screens. In the next room, Father and you
snore terribly, rattling the utensils in the kitchen cabinet. Then I kick
about in my bed, turn my swollen head on the pillow and hear the man
locked up in the hut banging furiously against the door. This goes on till
daybreak."

"You give me a terrible start," Mother said, "every time you come into
my room looking for things." She fixed her eyes on me as she backed toward the door. I saw the flesh of one of her cheeks contort ridiculously.

One day I decided to go up to the mountain to find out what on earth
was the trouble. As soon as the wind let up, I began to climb. I climbed
and climbed for a long time. The sunshine made me dizzy. Tiny white
flames were flickering among the pebbles.

I wandered about, coughing all the time. The salty sweat from my forehead was streaming into my eyes. I couldn't see or hear anything. When
I reached home, I stood outside the door for a while and saw that the
person reflected in the mirror had mud on her shoes and dark purple
pouches under her eyes.

"It's some disease," I heard them snickering in the dark.

When my eyes became adapted to the darkness inside, they'd hidden themselves—laughing in their hiding places. I discovered they had made a mess of my desk drawers while I was out. A few dead moths and dragon-flies were scattered on the floor—they knew only too well that these were treasures to me.

"They sorted the things in the drawers for you," little sister told me, "when you were out." She stared at me, her left eye turning green.

"I hear wolves howling," I deliberately tried to scare her. "They keep running around the house. Sometimes they poke their heads in through the cracks in the door. These things always happen after dusk. You get so scared in your dreams that cold sweat drips from the soles of your feet. Everyone in this house sweats this way in his sleep. You have only to see how damp the quilts are."

I felt upset because some of the things in my desk drawers were missing. Keeping her eyes on the floor, Mother pretended she knew nothing about it. But I had a feeling she was glaring ferociously at the back of my head since the spot would become numb and swollen whenever she did that. I also knew they had buried a box with my chess set by the well behind the house. They had done it many times, but each time I would dig the chess set out. When I dug for it, they would turn on the light and poke their heads out the window. In the face of my defiance they always tried to remain calm.

"Up there on the mountain," I told them at mealtime, "there is a hut."

They all lowered their heads, drinking soup noisily. Probably no one heard me.

"Lots of big rats were running wildly in the wind," I raised my voice and put down the chopsticks. "Rocks were rolling down the mountain and crashing into the back of our house. And you were so scared cold sweat dripped from your soles. Don't you remember? You only have to look at your quilts. Whenever the weather's fine, you're airing the quilts; the clothesline out there is always strung with them."

Father stole a glance at me with one eye, which, I noticed, was the all-too-familiar eye of a wolf. So that was it! At night he became one of the wolves running around the house, howling and wailing mournfully.

"White lights are swaying back and forth everywhere." I clutched Mother's shoulder with one hand. "Everything is so glaring that my eyes blear from the pain. You simply can't see a thing. But as soon as I return to my room, sit down in my armchair, and put my hands on my knees,

I can see the fir-bark roof clearly. The image seems very close. In fact, every one of us must have seen it. Really, there's somebody squatting inside. He's got two big purple pouches under his eyes, too, because he stays up all night."

Father said, "Every time you dig by the well and hit stone with a screeching sound, you make Mother and me feel as if we were hanging in mid-air. We shudder at the sound and kick with bare feet but can't reach the ground." To avoid my eyes, he turned his face toward the window, the panes of which were thickly specked with fly droppings.

"At the bottom of the well," he went on, "there's a pair of scissors which I dropped some time ago. In my dreams I always make up my mind to fish them out. But as soon as I wake, I realize I've made a mistake. In fact, no scissors have ever fallen into the well. Your mother says positively that I've made a mistake. But I will not give up. It always steals into my mind again. Sometimes while I'm in bed, I am suddenly seized with regret: the scissors lie rusting at the bottom of the well, why shouldn't I go fish them out? I've been troubled by this for dozens of years. See my wrinkles? My face seems to have become furrowed. Once I actually went to the well and tried to lower a bucket into it. But the rope was thick and slippery. Suddenly my hands lost their grip and the bucket flopped with a loud boom, breaking into pieces in the well. I rushed back to the house, looked into the mirror, and saw the hair on my left temple had turned completely white."

"How that north wind pierces!" I hunched my shoulders. My face turned black and blue with cold.

"Bits of ice are forming in my stomach. When I sit down in my arm-chair I can hear them clinking away."

I had been intending to give my desk drawers a cleaning, but Mother was always stealthily making trouble. She'd walk to and fro in the next room, stamping, stamping, to my great distraction. I tried to ignore it, so I got a pack of cards and played, murmuring "one, two, three, four, five. . . ."

The pacing stopped all of a sudden and Mother poked her small dark green face into the room and mumbled, "I had a very obscene dream. Even now my back is dripping cold sweat."

"And your soles, too," I added. "Everyone's soles drip cold sweat. You aired your quilt again yesterday. It's usual enough."

Little sister sneaked in and told me that Mother had been thinking of breaking my arms because I was driving her crazy by opening and shutting the drawers. She was so tortured by the sound that every time she heard it, she'd soak her head in cold water until she caught a bad cold.

"This didn't happen by chance." Sister's stares were always so pointed that tiny pink measles broke out on my neck. "For example, I've heard Father talking about the scissors for perhaps twenty years. Everything has its own cause from way back. Everything."

So I oiled the sides of the drawers. And by opening and shutting them carefully, I managed to make no noise at all. I repeated this experiment for many days and the pacing in the next room ceased. She was fooled. This proves you can get away with anything as long as you take a little precaution. I was very excited over my success and worked hard all night. I was about to finish tidying my drawers when the light suddenly went out. I heard Mother's sneering laugh in the next room.

"That light from your room glares so that it makes all my blood vessels throb and throb, as though some drums were beating inside. Look," she said, pointing to her temple, where the blood vessels bulged like fat earth-worms. "I'd rather get scurvy. There are throbbings throughout my body day and night. You have no idea how I'm suffering. Because of this ailment, your father once thought of committing suicide." She put her fat hand on my shoulder, an icy hand dripping with water.

Someone was making trouble by the well. I heard him letting the bucket down and drawing it up, again and again; the bucket hit against the wall of the well—boom, boom, boom. At dawn, he dropped the bucket with a loud bang and ran away. I opened the door of the next room and saw Father sleeping with his vein-ridged hand clutching the bedside, groaning in agony. Mother was beating the floor here and there with a broom; her hair was disheveled. At the moment of daybreak, she told me, a huge swarm of hideous beetles flew in through the window. They bumped against the walls and flopped onto the floor, which now was scattered with their remains. She got up to tidy the room, and as she was putting her feet into her slippers, a hidden bug bit her toe. Now her whole leg was swollen like a thick lead pipe.

"He," Mother pointed to Father, who was sleeping stuporously, "is dreaming it is he who is bitten. "

"In the little hut on the mountain, someone is groaning, too. The black wind is blowing, carrying grape leaves along with it."

"Do you hear?" In the faint light of morning, Mother put her ear against the floor, listening with attention. "These bugs hurt themselves in their fall and passed out. They charged into the room earlier, at the moment of daybreak."

I did go up to the mountain that day, I remember. At first I was sitting in the cane chair, my hands on my knees. Then I opened the door and walked into the white light. I climbed up the mountain, seeing nothing but the white pebbles glowing with flames. There were no grapevines, nor any hut.

 VLADIMIR NABOKOV,
Excerpt from *Pnin*—RUSSIA

Vladimir Vladimirovich Nabokov was born in 1899 in Saint Petersburg, Russia, into an aristocratic and trilingual household. Nabokov's father was politically active in Russia before the family fled to Western Europe in 1919, in the wake of the Russian Revolution of 1917. Nabokov attended school in England and graduated from the University of Cambridge in 1923. Nabokov's father was killed one year earlier, in a political rally in Berlin, while trying to shield the speaker from right-wing assassins. For the next eighteen years, Nabokov lived in Berlin and Paris, writing prolifically for the Russian émigré press under the pseudonym of Vladimir Sirin and supporting himself through translations, lessons in English and tennis, and by composing the first crossword puzzles in Russian. In 1940, he moved to the United States, where he was a professor of English literature at Wellesley College from 1941 to 1948 and a professor of Russian literature at Cornell University from 1948 to 1959. After the publication and success of *Lolita*, he eventually retired from teaching and moved to Switzerland to concentrate on his writing. Vladimir Nabokov died in Montreux, Switzerland, in 1977.

Pnin, the Russian expatriate professor of Nabokov's *Pnin* (1957), is distracted from a game of croquet with colleagues by the mention of Mira, a woman he once knew. Pnin "remembered the last day they had met, on the Neva embankment in Petrograd, and the tears, and the stars, and the warm rose-red-silk lining of her karakul muff. The Civil War of 1918–22 separated them; history broke their engagement." Since then, Pnin had avoided thinking about Mira, who had subsequently perished in a concentration camp. But at times, memories of the past envelop Pnin. "Since the exact form of her death had not been recorded," Nabokov writes, "Mira kept dying a great number of deaths in one's mind, and undergoing a great number of resurrections, only to die again and again. . . . He did not believe in an autocratic God. He did believe, dimly, in a democracy of ghosts. The souls of the dead, perhaps, formed committees, and these, in continuous session, attended to the destinies of the quick."

Dinner was served on the screened porch. As he sat down next to Bolotov and began to stir the sour cream in his red *botvinia* (chilled beet soup), wherein pink ice cubes tinkled, Pnin automatically resumed an earlier conversation.

"You will notice," he said, "that there is a significant difference between Lyovin's spiritual time and Vronski's physical one. In mid-book, Lyovin and Kitty lag behind Vronski and Anna by a whole year. When, on a Sunday evening in May 1876, Anna throws herself under that freight train, she has existed more than four years since the beginning of the novel, but in the case of the Lyovins, during the same period, 1872 to 1876, hardly three years have elapsed. It is the best example of relativity in literature that is known to me."

After dinner, a game of croquet was suggested. These people favored the time-honored but technically illegal setting of hoops, where two of the ten are crossed at the centre of the ground to form the so-called Cage or Mousetrap. It became immediately clear that Pnin, who teamed with Madam Bolotov against Shpolyanski and Countess Poroshin, was by far the best player of the lot. As soon as the pegs were driven in and the game started, the man was transfigured. From his habitual, slow, ponderous, rather rigid self, he changed into a terrifically mobile, scampering, mute, sly-visaged hunchback. It seemed to be always his turn to play. Holding his mallet very low and daintily swinging it between his parted spindly legs (he had created a minor sensation by changing into Bermuda shorts expressly for the game), Pnin foreshadowed every stroke with nimble aim-taking oscillations of the mallet head, then gave the ball an accurate tap, and forthwith, still hunched, and with the ball still rolling, walked rapidly to the spot where he had planned for it to stop. With geometrical gusto, he ran it through hoops, evoking cries of admiration from the onlookers. Even Igor Poroshin, who was passing by like a shadow with two cans of beer he was carrying to some private banquet, stopped for a second and shook his head appreciatively before vanishing in the shrubbery. Plaints and protests, however, would mingle with the applause when Pnin, with brutal indifference, croqueted, or rather rocketed, an adversary's ball. Placing it in contact with his own ball, and firmly putting his curiously small foot upon the latter, he would bang at his ball so as to drive the other up the country by the shock of the stroke. When appealed to, Susan said it was completely against the rules, but Madam Shpolyanski insisted it was perfectly acceptable and said that when she was a child her English governess used to call it a Hong Kong.

After Pnin had tolled the stake and all was over, and Varvara accompanied Susan to get the evening tea ready, Pnin quietly retired to a bench under the pines. A certain extremely unpleasant and frightening cardiac sensation, which he had experienced several times throughout his adult life, had come upon him again. It was not pain or palpitation, but rather an awful feeling of sinking and melting into one's physical surroundings—sunset, red boles of trees, sand, still air. Meanwhile, Roza Shpolyanski, noticing Pnin sitting alone, and taking advantage of this, walked over to him (*"sidite, sidite!"* don't get up) and sat down next to him on the bench.

"In 1916 or 1917," she said, "you may have had occasion to hear my maiden name—Geller—from some great friends of yours."

"No, I don't recollect," said Pnin.

"It is of no importance, anyway. I don't think we ever met. But you knew well my cousins, Grisha and Mira Belochkin. They constantly spoke of you. He is living in Sweden, I think—and, of course, you have heard of his poor sister's terrible end . . ."

"Indeed, I have," said Pnin.

"Her husband," said Madam Shpolyanski, "was a most charming man, Samuil Lvovich and I knew him and his first wife, Svetlana Chertok, the pianist, very intimately. He was interned by the Nazis separately from Mira, and died in the same concentration camp as did my elder brother Misha. You did not know Misha, did you? He was also in love with Mira once upon a time."

"*Tshay gotoff!* (tea's ready)," called Susan from the porch in her funny functional Russian. "Timofey, Rozochka! *Tshay!*"

Pnin told Madam Shpolyanski he would follow her in a minute, and after she had gone he continued to sit in the first dusk of the arbor, his hands clasped on the croquet mallet he still held.

Two kerosene lamps cozily illuminated the porch of the country house. Dr. Pavel Antonovich Pnin, Timofey's father, an eye specialist, and Dr.

Yakov Grigorievich Belochkin, Mira's father, a pediatrician, could not be torn away from their chess game in a corner of the veranda, so Madam Belochkin had the maid serve them there—on a special small Japanese table, near the one they were playing at—their glasses of tea in silver holders, the curd and whey with black bread, the Garden Strawberries, *zemlyanika,* and the other cultivated species, *klubnika* (Hautbois or Green Strawberries), and the radiant golden jams, and the various biscuits, wafers, pretzels, zwiebacks—instead of calling the two engrossed doctors to the main table at the other end of the porch, where sat the rest of the family and guests, some clear, some grading into a luminous mist.

Dr. Belochkin's blind hand took a pretzel; Dr. Pnin's seeing hand took a rook. Dr. Belochkin munched and stared at the hole in his ranks; Dr. Pnin dipped an abstract zwieback into the hole of his tea.

The country house that the Belochkins rented that summer was in the same Baltic resort near which the widow of General N— let a summer cottage to the Pnins on the confines of her vast estate, marshy and rugged, with dark woods hemming in a desolate manor. Timofey Pnin was again the clumsy, shy, obstinate, eighteen-year-old boy, waiting in the dark for Mira—and despite the fact that logical thought put electric bulbs into the kerosene lamps and reshuffled the people, turning them into aging emigrés and securely, hopelessly, forever wire-netting the lighted porch, my poor Pnin, with hallucinatory sharpness, imagined Mira slipping out of there into the garden and coming toward him among tall tobacco flowers whose dull white mingled in the dark with that of her frock. This feeling coincided somehow with the sense of diffusion and dilation within his chest. Gently he laid his mallet aside and, to dissipate the anguish, started walking away from the house, through the silent pine grove. From a car which was parked near the garden tool house and which contained presumably at least two of his fellow guests' children, there issued a steady trickle of radio music.

"Jazz, jazz, they always must have their jazz, those youngsters," muttered Pnin to himself, and turned into the path that led to the forest and river. He remembered the fads of his and Mira's youth, the amateur theatricals, the gypsy ballads, the passion she had for photography. Where were they now, those artistic snapshots she used to take—pets, clouds, flowers, an April glade with shadows of birches on wet-sugar snow, soldiers posturing on the roof of a boxcar, a sunset skyline, a hand holding a book? He remembered the last day they had met, on the Neva embankment in Petrograd, and the tears, and the stars, and the warm rose-red silk lining of her karakul muff. The Civil War of 1918–22 separated them: history broke their engagement. Timofey wandered southward, to join briefly the ranks of Denikin's army, while Mira's family escaped from the Bolsheviks to Sweden and then settled down in Germany, where eventually she married a fur dealer of Russian extraction. Sometime in the early thirties, Pnin, by then married too, accompanied his wife to Berlin, where she wished to attend a congress of psychotherapists, and one night, at a Russian restaurant on the Kurfurstendamm, he saw Mira again. They exchanged a few words, she smiled at him in the remembered fashion, from under her dark brows, with that bashful slyness of hers; and the contour of her prominent cheekbones, and the elongated eyes, and the slenderness of arm and ankle were unchanged, were immortal, and then she joined her husband who was getting his overcoat at the cloakroom, and that was all—but the pang of tenderness remained, akin to the vibrating outline of verses you know you know but cannot recall.

What chatty Madam Shpolyanski mentioned had conjured up Mira's image with unusual force. This was disturbing. Only in the detachment of an incurable complaint, in the sanity of near death, could one cope with this for a moment. In order to exist rationally, Pnin had taught himself, during the last ten years, never to remember Mira Belochkin—not because, in itself, the evocation of a youthful love affair, banal and brief, threatened his peace of mind (alas, recollections of his marriage to Liza were imperious enough to crowd out any former romance), but because, if one were quite sincere with oneself, no conscience, and hence no consciousness, could be expected to subsist in a world where such things as Mira's death were possible. One had to forget—because one could not live with the thought that this graceful, fragile, tender young woman with those eyes, that smile, those gardens and snows in the background, had been brought in a cattle car to an extermination camp and killed by an injection of phenol into the heart, into the gentle heart one had heard beating under one's lips in the dusk of the past. And since the exact form of her death had not been recorded, Mira kept dying a great number of deaths in one's mind, and undergoing a great number of resurrections, only to die again and again, led away by a trained nurse, inoculated with filth, tetanus bacilli, broken glass, gassed in a sham shower bath with prussic acid, burned alive in a pit on a gasoline-soaked pile of beechwood. According to the investigator Pnin had happened to talk to in Washington, the only certain thing was that being too weak to work (though still smiling, still able to help other Jewish women), she was selected to die

and was cremated only a few days after her   val in Buchenwald, in the
beautifully wooded Grosser Ettersberg, as the   ion is resoundingly called.
It is an hour's stroll from Weimar, where wa   Goethe, Herder, Schiller,
Wieland, the inimitable Kotzebue and other   *ber warum*—but why—"
Dr. Hagen, the gentlest of souls alive, would   "why had one to put that
horrid camp so near!" for indeed, it was ne   only five miles from the
cultural heart of Germany—"that nation of   /ersities," as the President
of Waindell College, renowned for his use of   *mot juste*, had so elegantly
phrased it when reviewing the European situ   n in a recent Commence-
ment speech, along with the compliment h   id another torture house,
"Russia—the country of Tolstoy, Stanislavski   kolnikov, and other great
and good men."

Pnin slowly walked under the solemn pines. The sky was dying. He did
not believe in an autocratic God. He did believe, dimly, in a democracy
of ghosts. The souls of the dead, perhaps, formed committees, and these,
in continuous session, attended to the destinies of the quick.

The mosquitoes were getting bothersome. Time for tea. Time for a game
of chess with Chateau. That strange spasm was over, one could breathe
again. On the distant crest of the knoll, at the exact spot where Grami-
neev's easel had stood a few hours before, two dark figures in profile were
silhouetted against the ember-red sky. They stood there closely, facing each
other. One could not make out from the road whether it was the Poroshin
girl and her beau, or Nina Bolotov and young Poroshin, or merely an em-
blematic couple placed with easy art on the last page of Pnin's fading day.

〜 TONI MORRISON,
   Excerpt from *Beloved*—UNITED STATES

See "Writing the Unspeakable and the Pressure of Emptiness"
for Toni Morrison's biography.

In Toni Morrison's novel *Beloved* (1987), Sethe's daughter,
Beloved, who has been killed by her mother, does indeed *come
back unappeased*, referring back to Lawrence's ghosts that Robert
Polito mentioned. Sethe cuts her daughter's neck in order to
ensure that she will not be enslaved and suffer the same torments
Sethe has endured. Beloved underscores the characters' struggle
with traumatic memories that both stifle and enrich their lives
years later. From a macrocosmic perspective, Morrison challenges

her readers to decide whether Beloved is simply another character or actually an embodied memory, returned to help Sethe process her grief. Beloved appears out of the blue (she is literally seen emerging from the water) and seeks refuge in Sethe's family. From the reader's external perspective, Beloved is as "real" as any other character in the text. She is one of the few characters with chapters written in her direct voice; and Morrison provides just enough narrative detail to rationalize Beloved's existence. (A rumor circulates in the community about a girl locked up in a house by a white man, who escaped some months prior to the novel's action.) Yet Morrison plants many more uncanny coincidences to suggest that Beloved is, in fact, Sethe's dead daughter, who has "come back home from the timeless place." Beloved spontaneously sings lullabies that Sethe invented and sang, only years ago, and Beloved has a telling scar on her neck. It is a meta-fictional exercise, and the proof for and against Beloved as a ghost doesn't stack up neatly. Yet Morrison uses our readerly troubles with Beloved in order to reflect the characters' struggle with vivid memories of slavery, which also refuse to be patly processed.

A fully dressed woman walked out of the water. She barely gained the dry bank of the stream before she sat down and leaned against a mulberry tree. All day and all night she sat there, her head resting on the trunk in a position abandoned enough to crack the brim in her straw hat. Everything hurt but her lungs most of all. Sopping wet and breathing shallow she spent those hours trying to negotiate the weight of her eyelids. The day breeze blew her dress dry; the night wind wrinkled it. Nobody saw her emerge or came accidentally by. If they had, chances are they would have hesitated before approaching her. Not because she was wet, or dozing or had what sounded like asthma, but because amid all that she was smiling. It took her the whole of the next morning to lift herself from the ground and make her way through the woods past a giant temple of boxwood to the field and then the yard of the slate-gray house. Exhausted again, she sat down on the first handy place—a stump not far from the steps of 124. By then keeping her eyes open was less of an effort. She could manage it for a full two minutes or more. Her neck, its circumference no wider than a parlor-service saucer, kept bending and her chin brushed the bit of lace edging her dress.

Women who drink champagne when there is nothing to celebrate can look like that: their straw hats with broken brims are often askew; they nod in public places; their shoes are undone. But their skin is not like that of the woman breathing near the steps of 124. She had new skin, lineless and smooth, including the knuckles of her hands.

By late afternoon when the carnival was over, and the Negroes were hitching rides home if they were lucky—walking if they were not—the woman had fallen asleep again. The rays of the sun struck her full in the face, so that when Sethe, Denver and Paul D rounded the curve in the road all they saw was a black dress, two unlaced shoes below it, and Here Boy nowhere in sight.

"Look," said Denver. "What is that?"

And, for some reason she could not immediately account for, the moment she got close enough to see the face, Sethe's bladder filled to capacity. She said, "Oh, excuse me," and ran around to the back of 124. Not since she was a baby girl, being cared for by the eight year-old girl who pointed out her mother to her, had she had an emergency that unmanageable. She never made the outhouse. Right in front of its door she had to lift her skirts, and the water she voided was endless. Like a horse, she thought, but as it went on and on she thought, No, more like flooding the boat when Denver was born. So much water Amy said, "Hold on, Lu. You going to sink us you keep that up." But there was no stopping water breaking from a breaking womb and there was no stopping now. She hoped Paul D wouldn't take it upon himself to come looking for her and be obliged to see her squatting in front of her own privy making a mudhole too deep to be witnessed without shame. Just about the time she started wondering if the carnival would accept another freak, it stopped. She tidied herself and ran around to the porch. No one was there. All three were inside—Paul D and Denver standing before the stranger, watching her drink cup after cup of water.

"She said she was thirsty," said Paul D. He took off his cap. "Mighty thirsty look like."

The woman gulped water from a speckled tin cup and held it out for more. Four times Denver filled it, and four times the woman drank as though she had crossed a desert. When she was finished a little water was on her chin, but she did not wipe it away. Instead she gazed at Sethe with sleepy eyes. Poorly fed, thought Sethe, and younger than her clothes suggested—good lace at the throat, and a rich woman's hat. Her skin was flawless except for three vertical scratches on her forehead so fine and thin they seemed at first like hair, baby hair before it bloomed and roped into the masses of black yarn under her hat.

"You from around here?" Sethe asked her.

She shook her head no and reached down to take off her shoes. She pulled her dress up to the knees and rolled down her stockings. When the hosiery was tucked into the shoes, Sethe saw that her feet were like her hands, soft and new. She must have hitched a wagon ride, thought Sethe. Probably one of those West Virginia girls looking for something to beat a life of tobacco and sorghum. Sethe bent to pick up the shoes.

"What might your name be?" asked Paul D.

"Beloved," she said, and her voice was so low and rough each one looked at the other two. They heard the voice first—later the name.

"Beloved. You use a last name, Beloved?" Paul D asked her.

"Last?" She seemed puzzled. Then "No," and she spelled it for them, slowly, as though the letters were being formed as she spoke them.

Sethe dropped the shoes; Denver sat down and Paul D smiled. He recognized the careful enunciation of letters by those, like himself, who could not read but had memorized the letters of their name. He was about to ask who her people were but thought better of it. A young colored woman drifting was drifting from ruin. He had been in Rochester four years ago and seen five women arriving with fourteen female children. All their men—brothers, uncles, fathers, husbands, sons—had been picked off one by one. They had a single piece of paper directing them to a preacher on DeVore Street. The War had been over four or five years then, but nobody white or black seemed to know it. Odd clusters and strays of Negroes wandered the back roads and cowpaths from Schenectady to Jackson. Dazed but insistent, they searched each other out for word of a cousin, an aunt, a friend who once said, "Call on me. Anytime you get near Chicago, just call on me." Some of them were running from family that could not support them, some to family; some were running from dead crops, dead kin, life threats, and took-over land. Boys younger than Buglar and Howard; configurations and blends of families of women and children, while elsewhere, solitary, hunted and hunting for, were men, men, men. Forbidden public transportation, chased by debt and filthy "talking sheets," they followed secondary routes, scanned the horizon for signs and counted heavily on each other. Silent, except for social courtesies, when they met one another they neither described nor asked about the sorrow that drove them from one place to another. The whites didn't bear speaking on. Everybody knew.

So he did not press the young woman with the broken hat about where from or how come. If she wanted them to know and was strong enough to get through the telling, she would. What occupied them at the moment was what it might be that she needed. Underneath the major question, each harbored another. Paul D wondered at the newness of her shoes. Sethe was deeply touched by her sweet name; the remembrance of glittering headstone made her feel especially kindly toward her. Denver, however, was shaking. She looked at this sleepy beauty and wanted more.

Sethe hung her hat on a peg and turned graciously toward the girl. "That's a pretty name, Beloved. Take off your hat, why don't you, and I'll make us something. We just got back from the carnival over near Cincinnati. Everything in there is something to see."

Bolt upright in the chair, in the middle of Sethe's welcome, Beloved had fallen asleep again.

"Miss. Miss." Paul D shook her gently. "You want to lay down a spell?"

She opened her eyes to slits and stood up on her soft new feet which, barely capable of their job, slowly bore her to the keeping room. Once there, she collapsed on Baby Sugg's bed. Denver removed her hat and put the quilt with two squares of color over her feet. She was breathing like a steam engine.

. . .

When Sethe wrapped her head and bundled up to go to town, it was already midmorning. And when she left the house she neither saw the prints nor heard the voices that ringed 124 like a noose.

Trudging in the ruts left earlier by wheels, Sethe was excited to giddiness by the things she no longer had to remember. I don't have to remember nothing. I don't even have to explain. She understands it all. I can forget how Baby Suggs' heart collapsed; how we agreed it was consumption without a sign of it in the world. Her eyes when she brought my food, I can forget that, and how she told me that Howard and Buglar were all right but wouldn't let go each other's hands. Played that way: stayed that way especially in their sleep. She handed me the food from a basket; things wrapped small enough to get through the bars, whispering news: Mr. Bodwin going to see the judge—in chambers, she kept on saying, in chambers, like I knew what it meant or she did. The Colored Ladies of Delaware, Ohio, had drawn up a petition to keep me from being hanged. That two white preachers had come round and wanted to talk to me, pray for me. That a newspaperman came too. She told me the news and I told her I needed something for the rats. She wanted Denver out and slapped her palms when I wouldn't let her go. "Where your earrings?" she said. "I'll hold em for you." I told her the jailer took them, to protect me from myself. He thought I could do some harm with the wire. Baby Suggs covered her mouth with her hand. "Schoolteacher left town," she said. "Filed a claim and rode on off. They going to let you out for the burial," she said, "not the funeral, just the burial," and they did. The sheriff came with me and looked away when I fed Denver in the wagon. Neither Howard nor Buglar would let me near them, not even to touch their hair. I believe a lot of folks were there, but I just saw the box. Reverend Pike spoke in a real loud voice, but I didn't catch a word—except the first two, and three months later when Denver was ready for solid food and they let me out for good, I went and got you a gravestone, but I didn't have money enough for the carving so I exchanged (bartered, you might say) what I did have and I'm sorry to this day I never thought to ask him for the whole thing: all I heard of what Reverend Pike said. Dearly Beloved, which is what you are to me and I don't have to be sorry about getting only one word, and I don't have to remember the slaughterhouse and the Saturday girls who worked its yard. I can forget that what I did changed Baby Sugg's life. No Clearing, no company. Just laundry and shoes. I can forget it all now because as soon as I got the gravestone in place you made your presence known in the house and worried us all to distraction. I didn't understand it then. I thought you were mad with me. And now I know that if you was, you ain't now because you came back here to me and I was right all along: there is no world outside my door. I only need to know one thing. How bad is the scar?

As Sethe walked back to work, late for the first time in sixteen years and wrapped in a timeless present, Stamp Paid fought fatigue and the habit of a lifetime. Baby Suggs refused to go to the Clearing because she believed *they* had won; he refused to acknowledge any such victory. Baby had no back door; so he braved the cold and a wall of talk to knock on the one she did have. He clutched the red ribbon in his pocket for strength. Softly at first, then harder. At the last he banged furiously—disbelieving it could happen. That the door of a house with colored people in it did not fly open in his presence. He went to the window and wanted to cry. Sure enough, there they were, not a one of them heading for the door. Worrying his scrap of ribbon to shreds, the old man turned and went down the steps. Now curiosity joined his shame and his debt. Two backs curled away from him as he looked in the window. One had a head he recognized; the other troubled him. He didn't know her and didn't know anybody it could be. Nobody, but nobody visited that house.

After a disagreeable breakfast he went to see Ella and John to find out what they knew. Perhaps there he could find out if, after all these years of clarity, he has misnamed himself and there was yet another debt he owed. Born Joshua, he renamed himself when he handed over his wife to his master's son. Handed her over in the sense that he did not kill anybody, thereby himself, because his wife demanded he stay alive. Otherwise, she reasoned, where and to whom could she return when the boy was through? With that gift, he decided that he didn't owe anybody anything. Whatever his obligations were, that act paid them off. He thought it would make him rambunctious, renegade—a drunkard even, the debtlessness, and in a way it did. But there was nothing to do with it. Work well; work poorly. Work a little; work not at all. Make sense; make none. Sleep, wake up; like somebody, dislike others. It didn't seem much of a way to live and it brought him no satisfaction. So he extended this debtlessness to other people by helping them pay out and off whatever they owed in misery. Beaten runaways? He ferried them out and rendered them paid for; gave them their own bill of sale, so to speak. "You paid it; now life owes you." And the receipt, as it were, was a welcome door that he never had to knock on, like John and Ella's in front of which he stood and said, "Who in there?" only once and she was pulling on the hinge.

"Where you been keeping yourself? I told John must be cold if Stamp stay inside."

"Oh, I been out." He took off his cap and massaged his scalp.

"Out where? Not by here." Ella hung two suits of underwear on a line behind the stove.

"Was over to Baby Suggs' this morning."

"What you want in there?" asked Ella. "Somebody invite you in?"

"That's Baby's kin. I don't need no invite to look after her people."

"Sth." Ella was unmoved. She had been Baby Suggs' friend and Sethe's too till the rough time. Except for a nod at the carnival, she hadn't given Sethe the time of day.

"Somebody new in there. A woman. Thought you might know who is she."

"Ain't no new Negroes in this town I don't know about," she said. "What she look like? You sure that wasn't Denver?"

"I know Denver. This girl's narrow."

"You sure?"

"I know what I see."

"Might see anything at all at 124."

"True."

PART III

REMEMBRANCE

NINE

SETTING THE RECORD STRAIGHT

The Polish–Canadian writer Eva Hoffman makes an important distinction between trauma and tragedy. A trauma is an undigested tragedy that emerges from violence against a group which has no means of resistance and is targeted not for its ideology or convictions but for its very identity. A trauma remains internalized; it has no means of outward expression. A trauma gains recognition as a tragedy when an individual or society that has survived the trauma begins to describe, understand, and frame what has happened in its own terms.

In this part, *Remembrance,* the trauma of large-scale violence has begun this process of recognition, moving toward a sense of tragedy, as mourning becomes remembrance and private grief becomes public memory. The writers in this section, "Setting the Record Straight," mark a death or an event that has been hidden under the carpet, correct an official record that has deliberately omitted or glossed over some killing, or recreate an event for those with no direct experience of it. In an interview with the Legacy Project, Chicano American poet Alfred Arteaga spoke of the relationship between poetry and history and the need to use poetry and literature to remember those on the fringes, those that History—the official record created by those in power—overlooked. Arteaga used the example of Victor Jara, one of the leaders of the Chilean Nueva Canción (New Song) Movement of the 1960s and '70s, which used song in political protest. Jara was killed by military police after the Pinochet regime assumed power in Chile. The police cut out his tongue and cut off his hands. But he became a hero for many Chileans. "At the very least we need to recite his name in poetry, so that people remember there was such a man as Victor Jara," said

Arteaga. "Names function as important markers for historical lessons that we cannot forget."

This section brings together the Nigerian Nobel Laureate Wole Soyinka, discussing violence in Kenya; Fang Li-Zhi, the Chinese writer, discussing government amnesia after the Tiananmen Square Massacres of 1989; Urvashi Butalia, addressing the official silence after the India-Pakistan Partition of 1947; American writer Tim O'Brien, filling in gaps of public knowledge of the Vietnam War (1965–1975); Argentine poet Juan Gelman, discussing violence to indigenous populations in the Americas; Khwaja Ahmad Abbas, reflecting on the multifaceted violence in India; and Nobel Laureate Czeslaw Milosz, ruminating on the power and futility of poetry in the face of violence.

ᕐᑲ URVASHI BUTALIA,
Excerpt from *The Other Side of Silence*—INDIA

Urvashi Butalia was born in Ambala, India, in 1952. She received a bachelor of arts and a masters in literature from Delhi University in 1971 and 1973, respectively, and a masters in South Asian studies from the University of London in 1977. She has worked as an editor at the Oxford University Press and ZedBooks. Butalia is now the director and co-founder of Kali for Women, India's first feminist publishing house. Her writing has appeared in several newspapers, including the *Guardian,* the *Statesmen,* the *Times of India,* and several magazines. Ms. Butalia is very active in India's women's movement, she is a consultant for Oxfam India, and she holds the position of reader at the College of Vocational Studies at the University of Delhi. Her main areas of research are the Partition and oral histories. She has also written on gender, communalism, fundamentalism, and media.

In this excerpt from *The Other Side of Silence,* Butalia examines how fifty-eight years after the Partition of India and Pakistan, there is still no institutional memory of the event. Indeed, in the streets of the largest cities, such as Delhi and Bombay, there are no public memorials to those who died in Partition since both parties on either side of the violence—Hindus and Muslims—continue living in close proximity, with periodic outbursts of violence between the groups. Memory of this event is still restricted to the private realm.

In India, there is no institutional memory of Partition: the State has not seen fit to construct any memorials, to mark any particular places—as has been done, say, in the case of Holocaust memorials or memorials for the Vietnam War. There is nothing at the border that marks it as a place where millions of people crossed, no plaque or memorial at any of the sites of the camps, nothing that marks a particular spot as a place where Partition memories are collected. Partition was the dark side of independence: the question then is, how can it be memorialized by the State without the State recognizing its own complicity? It is true that hundreds of thousands of people died as a result of Partition. A half century later, you might well be able to read them as martyrs to the cause of forging a new nation. But alongside there is also the other, inescapable reality that millions of people were killed and in many families where there were deaths there were probably also murders. How do you memorialize such a history? What do you commemorate? For people, for the State, what is at stake in remembering? To what do you have to be true in order to remember? It was not only that people killed those of the "other" religion, but in hundreds of instances they killed people of their own families; it was not only that men of one religion raped women of the other, but in hundreds of instances men of the same religion raped women of the same religion. What can you do to mark such a history as anything other than a history of shame? No matter how much Indian politicians, members of the Congress, tried to see themselves as reluctant players in the game, they could not escape the knowledge that they accepted Partition as the cost of freedom. Such histories are not easily memorialized.

In many countries in the world today there are memorials to moments of conflict and upheaval. Either with State support or otherwise, scholars have painstakingly built up meticulous archives of people's testimonies, of photographs, letters, documents, memoirs, books in which such historical moments are represented. Very little of this exists for Partition. Until recently, little attempt has been made even to collect people's accounts. Visual representations of Partition—despite the rich archive of photographs that must exist in many newspapers and magazines—remain limited, and while a half century of Indian independence has called for all manner of celebratory events, little has been done to mark this important event in the history of India.

But while there is no public memory of Partition, inside homes and families the memory is kept alive through remembrance rituals and stories that mark particular events. When Mangal Singh and his two brothers came away from their village carrying with them the burden of the death of seventeen of their family members, they built a commemorative plaque with all seventeen names on it, and had it placed in the Golden Temple in Amritsar. An annual forty-eight-hour reading of the Sikh scriptures was held to mark the occasion of their deaths, to commemorate their martyrdom. While they were alive, Mangal Singh's brothers attended the ritual with him each year. After their deaths he went to it, usually alone, and sometimes accompanied by Trilok Singh, the sole survivor of the family deaths. When I asked Mangal Singh, many years later, how he had lived with these memories, he pointed around him to the fertile fields of Punjab. He said: "All of us who came from there, Partition refugees, we have put all our forgetting into working this land, into making it prosper."

꩜ WOLE SOYINKA,
   Excerpt from "This Past Must Address Its Present"—NIGERIA

Wole Soyinka was born in western Nigeria in 1934. After graduating from the University of Leeds in 1957, Soyinka worked for several years as a script-reader, actor, and director at the Royal Court Theatre in London. During this time Soyinka wrote the plays *The Swamp Dwellers* and *The Lion and the Jewel,* staged in both London and Ibadan, Nigeria, where Soyinka was born. In 1960, Soyinka returned to Nigeria, where he created an acting company. He also produced a new play, *A Dance of the Forests,* and its opening coincided with Nigeria's official celebration of independence in October. At the beginning of the Nigerian Civil War (1967–1970), Soyinka wrote an article appealing for a cease-fire. He was arrested and accused of conspiring with Biafran rebels. He was held as a political prisoner for nearly two years until 1969. In 1973, Soyinka returned to the University of Leeds and completed his doctorate. Soyinka has taught drama and literature at various universities in Ibadan, Lagos, and Ife and has been a visiting professor at the universities of Cambridge, Sheffield, and Yale. He has published about twenty works of drama, novels, and poetry. Wole Soyinka won the Nobel Prize for Literature in 1986.

In the excerpt from Soyinka's Nobel speech (1986), he discusses a theatrical show in London in 1973 that dramatized two different versions of the events at Hola Camp, Kenya, during the Mau-Mau

Liberation struggle: the official record and what actually took place. From 1952 to 1960, the Kikuyu tribe of central Kenya, which had lost vast areas of their land to white settlers, revolted. Britain responded with a brutal counter-insurgency war in which over one thousand Africans were hanged and tens of thousands of Kikuyu were deported to detention camps, where violence was routine. Britain won the war that became known as Mau-Mau, and they dramatically downplayed the violence that occurred when Kenya was granted independence in 1963. Soyinka later participated as an actor in an experimental night of theater in London examining this event. Even in this guise, he cannot bring himself to act out the violent truth—the fatal beatings the guards dealt the inmates versus how the prisoners were supposed to have died according to official record: from drinking water from a poisoned water supply.

A rather curious scene, unscripted, once took place in the wings of a London theatre at the same time as the scheduled performance was being presented on the actual stage, before an audience. What happened was this: an actor refused to come on stage for his allocated role. Action was suspended. A fellow actor tried to persuade him to emerge, but he stubbornly shook his head. Then a struggle ensued. The second actor had hoped that, by suddenly exposing the reluctant actor to the audience in full glare of the spotlight, he would have no choice but to rejoin the cast. And so he tried to take the delinquent actor by surprise, pulling him suddenly towards the stage. He did not fully succeed, so a brief but untidy struggle began. The unwilling actor was completely taken aback and deeply embarrassed—some of that tussle was quite visible to a part of the audience.

The performance itself, it should be explained, was an improvisation around an incident. This meant that the actors were free, within the convention of the performance—to stop, re-work any part they wished, invite members of the audience on stage, assign roles and change costumes in full view of the audience. They therefore could also dramatize their wish to have that uncooperative actor join them—which they did with gusto. That actor had indeed left the stage before the contentious scene began. He had served notice during rehearsals that he would not participate in it. In the end, he had his way, but the incident proved very troubling to him for weeks afterwards. He found himself compelled to puzzle out this clash in attitudes between himself and his fellow writers and performers.

He experienced, on the one hand, an intense rage that he had been made to appear incapable of confronting a stark reality, made to appear to suffer from interpretative coyness, to seem inhibited by a cruel reality or perhaps to carry his emotional involvement with an event so far as to interfere with his professional will. Of course, he knew that it was none of these things. The truth was far simpler. Unlike his colleagues together with whom he shared, unquestionably, the same political attitude towards the event which was being represented, he found the mode of presentation at war with the ugliness it tried to convey, creating an intense disquiet about his very presence on that stage, in that place, before an audience whom he considered collectively responsible for that dehumanizing actuality.

And now let us remove some of the mystery and make that incident a little more concrete. The scene was the Royal Court Theatre, London, 1958. It was one of those Sunday nights which were given to experimentation, an innovation of that remarkable theatre manager-director, George Devine, whose creative nurturing radicalised British theatre of that period and produced later icons like John Osborne, N. F. Simpson, Edward Bond, Arnold Wesker, Harold Pinter, John Arden, etc., and even forced the then conservative British palate to sample stylistic and ideological pariahs like Samuel Beckett and Bertold Brecht. On this particular occasion, the evening was devoted to a form of "living" theatre, and the main fare was titled ELEVEN MEN DEAD AT HOLA. The actors were not all professional actors; indeed they were mostly writers who jointly created and performed these dramatic pieces. Those with a long political memory may recall what took place at Hola Camp, Kenya, during the Mau-Mau Liberation struggle. The British Colonial power believed that the Mau-Mau could be smashed by herding Kenyans into special camps, trying to separate the hard cases, the mere suspects and the potential recruits—oh, they had it all neatly worked out. One such camp was Hola Camp and the incident involved the death of eleven of the detainees who were simply beaten to death by camp officers and warders. The usual enquiry set up, and it was indeed the Report which provided the main text on which the performance was based.

We need now only to identify the reluctant actor, if you have not guessed that by now—it was none other than this speaker. I recall the occasion as vividly as actors are wont to recollect for ever and ever the frightening moment of a blackout, when the lines are not only forgotten but even the moment in the play. The role which I had been assigned was that of a camp guard, one of the killers. We were equipped with huge night-sticks and, while a narrator read the testimony of one of the guards, our task was to raise the cudgels slowly and, almost ritualistically, bring them down on the necks and shoulders of the prisoners, under orders of the white camp officers. A surreal scene. Even in rehearsals, it was clear that the end product would be a surrealist tableau. The Narrator at a lectern under a spot; a dispassionate reading, deliberately clinical, letting the stark facts reveal the states of mind of torturers and victims. A small ring of white officers, armed. One seizes a cudgel from one of the warders to demonstrate how to beat a human being without leaving visible marks. Then the innermost clump of detainees, their only weapon—non-violence. They had taken their decision to go on strike, refused to go to work unless they obtained better camp conditions. So they squatted on the ground and refused to move, locked their hands behind their knees in silent defiance. Orders were given. The inner ring of guards, the blacks, moved in, lifted the bodies by hooking their hands underneath the armpits of the detainees, carried them like toads in a state of petrification to one side, divided them in groups.

The faces of the victims are impassive; they are resolved to offer no resistance. The beatings begin: one to the left side, then the back, the arms—right, left, front, back. Rhythmically. The cudgels swing in unison. The faces of the white guards glow with professional satisfaction, their arms gesture languidly from time to time, suggesting it is time to shift to the next batch, or beat a little more severely on the neglected side. In terms of images, a fluid, near balletic scene.

Then the contrast, the earlier official version, enacting how the prisoners were supposed to have died. This claimed that the prisoners had collapsed, that they died after drinking from a poisoned water supply. So we staged that also. The prisoners filed to the water wagon, gasping with thirst. After the first two or three had drunk and commenced writhing with pain, these humane guards rushed to stop the others but no, they were already wild with thirst, fought their way past salvation and drank greedily the same source. The groans spread from one to the other, the writhing, the collapse—then agonized deaths. That was the version of the camp governors.

The motif was simple enough, the theatrical format a tried and tested one, faithful to a particular convention. What then was the problem? It was one, I believe, that affects most writers. When is playacting rebuked by reality? When is fictionalizing presumptuous? What happens after playacting? One of the remarkable properties of the particular theatrical convention I have just described is that it gives off a strong odour of perenniality, that feeling of "I have been here before." "I have been a witness to this." "The past enacts its presence." In such an instance, that sense of perenniality can serve both as exorcism, a certificate of release or indeed, especially for the audience, a soporific. We must bear in mind that at the time of presentation, and to the major part of that audience, every death of a freedom fighter was a notch on a gun, the death of a fiend, an animal, a bestial mutant, not the martyrdom of a patriot.

We know also, however, that such efforts can provoke changes, that an actualization of the statistical, journalistic footnote can arouse revulsion in the complacent mind, leading to the beginning of a commitment to change, redress. And on this occasion, angry questions had been raised in the Houses of Parliament. Liberals, humanitarians and reformists had taken up the cause of justice for the victims. Some had even travelled to Kenya to obtain details which exposed the official lie. This profound unease, which paralysed my creative will, therefore reached beyond the audience and, finally, I traced its roots to my own feelings of assaulted humanity, and its clamour for a different form of response. It provoked a feeling of indecency about that presentation, rather like the deformed arm of a leper which is thrust at the healthy to provoke a charitable sentiment. This, I believe, was the cause of that intangible, but totally visceral rejection which thwarted the demands of my calling, rendered it inadequate and mocked the empathy of my colleagues. It was as if the inhuman totality, of which that scene was a mere fragment, was saying to us: Kindly keep your comfortable sentiment to yourselves.

Of course, I utilize that episode only as illustration of the far deeper internalised processes of the creative mind, a process that endangers the writer in two ways: he either freezes up completely, or he abandons the pen for far more direct means of contesting unacceptable reality. And again, Hola Camp provides a convenient means of approaching that aspect of my continent's reality which, for us whom it directly affronts, constitutes the greatest threat to global peace in our actual existence. For there is a gruesome appropriateness in the fact that an African, a black man should stand here today, in the same year that the progressive Prime Minister of this host country was murdered, in the same year as Samora Machel was brought down on the territory of the desperate last-ditch guardians of the theory of racial superiority which has brought so much misery to our common humanity. Whatever the facts are about Olof Palme's death, there can be no question about his life. To the racial oppression of a large sector of humanity, Olof Palme pronounced, and acted, a decisive No!

Perhaps it was those who were outraged by this act of racial "treachery" who were myopic enough to imagine that the death of an individual would arrest the march of his convictions; perhaps it was simply yet another instance of the Terror Epidemic that feeds today on shock, not reason. It does not matter; an authentic conscience of the white tribe has been stilled, and the loss is both yours and mine. Samora Machel, the leader who once placed his country on a war footing against South Africa, went down in as yet mysterious circumstances. True, we are all still haunted by the Nkomati Accord which negated that earlier triumphant moment on the African collective will; nevertheless, his foes across the border have good reason to rejoice over his demise and, in that sense, his death is, ironically, a form of triumph for the black race.

Is that perhaps too stark a paradox? Then let me take you back to Hola Camp. It is cattle which are objects of the stick, or whip. So are horses, goats, donkeys etc. Their definition therefore involves being occasionally beaten to death. If, thirty years after Hola Camp, it is at all thinkable that it takes the ingenuity of the most sophisticated electronic interference to kill an African resistance fighter, the champions of racism are already admitting to themselves what they continue to deny to the world: that they, white supremacist breed, have indeed come a long way in their definition of their chosen enemy since Hola Camp. They have come an incredibly long way since Sharpeville when they shot unarmed, fleeing Africans in the back. They have come very far since 1930 when, at the first organized incident of the burning of passes, the South African blacks decided to turn Dingaan's Day, named for the defeat of the Zulu leader Dingaan, into a symbol of affirmative resistance by publicly destroying their obnoxious passes. In response to those thousands of passes burnt on Cartright Flats, the Durban police descended on the unarmed protesters killing some half dozen and wounding hundreds. They backed it up with scorched earth campaign which dispersed thousands of Africans from their normal environment, victims of imprisonment and deportation. And even that 1930 repression was a quantum leap from that earlier, spontaneous protest against the Native Pass law in 1919, when the police merely rode down the protesters on horseback, whipped and sjamboked them, chased and harried them, like stray goats and wayward cattle, from street corner to shanty lodge. Every act of racial terror, with its vastly increasing sophistication of style and escalation in human loss, is itself an acknowledgement of improved knowledge and respect for the potential of what is feared, an acknowledgement of the sharpening tempo of triumph by the victimized.

For there was this aspect which struck me most forcibly in that attempt to recreate the crime at Hola Camp: in the various testimonies of the white officers, it stuck out, whether overtly stated or simply through their efficient detachment from the ongoing massacre. It was this: at no time did these white overseers actually experience the human "otherness" of their victims. They clearly did not experience the reality of the victims as human beings. Animals perhaps, a noxious form of vegetable life maybe, but certainly not human.

∽ FANG LI-ZHI,
Excerpt from "The Chinese Amnesia"—CHINA

Dr. Fang Li-Zhi was born in Beijing in 1936. Upon receiving a degree in physics from Beijing University (1956), he began working there as a researcher and lecturer. He lectured about theoretical physics and the need for democracy in China. He was subsequently transferred to a teaching post at the University of Science and Technology (USTC) because of his outspoken political views. During the Cultural Revolution (1966–1976), he was sentenced to work in a coal mine. Fang Li-Zhi eventually returned to USTC as a full professor in 1978 and became an elected member of the Chinese Academy of Sciences in 1981 and vice president of the university in 1984. In 1986, he was again dismissed from his job for supporting pro-democracy student movements and began working at the Beijing Astronomical Observatory. Following the Tiananmen Square incident in 1989, he was labeled a counter-revolutionary by the Chinese government and was forced to seek asylum in the U.S. Embassy in Beijing. Fang Li-Zhi eventually left China for England, where he was a guest professor at Cambridge University for a year, then Princeton University, and he settled at the University of Arizona in 1992. In addition to his research and teaching, he has remained an active leader in human rights activities in China. His numerous awards include the Chinese National Award for Science and Technology (1978), the Robert F. Kennedy Human Rights Award (1989), and the International Rescue Committee Freedom Award (1991). He is currently a professor of physics and astronomy at the University of Arizona.

>   In Fang Li-Zhi's essay "The Chinese Amnesia," translated by
> Perry Link, he writes how a large "saturated" market of literature
> in response to the Tiananmen massacres is promising because
> "it signals the failure of the 'Technique of Forgetting History,' . . .
> an important device of rule by the Chinese Communists." Fang
> Li-Zhi lived under the Chinese Communist regime for four
> decades and watched how the true history of the country and
> the Chinese Communist Party was hidden from society.

There seems to be no accurate count of all the books that have appeared about the Tiananmen events of the spring of 1989. But certainly they have been many. A friend at Columbia University recently wrote me that she and one of her Chinese colleagues, both of whom were eyewitnesses at Tiananmen, had originally planned to write a book about it. But publishers told them that so many Tiananmen books were already available that the market had become "saturated." The two reluctantly dropped their plan. It seems that a new Tiananmen book, for now, can have only a modest circulation.

In my view, a large but "saturated" market is itself one of the most important consequences to emerge from the events at Tiananmen. It signals the failure of the "Technique of Forgetting History," which has been an important device of rule by the Chinese Communists. I have lived under the Chinese Communist regime for four decades, and have had many opportunities to observe this technique at work. Its aim is to force the whole of society to forget its history, and especially the true history of the Chinese Communist party itself.

In 1957 Mao Zedong launched an "Anti-Rightist Movement" to purge intellectuals, and 500,000 people were persecuted. Some were killed, some killed themselves, and some were imprisoned or sent for "labor reform." The lightest punishment was to be labeled a "Rightist." This was called "wearing a cap" and meant that one had to bear a powerful stigma. I had just graduated from college that year, and also in that year was purged for the first time.

After the 1957 Anti-Rightist purge, what worried me most was not that I had been punished, or that free thought had been curtailed. At that time, I was still a believer, or semibeliever, in Marxism, and felt that the criticism of free thought, including my own free thought, was not entirely unreasonable. But what worried me, what I just couldn't figure out, was why the Communist party in China would want to use such cruel methods against intellectuals who showed just a tiny bit (and some not even that) of independent thought. I had always assumed that the relationship between the Communist party and intellectuals, including intellectuals who had some independent views, was one of friendship—or at least not one of enmity.

Later I discovered that this worry of mine seemed ridiculous to teachers and friends who were ten or twenty years older than I. They laughed at my ignorance of history. They told me how, as early as 1942, before the Party had wrested control of the whole country, the same cruel methods against intellectuals were already being used at the Communist base in Yan'an. In college I had taken courses in Communist party history, and of course knew that in 1942 at Yan'an there had been a "rectification" movement aimed at "liberalism," "individualism," and other non-Marxist thought. But it was indeed true that I had had no idea that the methods of that "rectification" included "criticism and struggle"—which meant in practice forcing people to commit suicide, and even execution by beheading. People who had experienced the Yan'an "rectification" paled at the very mention of it. But fifteen years later my generation was completely ignorant of it. We deserved the ridicule we received.

After another thirteen years, in 1970, it became our turn to laugh at a younger generation. This was in the middle stage of the Cultural Revolution that took place between 1966 and 1976. In the early stage of the Cultural Revolution, Mao Zedong had used university students, many of whom supported him fanatically, to bring down his political opponents. But in the early 1970s these same students became the targets of attack. In 1970 all the students and teachers in the physics department of the Chinese University of Science and Technology were sent to a coal mine in Huainan, Anhui Province, for "re-education." I was a lecturer in physics at the time. The movement to "criticize and struggle" against the students' "counterrevolutionary words and deeds" reached its most intense point during the summer. Some students "struggled"; others were locked up "for investigation"; a good number could not endure the torment of the vile political atmosphere and fell ill. One of my assignments was to pull a plank-cart (like a horse cart, but pulled by a human being) to transport the ill students. Of the group of forty-some students working in the same mine as I did, two were driven to suicide—one by jumping off a building, the other by lying in front of a train.

Most of these students, as innocent as I had been in 1957, never imagined that the Communist government could be so cruel in its treatment of students who had followed them so loyally. Later one of the students, who became my co-worker in astrophysical research (and who is now in the US), confided to me that he had had no knowledge whatever of the true history of the Anti-Rightist Movement. It was not until he was himself detained and interrogated that he slowly began to appreciate why some of the older people he knew lived in such fear of the phrase Anti-Rightist. The whole story of the main actors and issues had, for this generation, become a huge blank.

∾ TIM O'BRIEN,
    "Speaking of Courage"—UNITED STATES

William Timothy O'Brien was born in Austin, Minnesota, in 1946. When he was in the fourth grade, his family moved to Worthington, Minnesota. At eighteen, O'Brien left Worthington for Macalaster College in St. Paul, Minnesota, where he majored in political science. As the Vietnam War escalated during O'Brien's college years, he took part in some minor anti-war demonstrations. The summer after O'Brien graduated from Macalaster, he received his draft notice, and in February 1969 he was sent to Vietnam. He served a thirteen-month tour of duty, during which he earned a Purple Heart, a Bronze Star (for rescuing a wounded comrade under fire), and the Combat Infantry Badge. After his discharge from the army, O'Brien studied American military history at Harvard, worked as a journalist for the *Washington Post,* and continued writing about his war experiences, which he had begun to do while still in Vietnam. Most recently, he was a visiting professor of creative writing at Texas State University, San Marcos, between 2005 and 2006.

The excerpt from "Speaking of Courage" evolved out of an exchange, as O'Brien writes, with his friend and fellow soldier Norman Bowker, who wrote O'Brien to lament the difficulties of finding meaningful uses for his time after returning from the Vietnam War. In the story Bowker drives around a lake in a small town imagining how he would have told his father about one of his combat moments he most regretted, when he lost hold of a buddy's boot who was sinking into a fecal field. O'Brien writes, "He wished he could've explained some of this.

How he had been braver than he ever thought possible, but how
he had not been so brave as he wanted to be."

The war was over and there was no place in particular to go. Norman
Bowker followed the tar road on its seven-mile loop around the lake, then
he started all over again, driving slowly, feeling safe inside his father's big
Chevy, now and then looking out on the lake to watch the boats and water-
skiers and scenery. It was Sunday and it was summer, and the town seemed
pretty much the same. The lake lay flat and silvery against the sun. Along
the road the houses were all low-slung and split-level and modern, with
big porches and picture windows facing the water. The lawns were spa-
cious. On the lake side of the road, where real estate was most valuable,
the houses were handsome and set deep in, well kept and brightly painted,
with docks jutting out into the lake, and boats moored and covered with
canvas, and neat gardens, and sometimes even gardeners, and stone patios
with barbecue spits and grills, and wooden shingles saying who lived where.
On the other side of the road, to his left, the houses were also handsome,
though less expensive and on a smaller scale and with no docks or boats
or gardeners. The road was a sort of boundary between the affluent and
the almost affluent, and to live on the lake side of the road was one of the
few natural privileges in a town of the prairie—the difference between
watching the sun set over cornfields or over water.

It was a graceful, good-sized lake. Back in high school, at night, he had
driven around and around it with Sally Kramer, wondering if she'd want
to pull into the shelter of Sunset Park, or other times with his friends,
talking about urgent matters, worrying about the existence of God and
theories of causation. Then, there had not been a war. But there had always
been the lake, which was the town's first cause of existence, a place for
immigrant settlers to put down their loads. Before the settlers were the
Sioux, and before the Sioux were the vast open prairies, and before the
prairies there was only ice. The lake bed had been dug out by the south-
ernmost advance of the Wisconsin glacier. Fed by neither streams nor
springs, the lake was often filthy and algaed, relying on fickle prairie rains
for replenishment. Still, it was the only important body of water within
forty miles, a source of pride, nice to look at on bright summer days, and
later that evening it would color up with fireworks. Now, in the late afternoon, it lay calm and smooth, a good audience for silence, a seven-mile
circumference that could be traveled by slow car in twenty-five minutes.
It was not such a good lake for swimming. After high school, he'd caught

an ear infection that had almost kept him out of the war. And the lake had drowned his friend Max Arnold, keeping him out of the war entirely. Max had been the one who liked to talk about the existence of God. "No, I'm not saying *that*," he'd argue against the drone of the engine. "I'm saying that it's possible as an *idea*, even necessary as an idea, a final cause in the whole structure of causation." Now he knew, perhaps. Before the war, they'd driven around the lake as friends, but now Max was just an idea, and most of Norman Bowker's other friends were living in Des Moines or Sioux City, or going to school somewhere, or holding down jobs. The high school girls were mostly gone or married. Sally Kramer, whose pictures he had once carried in his wallet, was one who had married. Her name was now Sally Gustafson and she lived in a pleasant blue house on the less expensive side of the lake road. On his third day home he'd seen her out mowing the lawn, still pretty in a lacy red blouse and white shorts. For a moment he'd almost pulled over, just to talk, but instead he'd pushed down hard on the gas pedal. She looked happy. She had her house and her new husband, and there was really nothing he could say to her.

The town seemed remote somehow. Sally was married and Max was drowned and his father was at home watching baseball on national TV.

Norman Bowker shrugged. "No problem," he murmured.

Clockwise, as if in orbit, he took the Chevy on another seven-mile turn around the lake.

Even in late afternoon the day was hot. He turned on the air conditioner, then the radio, and he leaned back and let the cold air and music blow over him. Along the road, kicking stones in front of them, two young boys were hiking with knapsacks and toy rifles and canteens. He honked going by, but neither boy looked up. Already he had passed them six times, forty-two miles, nearly three hours without stop. He watched the boys recede in his rearview mirror. They turned a soft grayish color, like sand, before finally disappearing.

He tapped down lightly on the accelerator.

Out on the lake a man's motorboat had stalled; the man was bent over the engine with a wrench and a frown. Beyond the stalled boat there were other boats, and a few water-skiers, and the smooth July waters, and an immense flatness everywhere. Two mud hens floated stiffly beside a white dock.

The road curved west, where the sun had now dipped low. He figured it was close to five o'clock—twenty after, he guessed. The war had taught him to tell time without clocks, and even at night, waking from sleep, he could usually place it within ten minutes either way. What he should do, he thought, is stop at Sally's house and impress her with this new time-telling trick of his. They'd talk for a while, catching up on things, and then he'd say, "Well, better hit the road, it's five thirty-four," and she'd glance at her wristwatch and say, "Hey! How'd you *do* that?" and he'd give a casual shrug and tell her it was just one of those things you pick up. He'd keep it light. He wouldn't say anything about anything. "How's it being married?" he might ask, and he'd nod at whatever she answered with, and he would not say a word about how he'd almost won the Silver Star for valor.

He drove past Slater Park and across the causeway and past Sunset Park. The radio announcer sounded tired. The temperature in Des Moines was eighty-one degrees, and the time was five thirty-five, and "All you on the road, drive extra careful now on this fine Fourth of July." If Sally had not been married, or if his father were not such a baseball fan, it would have been a good time to talk.

"The Silver Star?" his father might have said.

"Yes, but I didn't get it. Almost, but not quite."

And his father would have nodded, knowing full well that many brave men do not win medals for their bravery, and that others win medals for doing nothing. As a starting point, maybe, Norman Bowker might then have listed the seven medals he did win: the Combat Infantryman's Badge, the Air Medal, the Army Commendation Medal, the Good Conduct Medal, the Vietnam Campaign Medal, the Bronze Star, and the Purple Heart, thought it wasn't much of a wound and did not leave a scar and did not hurt and never had. He would've explained to his father that none of these decorations was for uncommon valor. They were for common valor. The routine, daily stuff—just humping, just enduring—but that was worth something, wasn't it? Yes, it was. Worth plenty. The ribbons looked good on the uniform in his closet, and if his father were to ask, he would've explained what each signified and how he was proud of all of them, especially the Combat Infantryman's Badge, because it meant he had been there as a real soldier and had done all the things soldiers do, and therefore it wasn't such a big deal that he could not bring himself to be uncommonly brave.

And then he would have talked about the medal he did not win and why he did not win it.

"I almost won the Silver Star," he would have said.

"How's that?"

"Just a story."

"So tell me," his father would have said.

Slowly then, circling the lake, Norman Bowker would have started by describing the Song Tra Bong. "A river," he would've said, "this slow flat muddy river." He would've explained how during the dry season it was exactly like any other river, nothing special, but how in October the monsoons began and the whole situation changed. For a solid week the rains never stopped, not once, and so after a few days the Song Tra Bong overflowed its banks and the land turned into a deep, thick muck for a half mile on either side. Just muck—no other word for it. Like quicksand, almost, except the stink was incredible. "You couldn't even sleep," he'd tell his father. "At night you'd find a high spot, and you'd doze off, but then later you'd wake up because you'd be buried in all that slime. You'd just sink in. You'd feel it ooze up over your body and sort of suck you down. And the whole time there was that constant rain. I mean, it never stopped, not ever."

"Sounds pretty wet," his father would've said, pausing briefly. "So what happened?"

"You really want to hear this?"

"Hey, I'm your *father*."

Norman Bowker smiled. He looked out across the lake and imagined the feel of his tongue against the truth. "Well, this one time, this one night out by the river . . . I wasn't very brave."

"You have seven medals."

"Sure."

"Seven. Count 'em. You weren't a coward either."

"Well, maybe not. But I had the chance and I blew it. The stink, that's what got to me. I couldn't take that goddamn awful *smell*."

"If you don't want to say anymore—"

"I do want to."

"All right then. Slow and sweet, take your time."

The road descended into the outskirts of town, turning northwest past the junior college and the tennis courts, then past Chautauqua Park, where the picnic tables were spread with sheets of colored plastic and where picnickers sat in lawn chairs and listened to the high school band playing Sousa marches under the band shell. The music faded after a few blocks. He drove beneath a canopy of elms, then along a stretch of open shore, then past the municipal docks, where a woman in pedal pushers stood casting for bullheads. There were no other fish in the lake except for perch and a few worthless carp. It was a bad lake for swimming and fishing both.

He drove slowly. No hurry, nowhere to go. Inside the Chevy the air was cool and oily-smelling, and he took pleasure in the steady sounds of the engine and air-conditioning. A tour bus feeling, in a way, except the town he was touring seemed dead. Through the windows, as if in a stop-motion photograph, the place looked as if it had been hit by nerve gas, everything still and lifeless, even the people. The town could not talk, and would not listen. "How'd you like to hear about the war?" he might have asked, but the place could only blink and shrug. It had no memory, and therefore no guilt. The taxes got paid and the votes got counted and the agencies of government did their work briskly and politely. It was a brisk, polite town. It did not know shit about shit, and did not care to know.

Norman Bowker leaned back and considered what he might have said on the subject. He knew shit. It was his specialty. The smell, in particular, but also the numerous varieties of texture and taste. Someday he'd give a lecture on the topic. Put on a suit and tie and stand up in front of the Kiwanis club and tell the fuckers about all the wonderful shit he knew. Pass out samples, maybe.

Smiling at this, he clamped the steering wheel slightly right of center, which produced a smooth clockwise motion against the curve of the road. The Chevy seemed to know its own way.

The sun was lower now. Five fifty-five, he decided—six o'clock, tops.

Along an unused railway spur, four workmen labored in the shadowy red heat, setting up a platform and steel launchers for the evening fireworks. They were dressed alike in khaki trousers, work shirts, visored caps, and brown boots. Their faces were dark and smudgy. "Want to hear about the Silver Star I almost won?" Norman Bowker whispered, but none of the workmen looked up. Later they would blow color into the sky. The lake would sparkle with reds and blues and greens, like a mirror, and the picnickers would make low sounds of appreciation.

"Well, see, it never stopped raining," he would've said. "The muck was everywhere, you couldn't get away from it."

He would have paused a second.

Then he would have told about the night they bivouacked in a field along the Song Tra Bong. A big swampy field beside the river. There was a ville nearby, fifty meters downstream, and right away a dozen old mama-sans ran out and started yelling. A weird scene, he would've said. The mama-sans just stood there in the rain, soaking wet, yapping away about how this field was bad news. Number ten, they said. Evil ground. Not a good spot for good GIs. Finally Lieutenant Jimmy Cross had to get out his pistol and fire off a few rounds just to shoo them away. By then it was almost dark. So they set up a perimeter, ate chow, then crawled under their ponchos and tried to settle in for the night.

But the rain kept getting worse. And by midnight the field turned into soup.

"Just this deep, oozy soup," he would've said. "Like sewage or something. Thick and mushy. You couldn't sleep. You couldn't even lie down, not for long, because you'd start to sink under the soup. Real clammy. You could feel the crud coming up inside your boots and pants."

Here, Norman Bowker would have squinted against the low sun. He would have kept his voice cool, no self-pity.

"But the worst part," he would've said quietly, "was the smell. Partly it was the river—a dead-fish smell—but it was something else, too. Finally somebody figured it out. What this was, it was a shit field. The village toilet. No indoor plumbing, right? So they used the field. I mean, we were camped in a goddamn *shit* field."

He imagined Sally Kramer closing her eyes.

If she were here with him, in the car, she would've said, "Stop it. I don't like that word."

"That's what it *was*."

"All right, but you don't have to use that word."

"Fine. What should we call it?"

She would have glared at him. "I don't know. Just stop it."

Clearly, he thought, this was not a story for Sally Kramer. She was Sally Gustafson now. No doubt Max would've liked it, the irony in particular, but Max had become a pure idea, which was its own irony. It was just too bad. If his father were here, riding shotgun around the lake, the old man might have glanced over for a second, understanding perfectly well that it was not a question of offensive language but of fact. His father would have sighed and folded his arms and waited.

"A shit field," Norman Bowker would have said. "And later that night I could've won the Silver Star for valor."

"Right," his father would've murmured, "I hear you."

The Chevy rolled smoothly across a viaduct and up the narrow tar road. To the right was open lake. To the left, across the road, most of the lawns were scorched dry like October corn. Hopelessly, round and round, a rotating sprinkler scattered lake water on Dr. Mason's vegetable garden. Already the prairie had been baked dry, but in August it would get worse. The lake would turn green with algae, and the golf course would burn up, and the dragonflies would crack open for want of good water.

The big Chevy curved past Centennial Beach and the A&W root beer stand.

It was his eighth revolution around the lake.

He followed the road past the handsome houses with their docks and wooden shingles. Back to Slater Park, across the causeway, around to Sunset Park, as though riding on tracks.

The two little boys were still trudging along on their seven-mile hike.

Out on the lake, the man in the stalled motorboat still fiddled with his engine. The pair of mud hens floated like wooden decoys, and the water-skiers looked tanned and athletic, and the high school band was packing up its instruments, and the woman in pedal pushers patiently rebaited her hook for one last try.

Quaint, he thought.

A hot summer day and it was all very quaint and remote. The four workmen had nearly completed their preparations for the evening fireworks.

Facing the sun again, Norman Bowker decided it was nearly seven o'clock. Not much later the tired radio announcer confirmed it, his voice rocking itself into a deep Sunday snooze. If Max Arnold were here, he would say something about the announcer's fatigue, and relate it to the bright pink in the sky, and the war, and courage. A pity that Max was gone. And a pity about his father, who had had his own war and who now preferred silence.

Still, there was so much to say.

How the rain never stopped. How the cold worked into your bones. Sometimes the bravest thing on earth was to sit through the night and feel the cold in your bones. Courage was not always a matter of yes or no. Sometimes it came in degrees, like the cold; sometimes you were very brave up to a point and then beyond that point you were not so brave. In certain situations you could do incredible things, you could advance toward enemy fire, but in other situations, which were not nearly so bad, you had trouble keeping your eyes open. Sometimes, like that night in the shit field, the difference between courage and cowardice was something small and stupid.

The way the earth bubbled. And the smell.

In a soft voice, without flourishes, he would have told the exact truth.

"Late in the night," he would've said, "we took some mortar fire."

He would've explained how it was still raining, and how the clouds were pasted to the field, and how the mortar rounds seemed to come right out of the clouds. Everything was black and wet. The field just exploded. Rain and slop and shrapnel, nowhere to run, and all they could do was worm down into the slime and cover up and wait. He would've described the crazy things he saw. Weird things. Like how at one point he noticed a guy lying next to him in the sludge, completely buried except for his face, and how after a moment the guy rolled his eyes and winked at him. The noise was fierce. Heavy thunder, and mortar rounds, and people yelling. Some of the men began shooting up flares. Red and green and silver flares, all colors, and the rain came down in Technicolor.

The field was boiling. The shells made deep slushy craters, opening up all those years of waste, centuries worth, and the smell came bubbling out of the earth. Two rounds hit close by. Then a third, even closer, and immediately off to his left, he heard somebody screaming. It was Kiowa— he knew that. The sound was ragged and clotted up, but even so he knew the voice. A strange gargling noise. Rolling sideways, he crawled toward the screaming in the dark. The rain was hard and steady. Along the perimeter there were quick bursts of gunfire. Another round hit nearby, spraying up shit and water, and for a few moments he ducked down beneath the mud. He heard the valves in his heart. He heard the quick, feathering action of the hinges. Extraordinary, he thought. As he came up, a pair of red flares puffed open, a soft fuzzy glow, and in the glow he saw Kiowa's wide-open eyes settling down into the scum. Briefly, all he could do was watch. He heard himself moan. Then he moved again, crabbing forward, but when he got there Kiowa was almost completely under. There was a knee. There was an arm and a gold wristwatch and part of a boot.

He could not describe what happened next, not ever, but he would've tried anyway. He would've spoken carefully so as to make it real for anyone who would listen.

There were bubbles where Kiowa's head should've been.

The left hand was curled open; the fingernails were filthy; the wristwatch gave off a green phosphorescent shine as it slipped beneath the thick waters.

He would've talked about this, and how he grabbed Kiowa by the boot and tried to pull him out. He pulled hard but Kiowa was gone, and then suddenly he felt himself going, too. He could taste it. The shit was in his nose and eyes. There were flares and mortar rounds, and the stink was everywhere—it was inside him, in his lungs—and he could no longer tolerate it. Not here, he thought. Not like this. He released Kiowa's boot and watched it slide away. Slowly, working his way up, he hoisted himself out of the deep mud, and then he lay still and tasted the shit in his mouth and closed his eyes and listened to the rain and explosions and bubbling sounds.

He was alone.

He had lost his weapon but it did not matter. All he wanted was a bath. Nothing else. A hot soapy bath.

Circling the lake, Norman Bowker remembered how his friend Kiowa had disappeared under the waste and water.

"I didn't flip out," he would've said. "I was cool. If things had gone right, if it hadn't been for that smell, I could've won the Silver Star."

A good war story, he thought, but it was not a war for war stories, nor for talk of valor, and nobody in town wanted to know about the terrible stink. They wanted good intentions and good deeds. But the town was not to blame, really. It was a nice little town, very prosperous, with neat houses and all the sanitary conveniences.

Norman Bowker lit a cigarette and cranked open his window. Seven thirty-five, he decided.

The lake had divided into two halves. One half still glistened, the other was caught in shadow. Along the causeway, the two little boys marched on. The man in the stalled motorboat yanked frantically on the cord to his engine, and the two mud hens sought supper at the bottom of the lake, tails bobbing. He passed Sunset Park once again, and more houses, and the junior college and the tennis courts, and the picnickers, who now sat waiting for the evening fireworks. The high school band was gone. The woman in pedal pushers patiently toyed with her line.

Although it was not yet dusk, the A&W was already awash in neon lights.

He maneuvered his father's Chevy into one of the parking slots, let the engine idle, and sat back. The place was doing a good holiday business. Mostly kids, it seemed, and a few farmers in for the day. He did not recognize any of the faces. A slim, hipless young carhop passed by, but when he hit the horn, she did not seem to notice. Her eyes slid sideways. She hooked a tray to the window of a Firebird, laughing lightly, leaning forward to chat with the three boys inside.

He felt invisible in the soft twilight. Straight ahead, over the take-out counter, swarms of mosquitoes electrocuted themselves against an aluminum Pest-Rid machine.

It was a calm, quiet summer evening.

He honked again, this time leaning on the horn. The young carhop turned slowly, as if puzzled, then said something to the boys in the

Firebird and moved reluctantly toward him. Pinned to her shirt was a badge that said EAT MAMA BURGERS.

When she reached his window, she stood straight up so that all he could see was the badge.

"Mama Burger," he said. "Maybe some fries, too."

The girl sighed, leaned down and shook her head. Her eyes were as fluffy and airy-light as cotton candy.

"You blind?" she said.

She put out her hand and tapped an intercom attached to a steel post.

"Punch the button and place your order. All I do is carry the dumb trays."

She stared at him for a moment. Briefly, he thought, a question lingered in her fuzzy eyes, but then she turned and punched the button for him and returned to her friends in the Firebird.

The intercom squeaked and said, "Order."

"Mama Burger and fries," Norman Bowker said.

"Affirmative, copy clear. No rootie-tootie?"

"Rootie-tootie?"

"You know, man—*root* beer."

"A small one."

"Roger-dodger. Repeat: one Mama, one fries, one small beer. Fire for effect. Stand by."

The intercom squeaked and went dead.

"Out," said Norman Bowker.

When the girl brought his tray, he ate quickly, without looking up. The tired radio announcer in Des Moines gave the time, almost eight-thirty. Dark was pressing in tight now, and he wished there were somewhere to go. In the morning he'd check out some job possibilities. Shoot a few buckets down at the Y, maybe wash the Chevy.

He finished his root beer and pushed the intercom button.

"Order," said the tinny voice.

"All done."

"That's *it*?"

"I guess so."

"Hey, loosen up," the voice said. "What you really need, friend?"

Norman Bowker smiled.

"Well," he said, "how'd you like to hear about—"

He stopped and shook his head.

"Hear *what*, man?"

"Nothing."

"Well, hey," the intercom said, "I'm sure as fuck not *going* anywhere. Screwed to a post, for God's sake. Go ahead, try me."

"Nothing."

"You sure?"

"Positive. All done."

The intercom made a light sound of disappointment. "Your choice, I guess. Over an' out."

"Out," Norman Bowker said.

On his tenth turn around the lake he passed the hiking boys for the last time. The man in the stalled motorboat was gone; the mud hens were gone. Beyond the lake, over Sally Gustafson's house, the sun had left a smudge of purple on the horizon. The band shell was deserted, and the woman in pedal pushers quietly reeled in her line, and Dr. Mason's sprinkler went round and round.

On his eleventh revolution he switched off the air-conditioning, opened up his window, and rested his elbow comfortably on the sill, driving with one hand.

There was nothing to say.

He could not talk about it and never would. The evening was smooth and warm.

If it had been possible, which it wasn't, he would have explained how his friend Kiowa slipped away that night beneath the dark swampy field. He was folded in with the war; he was part of the waste.

Turning on his headlights, driving slowly, Norman Bowker remembered how he had taken hold of Kiowa's boot and pulled hard, but how the smell was simply too much, and how he'd backed off and in that way had lost the Silver Star.

He wished he could've explained some of this. How he had been braver than he ever thought possible, but how he had not been so brave as he wanted to be. The distinction was important. Max Arnold, who loved fine lines, would've appreciated it. And his father, who already knew, would've nodded.

"The truth," Norman Bowker would've said, "is I let the guy go."

"Maybe he was already gone."

"He wasn't."

"But maybe."

"No, I could feel it. He wasn't. Some things you can feel."

His father would have been quiet for a while, watching the headlights against the narrow tar road.

"Well, anyway," the old man would've said, "there's still the seven medals."

"I suppose."

"Seven honeys."

"Right."

On his twelfth revolution, the sky went crazy with color.

He pulled into Sunset Park and stopped in the shadow of a picnic shelter. After a time he got out, walked down to the beach, and waded into the lake without undressing. The water felt warm against his skin. He put his head under. He opened his lips, very slightly, for the taste, then he stood up and folded his arms and watched the fireworks. For a small town, he decided, it was a pretty good show.

Notes:

"Speaking of Courage" was written in 1975 at the suggestion of Norman Bowker, who three years later hanged himself in the locker room of YMCA in his hometown in central Iowa.

In the spring of 1975, near the time of Saigon's final collapse, I received a long, disjointed letter in which Bowker described the problem of finding a meaningful use for his life after the war. He had worked briefly as an automotive parts salesman, a janitor, a car wash attendant, and a short-order cook at the local A&W fast-food franchise. None of these jobs, he said, had lasted more than ten weeks. He lived with his parents, who supported him, and who treated him with kindness and obvious love. At one point he had enrolled in the junior college in his hometown, but the course work, he said, seemed too abstract, too distant, with nothing real or tangible at stake, certainly not the stakes of a war. He dropped out after eight months. He spent his mornings in bed. In the afternoons he played pickup basketball at the Y, and then at night he drove around town in his father's car, mostly alone, or with a six-pack of beer, cruising.

"The thing is," he wrote, "there's no place to go. Not just in this lousy little town. In general. My life, I mean. It's almost like I got killed over in Nam . . . Hard to describe. That night when Kiowa got wasted, I sort of sank down into the sewage with him . . . Feels like I'm still in deep shit."

The letter covered seventeen handwritten pages, its tone jumping from self-pity to anger to irony to guilt to a kind of feigned indifference. He didn't know what to feel. In the middle of the letter, for example, he re-proached himself for complaining too much:

> God, this is starting sound like some jerkoff vet crying in his beer. Sorry
> about that. I'm no basket case—not even any bad dreams. And I don't feel
> like anybody mistreats me or anything, except sometimes people act *too*
> nice, too polite, like they're afraid they might ask the wrong question . . .
> But I shouldn't bitch. One thing I hate—really hate—is all those whiner-
> vets. Guys sniveling about how they didn't get any parades. Such absolute
> crap. I mean, who in his right mind wants a *parade?* Or getting his back
> clapped by a bunch of patriotic idiots who don't know jack about what it
> feels like to kill people or get shot at or sleep in the rain or watch your
> buddy go down underneath the mud? Who *needs* it?
>
> Anyhow, I'm basically A-Okay. Home free!! So why not come down for
> a visit sometime and we'll chase pussy and tell each other old war lies? A
> good long bull session, you know?

I felt it coming, and near the end of the letter it came. He explained that he had read my first book, *If I Die in a Combat Zone,* which he liked except for the "bleeding-heart political parts." For half a page he talked about how much the book had meant to him, how it brought back all kinds of memories, the villes and paddies and rivers, and how he recognized most of the characters, including himself, even though almost all of the names were changed.

Then Bowker came straight out with it:

> What you should do, Tim, is write a story about a guy who feels like he
> got zapped over in that shithole. A guy who can't get his act together and
> just drives around town all day and can't think of any damn place to go
> and doesn't know how to get there anyway. This guy wants to talk about
> it, but he *can't* . . . If you want, you can use the stuff in this letter. (But not
> my real name, okay?) I'd write it myself except I can't ever find any words,
> if you know what I mean, and I can't figure out exactly what to *say.* Some-
> thing about the field that night. The way Kiowa just disappeared into the
> crud. You were there—you can tell it.

Norman Bowker's letter hit me hard. For years I'd felt a certain smug-ness about how easily I had made the shift from war to peace. A nice smooth glide—no flashbacks or midnight sweats. The war was over, after all. And the thing to do was go on. So I took pride in sliding gracefully from Vietnam to graduate school, from Chu Lai to Harvard, from one world to another. In ordinary conversation I never spoke much about the war, certainly not in detail, and yet ever since my return I had been talking about it virtually nonstop through my writing. Telling stories seemed a natural, inevitable process, like clearing the throat. Partly catharsis, partly communication, it was a way of grabbing people by the shirt and explaining exactly what had happened to me, how I'd allowed myself to get dragged into a wrong war, all the mistakes I'd made, all the terrible things I had seen and done.

I did not look on my work as therapy, and still don't. Yet when I received Norman Bowker's letter, it occurred to me that the act of writing had led me through a swirl of memories that might otherwise have ended in paralysis or worse. By telling stories, you objectify your own experience. You separate it from yourself. You pin down certain truths. You make up others. You start sometimes with an incident that truly happened, like the night in the shit field, and you carry it forward by inventing incidents that did not in fact occur but that nonetheless help to clarify and explain.

In any case, Norman Bowker's letter had an effect. It haunted me for more than a month, not the words so much as its desperation, and I resolved finally to take him up on his story suggestion. At the time I was at work on a new novel, *Going After Cacciato,* and one morning I sat down and began a new chapter titled "Speaking of Courage." The emotional core came directly from Bowker's letter: the simple need to talk. To provide a dramatic frame, I collapsed events into a single time and place, a car circling a lake on a quiet afternoon in midsummer, using the lake as a nucleus around which the story would orbit. As he'd requested, I did not use Norman Bowker's name, instead substituting the name of my novel's main character, Paul Berlin. For the scenery I borrowed heavily from my own hometown. Wholesale thievery, in fact. I lifted up Worthington, Minnesota—the lake, the road, the causeway, the woman in pedal pushers, the junior college, the handsome houses and docks and boats and public parks—and carried it all a few hundred miles south and transplanted it onto the Iowa prairie.

The writing went quickly and easily. I drafted the piece in a week or two, fiddled with it for another week, then published it as a separate short story.

Almost immediately, thought, there was a sense of failure. The details of Norman Bowker's story were missing. In this original version, which

I still conceived as part of the novel, I had been forced to omit the shit field and the rain and the death of Kiowa, replacing this material with events that better fit the book's narrative. As a consequence I'd lost the natural counterpoint between the lake and the field. A metaphoric unity was broken. What the piece needed, and did not have, was the terrible killing power of the shit field.

As the novel developed over the next year, and as my own ideas clarified, it became apparent that the chapter had no proper home in the larger narrative. *Going After Cacciato* was a war story; "Speaking of Courage" was a postwar story. Two different time periods, two different sets of issues. There was no choice but to remove the chapter entirely. The mistake, in part, had been in trying to wedge the piece into a novel. Beyond that, though, something about the story had frightened me—I was afraid to speak directly, afraid to remember—and in the end the piece had been ruined by a failure to tell the full and exact truth about our night in the shit field.

Over the next several months, as it often happens, I managed to erase the story's flaws from my memory, taking pride in a shadowy, idealized recollection of its virtues. When the piece appeared in an anthology of short fiction, I sent a copy off to Norman Bowker with the thought that it might please him. His reaction was short and somewhat bitter.

"It's not terrible," he wrote me, "but you left out Vietnam. Where's Kiowa? Where's the shit?"

Eight months later he hanged himself.

In August of 1978 his mother sent me a brief note explaining what had happened. He'd been playing pickup basketball at the Y; after two hours he went off for a drink of water; he used a jump rope; his friends found him hanging from a water pipe. There was no suicide note, no message of any kind. "Norman was a quiet boy," his mother wrote, "and I don't suppose he wanted to bother anybody."

Now, a decade after his death, I'm hoping that "Speaking of Courage" makes good on Norman Bowker's silence. And I hope it's a better story. Although the old structure remains, the piece has been substantially revised, in some places by severe cutting, in other places by the addition of new material. Norman is back in the story, where he belongs, and I don't think he would mind that his real name appears. The central incident—our long night in the shit field along the Song Tra Bong—has been restored to the piece. It was hard stuff to write. Kiowa, after all, had been a close friend, and for years I've avoided thinking about his death and my own complicity in it. Even here it's not easy. In the interest of truth, however, I want to make it clear that Norman Bowker was in no way responsible for what happened to Kiowa. Norman did not experience a failure of nerve that night. He did not freeze up or lose the Silver Star for valor. That part of the story is my own.

∾ JUAN GELMAN,
   "Under Foreign Rain (Footnotes to Defeat): XXV"—ARGENTINA

Juan Gelman was born in 1930 in Buenos Aires, the son of Russian Jewish immigrants. Gelman worked as a journalist and was a political activist until 1975, when he was forced to leave Argentina. One year later, his son and his daughter-in-law became part of the *desaparecidos,* the estimated thirty thousand mostly young people who vanished without a trace under the military regime. Gelman lived in Europe until 1988 when he returned to Argentina and began working as a columnist for the Buenos Aires daily newspaper *Página 12.* Upon his return, he began investigating the fate of his family, confirming the death of his son and his son's wife and the birth of a granddaughter after making his appeal public through a published letter. He has published more than twenty books of poetry since 1956 and is widely considered to be Argentina's leading contemporary poet. His poems, which have been translated into fourteen languages, contain themes touching on his Jewish heritage, family, Argentina, exile, and the tango. Juan Gelman currently lives in Mexico, where he continues to contribute to the newspaper *Página 12.*

Gelman's poem "Under Foreign Rain (Footnotes to Defeat): XXV" (1980), translated by Joan Lindgren, addresses the theme of the plundering of the Americas—of land, resources, and people— for the benefit of Europe. He addresses the fate of indigenous residents who have been largely ignored. "You don't smell old, Europe," writes Gelman, "You smell of double humanity, the one that murders and the one murdered."

Europe was the cradle of capitalism, and the child in the cradle was fed
on gold and silver from Peru, Mexico, and Bolivia. Millions of
Americans had to die to fatten the kid, who grew strong, developed

languages, arts, sciences, methods of loving and living, further
dimensions of being human.

Who says culture has no odor?

I stroll through Rome, Paris—what beautiful cities. On the via
Corso on the Bulmish suddenly I catch a whiff of Tainos devoured by
Andalusian dogs, of Ona ears mutilated, of Aztecs destroying themselves
in Lake Tenochtitlán, of the diminuitive Incas broken in Potosí, of
Querandí, Araucan, Congo, Carabalí, enslaved, massacred.

You don't smell old, Europe.

You smell of double humanity, the one that murders and the one
murdered.

Centuries have passed, and the beauty of the conquered still rots
upon your brow.

ROME / 9–14–80

ℭ KHWAJA AHMAD ABBAS,
Excerpt from "Who Killed India"—INDIA

Khwaja Ahmad Abbas was born in 1914 in Panipat, Haryana, and
graduated from Aligarh Muslim University in 1933. He began his
career as a journalist, writing for a newspaper based in New Delhi
called the *Aligargh Opinion,* while studying for a law degree which
he received in 1935. He worked as a film critic for the *Bombay
Chronicle* from 1935 to 1947. Between 1941 and 1986, he wrote the
longest-running political column in India's history, known as
"The Last Page." Abbas was also a prolific novelist, director, and
screenwriter. In 1951, he founded his own production company,
which became known for producing films with socially relevant
themes. Abbas directed, wrote, or produced over three dozen films.

In the essay "Who Killed India," Abbas examines how Indian
society has been destroyed from within. While British imperialists
and their *divide and rule* policy set the violence in motion, Abbas
writes how religious violence between Hindus and Muslims and
violence between different political factions has frayed the fabric
of civil society and constitutes a type of mass suicide.

Was it the work of an insane individual, a stab in the back as in a communal riot; or the diabolical conspiracy of a gang? Was it a case of slow

poisoning? Or, as it might be, was it a more diabolical, a more cunning master plan, in which the victim himself was hypnotically induced to commit suicide . . .

India was killed by Britain. The first blow was struck when the British (after ignoring and neglecting them for half a century after the events of 1857) instigated and encouraged the Muslims to demand separate electorates and then conceded it. That was the first step towards Pakistan, however copious tears Lord Mountbatten may now shed over the mortal remains of United India.

India was killed by the British and their "Divide and Rule" policy. But not by the British alone. India was killed by fanatical Muslim Leaguers who played upon the community's apprehensions and fears to produce in them a peculiar psychosis which was a dangerous combination of inferiority complex, aggressive jingoism, religious fanaticism, and fascistic Herrenvolk legends.

India was killed by the fanatical Hindus, the Hindu fascists and Hindu imperialists, the dreamers of a Hindu empire, the crusaders of Hindu Sangathan, who provided the ideological fuel for the fire of Hindu communalism and fanaticism.

India was killed by the Hindu communalists, the believers and supporters of Hindu exclusiveness . . . who yet masqueraded as Nationalists and Congressmen, who prevented the National congressmen and the National Movement from becoming a fully representative, completely non-communal front of all Indian patriots.

India was killed by the Communist Part of India which (during the days of its "People's War" and "pro-Pakistan" policies) provided the Muslim separatists with an ideological basis for the irrational and anti-national demand for Pakistan. (Phrases like "homeland," "nationalities," "self-determination" etc. were all ammunition supplied by the Communists to the legions of Pakistan.)

India was killed, and stabbed in the heart, by every Hindu who killed a Muslim, by every Muslim who killed a Hindu, by every Hindu or Muslim who committed or abetted, or connived at, arson, rape and murder during the recent (and earlier) communal riots.

That an imperialist power planned the dismemberment of our country in the very hour of our freedom is not surprising. The wonder, and the tragedy is that India should have been killed by the children of India . . .

ᚖ Czeslaw Milosz,
"Dedication"—LITHUANIA, UNITED STATES, AND POLAND

Czeslaw Milosz was born June 30, 1911, in Seteiniai, Lithuania. Milosz received a master of law degree from the University of Vilnius in 1934 and then spent a year in Paris. There he formed a close relationship with his distant uncle, Oscar Milosz, who was a diplomat and a noteworthy French poet. Milosz made his literary début in 1930, published two volumes of poetry in the 1930s, and worked for the Polish Radio. During World War II, Milosz was active as a writer in the Resistance movement and witnessed the Holocaust firsthand. In 1951 he settled in France, where he wrote several books in prose. In 1960, the University of California invited Milosz to Berkeley, where he was a professor of Slavic languages and literatures from 1960 to 1978. In 1970 he became a U.S. citizen, in 1974 he received an award for poetry translations from the Polish P.E.N. Club in Warsaw, and in 1976 he was made a Guggenheim fellow for poetry. In 1980 Milosz received the Nobel Prize in Literature, and in 1989 he accepted the National Medal of Arts. Czeslaw Milosz died in his home in Cracow on August 14, 2004.

In his poem "Dedication," Milosz addresses those beyond the grave, whom he could not save. He wrestles with the genre of poetry itself that cannot save physical lives but which has a "salutary aim." He ends by offering the book of poems to the dead, "So that you should visit us no more," yet his work of writing also preserves a record of them for eternity.

You whom I could not save
Listen to me.
Try to understand this simple speech
as I would be ashamed of another.
I swear, there is in me no wizardry of words.
I speak to you with silence like a cloud or a tree.

What strengthened me, for you was lethal.
You mixed up farewell to an epoch with the beginning of a new one,
Inspiration of hatred with lyrical beauty,
Blind force with accomplished shape.

Here is the valley of shallow Polish rivers. And an immense bridge
Going into white fog. Here is a broken city,
And the wind throws the screams of gulls on your grave
When I am talking with you.

What is poetry which does not save
Nations or people?
A connivance with official lies,
A song of drunkards whose throats will be cut in a moment,
Readings for sophomore girls.
That I wanted good poetry without knowing it,
That I discovered, late, its salutary aim,
In this and only this I find salvation.

They used to pour millet on graves or poppy seeds
To feed the dead who would come disguised as birds.
I put this book here for you, who once lived
So that you should visit us no more.

TEN

ROSE-COLORED MEMORY

In 1994, photographer Henning Langenheim returned to a Holocaust massacre site along the Baltic Coast of northern Europe. The empty spaces in his black-and-white photographs seem innocent of all evil usage, until the photograph's caption recalls the actual history of the place. This photo—and others made in different historical sites of violence—are not documents of the events as they occurred. Rather, they are contemporary documents of the memory of these historical traumas that ask the spectator decades later to repopulate the empty images with the people who were killed there.

Does memory have color? In the visual realm, for instance, black-and-white photographs of sites where people were killed are the first documentary responses. Even years later, photographers rely on the fact that black-and-white images seem automatically to put a historical frame around the photos.

Yet as even more time passes, artists begin to revisit historical places in color, first perhaps through sepia, then in brighter tones. For instance, the Czech photographer Petra Ruzickova has a series of photos of the Terezin concentration camp that incorporate vibrant shades of blue, green, and red. The color brings our reactions into real time, emphasizing our distance from the Holocaust and the continuing vitality of our own lives, especially compared to the historical lives cut so gruesomely short. If, with the passage of time, it is possible to again find physical beauty in places where killing was done, has our resolve to remember the crime been reduced? Or, instead, is this an acknowledgment that we are no longer living in a time of mayhem, and our more normal appreciation of landscape may mix with our commitment to remembrance. Such photographs raise questions and unsettle us because the conventions of historical documentation have been removed, replaced by the conventions of normality, which include both attraction and rejection.

Moving from the visual realm to the literary realm, the writers in this chapter describe how even the most violent events can become rose-colored in memory, so that there is also an element of attraction and rejection as well. Italo Calvino reflects on memories of battle in Italy in the closing days of World War II and how these have begun to change color; Leslie Marmon Silko touches on the memories of indigenous populations fighting for the American forces in World War II; Ayi Kwei Armah remembers violence in Ghana in the twentieth century; Edmond Jabès recalls his experience as an officer in the British army in Palestine in World War II; and Joyce Carol Oates charts the changing memories of New Yorkers of 9/11 in the days and months that followed.

ᕰ ITALO CALVINO,
"Memories of a Battle"—ITALY

Journalist, short-story writer, and novelist Italo Calvino was born in 1923 in Santiago de las Vegas, Cuba. He left Cuba for Italy in his youth and grew up in San Remo, Italy. Calvino studied at the University of Turin (1941–47) and Royal University in Florence (1943). Early on in World War II, he was drafted into the Young Fascists, a boy scout–like organization that Mussolini created to form future fascists. But Calvino left and sought refuge in the Alps, where he joined the Communist Resistance. After the war, Calvino graduated from the University of Turin and worked as a journalist, in a publishing house, and as an editor at different points in his career. In 1952 he traveled to the Soviet Union and in 1959–60 to the United States. In 1964 he married Ester Judith Singer, and in 1967 he moved to Paris, and then in 1979 to Rome. Italo Calvino died of cerebral hemorrhage in Siena, in September 1985.

In "Memories of a Battle," (1993) translated by Tim Parks, Calvino reflects on one particular battle in the Alps when he was part of the Partisans in the Italian Resistance, in the Garibaldi brigade. Calvino ponders why memory retains certain things and not others. He forgets details he would like to recall and can't erase images which haunt him: "I continue to gaze into the valley bottom of the memory. And my fear now is that as soon as a memory forms it immediately takes on the wrong light, mannered, sentimental as war and youth always are, becomes a piece of narrative written in the style of the time, which can't tell us how things really are but only how we thought we saw them, thought we said them."

It's not true that I've forgotten everything, the memories are still there, hidden in the grey tangle of the brain, in the damp bed of sand deposited on the bottom of the stream of thought: assuming it's true, that is, that every grain of this mental sand preserves a moment of our lives fixed in such a way that it can never be erased yet buried under billions and billions of other grains. I am trying to bring a day, a morning, back to the surface, moments between dark and light at the dawning of that day. It's years since I stirred up these memories, lurking like eels in the pools of the mind. I was sure that whenever I wanted I had only to poke about in the shallows to see them rise to the surface with a flick of their tails. At most I would have to lift one or two of the big stones that form a barrier between present and past to uncover the little caves behind the forehead where things forgotten lie low. But why that morning? Why not another? Here and there bumps protrude from the sandy bottom, suggesting that a sort of vortex used to whirl around them, and when memories awake after a long sleep it is from the centre of one of these vortices that time's spiral unravels.

Yet almost thirty years later, now that I've finally decided to haul in memory's nets and see what's inside, I find myself groping in the dark, as if that morning didn't want to begin again, as if I were able to unglue the sleep from my eyes, and perhaps it is precisely this imprecision that guarantees that the memory is precise, what now seems half erased was so then too, that morning they woke us at four, and immediately the Olmo detachment was on the march down through the woods in the dark, almost running through the shortcuts where you can't see where you're putting your feet, not paths at all perhaps, just steep gorges, beds of dry streams overrun by brambles and ferns, smooth pebbles your hobnail shoes slither on, and we're still at the beginning of the approach march, just as it's an approach march I'm trying to make now on the trail of memories that crumble under pressure, not visual memories because it was a moonless starless night, memories of my body slithering in the dark, with half a plate of chestnuts in my stomach that haven't warmed me up and are just weighing me down like an acid handful of gravel that squeezes and jolts, with the weight of the machine-gun ammunition box banging on my back and every time my foot slips there's the danger the thing will topple me facedown or pull me over backwards my back against the stones. Maybe all that's left in my memory of the whole descent are these falls, which could equally be those of some other night or dawn. Morning marches before action are all the same, I'm one of the group carrying ammunition for my squad, always humping that hard square box with the straps that dig into my shoulders, but in this memory my curses and those of the men behind me are kept down to a crackle of whispers, as if our moving in silence were the key factor this time even more so than other times, because at the same moment on the same night lines of armed men like our own are coming down along all the ridges in the wood, all the detachments of the Figaro battalion billeted in hidden farmhouses have set out on time, all the battalions of Gino's brigade are pouring down from the valleys, and along the mule tracks they run in to other lines on the march since the evening before from mountains far away, since the moment they got that order from Vitto, who's commanding the division: all partisans of the area to gather at dawn around Baiardo.

The air is slow to brighten. Yet it should be March by now, spring should be beginning, the last (can it be true?) of the war or the last (for how many more of us?) of our lives. The uncertainty of the memory is surely the uncertainty of the light and the season and what was to follow. The important thing is that this descent into an uncertain memory swarming with shadows should lead me to set foot on something solid, as when I felt the crushed stones beneath my feet, and recognized that stretch of the big road to Baiardo that goes past the bottom of the cemetery, and at the turn, even though I can't see it, I know that opposite us is the village rising to a point at the top of the hill. Now that I have wrenched a specific place from the shadows of my forgetfulness, a place I've known since childhood, immediately the darkness begins to grow transparent letting shapes and colours filter through: all of a sudden we're not alone anymore, our column is marching alongside another column stopped along the road, or rather we're walking between two lines like our own shuffling their feet, their rifles propped on the ground. "Who are you with?" someone asks us. "With Figaro. And you?" "With Pelletta."

"We're with Gori," names of commanders with bases in other valleys, other mountains.

And passing by we watch each other, because it's always strange when one unit meets another, when you see how many different things we are all wearing, clothes of every colour, odd bits of uniforms, but how recognizable and alike we are too, the same tears where our clothes tend to come apart (where the rifle strap rests on the shoulder, where the brass magazines wear out the pockets, where branches and bushes have torn our trousers to shreds), alike and unlike in the weapons we have, a sad collection of battered old "ninety-ones" and German hand grenades with their wooden handles tucked in our belts, in the midst of which the eye settles on examples of light, faster, more modern weapons that the war has scattered across the fields of Europe and that every battle redistributes on one side and the other. Some of us are bearded, some callow, longhaired or shorn, with the spots you get from eating nothing but chestnuts and potatoes for months on end. We size each other up coming out of the dark as though surprised to find that so many of us have survived the terrible winter, to see so many of us together as happens only on days of great victory or great defeat. And unanswered in our eyes as we look at each other are our questions about the day that is dawning, a day being planned in a back-and-forth of commanders with binoculars round their necks hurriedly sorting out the squads along the dusty road, deciding positions and assignments for the attack on Baiardo.

Here I should open a parenthesis to tell you that this village of the Maritime Pre-Alps, clinging to the rocks like an old castle, was held at the time by the Republican *bersaglieri,* students for the most part, a well-armed, well-equipped, well-trained body of men controlling the whole olive-green valley right down as far as Ceriana, and that for months a ferocious unrelenting war had been going on between us partisans of the "Garibaldi" brigades and these *bersaglieri* of Graziani's army. I would have to add all kinds of other things to explain what the war was like there in those months, but rather than awakening memories this would bury them again under the sedimentary crust of hindsight, the kind of reflections that put things in order and explain everything according to history, whereas what I want to bring to light now is the moment when we struck off along a path that winds downwards around the village, in single file through a sparse reddish wood, and got the order: "Take your shoes off your feet and tie them round your necks, heaven help us if they hear footsteps, heaven help us if the dogs start barking in the village; pass the word along and forward in silence."

Good, this is exactly the moment I wanted to start my story from. For years I've been telling myself, not now, later, when I want to remember, all I'll have to do is conjure up the relief I felt on untying my stiff boots, the feeling of the ground under the soles of my feet, the twinges from chestnut husks and wild thistles, the circumspect way feet have of settling on the ground when at every step prickles are sinking through wool into the skin, see myself stopping to pull the husks from the felt-padded bottoms of my socks which immediately pick up others, I thought all I'd have to do was remember this moment and all the rest would follow on naturally like a ball of wool unwinding, like the unravelling of those socks with their holes at the big toe and the heel, over other layers of socks likewise with holes and inside all the prickles the grass spikes the twigs, the vegetable dusting of undergrowth caught in wool.

If I concentrate on this magnified detail I do it so as not to recognize how many holes there are in my memory. What had been night's shadows earlier on are bright blurred stains now. Every sign is interpreted, like the crowing of the cocks in Baiardo breaking the dawn silence all together, which could be a sign that all is proceeding normally or that the village is already in a state of alert. Our squad has taken up position with the machine gun in the olive groves at the bottom of the hill. We can't see the village. There is a pole carrying the telephone wire that links Baiardo to (I think) Ceriana. I remember the objectives assigned to us very well: to cut the telephone wires as soon as we hear the attack begin, to cut off the Fascists if they try to escape down the hill through the fields, to be ready to climb up to the villages to reinforce the attack as soon as we get the order.

What I would like to know is why the broken net of memory holds some things and not others: I remember one by one these orders that were never carried out, but now I would like to remember the faces and names of my companions in the squad, the voices, the dialect phrases, and how we managed to cut the wires without pincers. I even remember the battle plan, how it was supposed to unfold in various phases, and how it didn't unfold. But to follow the thread of my story I'll have to remember it all through my ears: the special silence of a country morning full of men moving in silence, rumblings, shots filling the sky. A silence that was expected but lasted longer than expected. The shots, every kind of explosion and machine-gun fire, a muddle of sound we can't make sense of because it doesn't take shape in space but only in time, a time of waiting for us stationed at the valley bottom where we can't see a damn thing.

I continue to gaze into the valley bottom of the memory. And my fear now is that as soon as a memory forms it immediately takes on the wrong light, mannered, sentimental as war and youth always are, becomes a piece of narrative written in the style of the time, which can't tell us how things really were but only how we thought we saw them, thought we said them. I don't know if I am destroying the past or saving it, the past hidden in that besieged village.

The village is up there, near and unapproachable, a village where there wasn't very much worth capturing in the end, but which for us nomads out in the woods for months had become the focus of notions of home, streets, people. A girl evacuee who the previous August (when we held Baiardo) had looked at me in amazement on recognizing me among the partisans. You see, memories of war and youth couldn't help but include at least one woman's glance, in the middle of the village besieged in its circle of death. Now the circle is just isolated shots. An occasional burst of fire still. Silence. We are on the alert, ready to cut off some lost enemy. But nobody comes. We wait. However things have gone, surely now one of our people will come to get us. We've been here a long time on our own, cut off from everything.

Again it's sound, not sight, that holds the reins of this memory: from the village comes a din of voices, singing now. Our boys celebrating victory! We head towards the village, almost at a run. We're right by the first houses already. What are they singing? It's not "Fischia il vento . . ." We stop. It's "Giovinezza" they're singing! The Fascists have won. Immediately we leap down through the olive terraces, trying to put as much distance as we can between us and the village. Heaven knows how long our lot have been retreating already. Heaven knows how we are going to catch up with them. We've been left stranded in enemy territory.

My memories of the battle end here. Now all I can do is cast about for my memories of the flight over a carpet of hazelnuts along the dry streambed we try to climb up to avoid the roads, go back and make my way once again through the night and the woods (a human shadow ran across our path, seized by panic it seemed, we never found out who), sift through the cold ashes of the deserted camp trying to find traces of the Olmo squad.

Or I could bring into focus everything I later found out about the battle: how our men ran into the village shooting and were pushed back

leaving three dead. And immediately I try to describe the battle in a way
I didn't see it, the memories that have so far lingered behind vague shadows suddenly pick up speed and direction: I see the column opening up
the way to the piazza while the others who went around the village are
climbing the steps of the narrow streets. I could give them all their names,
their places their gestures. Memories of what I didn't see in the battle take
on a more precise order and sense than what I really experienced, because
free from the confused sensations that clutter my memory of the whole.
Of course even here there are blanks I can't fill. I concentrate on the faces
I know best: Gino is in the piazza: a thickset boy commanding our brigade,
he looks into the square and crouches shooting from a balustrade, black
tufts of beard round his tense jaw, small eyes shining under the peak of
his Mexican hat. I know that Gino had taken to wearing a different hat
at the time but I can't remember now if it was a bearskin or a wool cap,
or a mountain cap.

I keep seeing him with that big straw hat that belongs to a memory of
the previous summer.

But there's no time left for imagining details because the boys have to
get out fast if they're not to be trapped inside the village. Tritolo jumps
forward from a low wall and throws a grenade as if he were playing a joke.
Cardil is near him covering the others as they retreat, waving to them to
say the way is clear now. Some of the *bersaglieri* have already recognized
the Milan squad, ex-comrades of theirs who came over to us a year ago.
And here I'm getting close to the point that's been on my mind right from
the beginning, the moment when Cardil dies.

This imagined memory is actually a real memory from that time
because I am recovering things I first imagined back then. It wasn't the
moment of Cardu's death I saw, but afterwards, when our men had already
left the village and one of the *bersaglieri* turns over a body on the ground
and sees the reddish-brown moustache and the big chest torn open and
says, "Hey, look who's dead," and then everybody gathers round this dead
man who instead of being the best of theirs had become the best of ours,
Cardu who ever since he had left them had been in their thoughts, their
conversation, their fears, their myths, Cardu who many of them would
have liked to emulate if only they'd had the courage, Cardil who carried
the secret of his strength in that calm bold smile.

Everything I've written so far serves to show me that I remember almost
nothing of that morning now, and there would be other pages to write
to tell of the evening, the night. The night, of the dead man in the enemy

village watched over by the living who no longer know who is living and who is dead. My own night as I search for my comrades in the mountains to have them tell me if I have won or if I have lost. The distance that separates that night then from this night I'm writing in now. The sense of everything appearing and disappearing.

ॐ LESLIE MARMON SILKO,
     Excerpt from *Ceremony*—UNITED STATES

> Leslie Marmon Silko was born in Albuquerque, New Mexico, in 1948, of mixed ancestry—Laguna Pueblo, Mexican, and white—and grew up on the Laguna Pueblo Reservation. Silko received her BA from the University of New Mexico in 1969. In addition to her writing, Silko has taught at the Navajo Community College, the University of New Mexico, and the University of Arizona. She received a MacArthur Foundation "genius" grant in 1981. She now lives in Tucson, Arizona.
>
> *Ceremony* (1977) tells the story of a Native American of mixed ancestry who returns as a veteran of World War II to his Laguna reservation. Silko touches on the sense of belonging that service in the U.S. Army in the Second World War brought many Native Americans. The character Tayo annoys his friends, also former veterans, on a boozy night out when he suggests that their belonging was illusory: "They spent all their checks trying to get back the good times. . . . Here they were, trying to bring back that old feeling, that feeling they belonged to America the way they felt during the war." Native Americans' historic exclusion and daily discrimination overshadow the larger life-and-death threat posed by war.

The room was almost dark. Tayo wondered where Auntie and old Grandma had been all this time. The old man put his sack on his lap and began to feel around inside it with both hands. He brought out a bundle of dry green stalks and a small paper bag full of blue cornmeal. He laid the bundle of Indian tea in Tayo's lap. He stood up then and set the bag of cornmeal on the chair.

"There are some things we can't cure like we used to," he said, "not since the white people came. The others who had the Scalp Ceremony, some of them are not better either."

He pulled the blue wool cap over his ears. "I'm afraid of what will happen to all of us if you and the others don't get well," he said.

Old man Ku'oosh left that day, and as soon as he had closed the door Tayo rolled over on his belly and knocked the stalks of Indian tea on the floor. He pressed his face into the pillow and pushed his head hard against the bed frame. He cried, trying to release the great pressure that was swelling inside his chest, but he got no relief from crying any more. The pain was solid and constant as the beating of his own heart. The old man only made him certain of something he had feared all along, something in the old stories. It took only one person to tear away the delicate strands of the web, spilling the rays of sun into the sand, and the fragile world would be injured. Once there had been a man who cursed the rain clouds, a man of monstrous dreams. Tayo screamed, and curled his body against the pain.

Auntie woke him up and gave him a cup of Indian tea brewed dark as coffee. It was late and they had already eaten supper. Robert was sitting at the kitchen table saddle-soaping a bridle. Old Grandma was dozing beside her stove. The tea was mild, tasting like the air after a rainstorm, when all the grass and plants smell green and earth is damp. She brought him a bowl of blue cornmeal mush. He shook his head when he looked at it, but she sat down on the chair by the bed and fed him spoonful by spoonful. He looked at her while she fed him; he knew she had asked Ku'oosh not to mention the visit, except to the old men. He knew she was afraid people would find out he was crazy. The cornmeal mush tasted sweet; his stomach did not cramp around it like it did with other food. She took the empty bowl and cup away. He slid down under the blankets and waited for the nausea to come. He let himself go limp; he did not brace himself against the nausea. He didn't care anymore if it came; he didn't care anymore if he died.

He was sitting in the sun outside the screen door when they came driving into the yard. He had been looking at the apple tree by the woodshed, trying to see the tiny green fruits that would grow all summer until they became apples. He had been thinking about how easy it was to stay alive now that he didn't care about being alive anymore. The tiny apples hung on that way; they didn't seem to fall, even in strong wind. He could eat regular food. He seldom vomited anymore. Some nights he even slept all night without the dreams.

He went with them in the old Ford coupe. He laid his head back on the dusty seat and felt the sun getting hot on his shoulders and neck. He didn't listen to them while they laughed and talked about how Emo bought the car. He didn't hear where they said they were going. He didn't care.

It was already getting hot, and it was still springtime. The sky was empty. The sun was too hot and it made the color of the sky too pale blue. He was the last one through the screen door at Dixie Tavern.

Harley pushed a bottle of beer in front of him. Harley said something to Tayo, and the others all laughed. These good times were courtesy of the U.S. Government and the Second World War. Cash from disability checks earned with shrapnel in the neck at Wake Island or shell shock on Iwo Jima; rewards for surviving the Bataan Death March.

"Hey, Tayo, you cash your check yet?"

Tayo pushed a ten dollar bill across the table. "More beer," he said.

Emo was getting drunk on whiskey; his face was flushed and his forehead sweaty. Tayo watched Harley and Leroy flip quarters to see who was buying the next round, and he swallowed the beer in big mouthfuls like medicine. He could feel something loosening up inside. He had heard Auntie talk about the veterans—drunk all the time, she said. But he knew why. It was something the old people could not understand. Liquor was the medicine for the anger that made them hurt, for the pain of the loss, medicine for tight bellies and choked-up throats. He was beginning to feel a comfortable place inside himself, close to his own beating heart, near his own warm belly; he crawled inside and watched the storm swirling on the outside and he was safe there; the winds of rage could not touch him.

They were all drunk now, and they wanted him to talk to them; they wanted him to tell stories with them. Someone kept patting him on the back. He reached for another bottle of beer.

White women never looked at me until I put on that uniform, and then by God I was a U.S. Marine and they came crowding around. All during the war they'd say to me, "Hey, soldier, you sure are handsome. All that black thick hair." "Dance with me," the blond girl said. You know Los Angeles was the biggest city I ever saw. All those streets and tall buildings. Lights at night everywhere. I never saw so many bars and juke boxes— all the people coming from everywhere, dancing and laughing. They never asked me if I was Indian; sold me as much beer as I could drink. I was a big spender then. Had my military pay. Double starch in my uniform and my boots shining so good. I mean those white women fought over me. Yeah, they did really! I went home with a blonde one time. She had a big '38 Buick. Good car. She let me drive it all the way.

Hey, whose turn to buy?

The first day in Oakland he and Rocky walked down the street together and a big Chrysler stopped in the street and an old white woman rolled down the window and said, "God bless you, God bless you," but it was the uniform, not them, she blessed.

"Come on, Tayo! They didn't keep you on latrine duty the whole war, did they? You talk now!"

"Yeah! Come on!"

Someone jerked the bottle out of his hand. His hand was cold and wet; he clenched it into a fist. They were outside him, in the distance; his own voice sounded far away too.

"America! America!" he sang, "God shed his grace on thee." He stopped and pulled a beer away from Harley.

"One time there were these Indians, see. They put on uniforms, cut their hair. They went off to a big war. They had a real good time too. Bars served them booze, old white ladies on the street smiled at them. At Indians, remember that, because that's all they were. Indians. These Indians fucked white women, they had as much as they wanted too. They were MacArthur's boys; white whores took their money same as anyone. These Indians got treated the same as anyone: Wake Island, Iwo Jima. They got the same medals for bravery, the same flag over the coffin." Tayo stopped. He realized the others weren't laughing and talking anymore. They were listening to him, and they weren't smiling. He took another beer from Harley's hand and swallowed until the bottle was empty. Harley yelled, "Hey, Mannie!" to the bartender. "Plug in the jukebox for us!" But Tayo yelled, "No! No. I didn't finish this story yet. See these dumb Indians thought these good times would last. They didn't ever want to give up the cold beer and the blond cunt. Hell no! They were America the Beautiful too, this was the land of the free just like teachers said in school. They had the uniform and they didn't look different no more. They got respect." He could feel the words coming out faster and faster, the momentum building inside him like the words were all going to explode and he wanted to finish before it happened.

"I'm half-breed. I'll be the first to say it. I'll speak for both sides. First time you walked down the street in Gallup or Albuquerque, you knew. Don't lie. You knew right away. The war was over, the uniform was gone. All of a sudden that man at the store waits on you last, makes you wait till all the white people bought what they wanted. And the white lady at the bus depot, she's real careful now not to touch your hand when she counts out your change. You watch it slide across the counter at you, and you know. Goddamn it! You stupid sonofabitches! You know!"

The bartender came over. He was a fat Mexican from Cubero who was losing his hair. He looked at them nervously. Harley and Leroy were holding Tayo's arms gently. They said something to the bartender and he went away. The juke box lit up, and Hank Williams started singing. Tayo got quiet. He looked across at Emo, and he saw how much Emo hated him. Because he had spoiled it for them. They spent all their checks trying to get back the good times, and a skinny light-skinned bastard had ruined it. That's what Emo was thinking. Here they were, trying to bring back that old feeling, that feeling they belonged to America the way they felt during the war. They blamed themselves for losing the new feeling; they never talked about it, but they blamed themselves just like they blamed themselves for losing the land the white people took. They never thought to blame the white people for any of it; they wanted white people for their friends. They never saw that it was the white people who gave them that feeling and it was white people who took it away again when the war was over.

Belonging was drinking and laughing with the platoon, dancing with blond women, buying drinks for buddies born in Cleveland, Ohio. Tayo knew what they had been trying to do. They repeated the stories about good times in Oakland and San Diego; they repeated them like long medicine chants, the beer bottles pounding on the counter tops like drums. Another round, and Harley tells his story about two blondes in bed with him. They forget Tayo's story. They give him another beer. Two bottles in front of him now. They go on with it, with their good old times. Tayo starts crying. They think maybe he's crying about what the Japs did to Rocky because they are to that part of the ritual where they damn those yellow Jap bastards.

Someone pats Tayo on the back. Harley wants to comfort him. They don't know he is crying for them. They don't know that he doesn't hate the Japanese, not even the Japanese soldiers who were grim-faced watching Tayo and the corporal stumble with the stretcher.

The short one had stopped and looked at Rocky in the blanket; he called the tall one over. The tall one looked like a Navajo guy from Fort Defiance that Tayo had known at Indian School. They looked tired too, those Japanese soldiers. Like they wanted this march to be over too. That tall one, he even shook his head like Willie Begay did: two abrupt movements, almost too quick to see, and then he pulled the corporal to his feet. But when Tayo tried to give the corporal his end of the blanket again, the tall soldier pushed Tayo away, not hard, but the way a small child would be pushed away by an older brother. It was then Tayo got confused, and he called this tall Jap soldier Willie Begay; "You remember him, Willie, he's my brother, best football player Albuquerque Indian School ever had."

The tall soldier looked at him curiously. He pushed Tayo out of the way, into the ditch running full of muddy water. He pulled the blanket over Rocky as if he were already dead, and then he jabbed the rifle butt into the muddy blanket. Tayo never heard the sound, because he was screaming. Later on, he regretted that he had not listened, because it became an uncertainty, loose inside his head, wandering into his imagination, so that any hollow crushing sound he heard—children smashing gourds along the irrigation ditch or a truck tire running over a piece of dry wood—any of these sounds took him back to that moment. Screaming, with mud in his mouth and in his eyes, screaming until the others dragged him away before the Japs killed him too. He fought them, trying to lie down in the ditch beside the blanket already partially buried in the mud. He had never planned to go any farther than Rocky went. They tried to help him. The corporal who had helped carry Rocky for so long put his arm around Tayo and kept him on his feet. "Easy, easy, it's okay. Don't cry. Your brother was already dead. I heard them say it. Jap talk for dead. He was already gone anyway. There was nothing anyone could do."

At the prison camp, behind the barbed wire enclosed in many more layers of barbed wire, Tayo thought he saw the tall soldier come each day to stand beside the guard at the south fence and stare for a long time in his direction. But the soldier was too far away, and the fever was too severe for Tayo to be sure of anything he had seen.

"How's your sunstroke?" Harley said when he saw that Tayo was awake. Harley had a handful of wild grapes not much bigger than blueberries; he reached over and gave Tayo some. The leaves were small and dark green. Tayo looked up at the big orange sandrock where the wild grape vine grew out of the sand and climbed along a fissure in the face of the boulder. Harley picked some more. He ate them in big mouthfuls, chewing the seeds because most of the grape was seed anyway. Tayo could not bite down on the seeds. Once he had loved to feel them break between his teeth, but not any more. The sound of crushing made him sick. He got up and walked the sandy trail to the spring. He didn't want to hear Harley crush the seeds.

The canyon was the way he always remembered it; the beeweed plants made the air smell heavy and sweet like wild honey, and the bumblebees were buzzing around waxy yucca flowers. The leaves of the cottonwood trees that crowded the canyon caught reflections of the afternoon sun, hundreds of tiny mirrors flashing. He blinked his eyes and looked away to the shade below the cliffs where the rabbit brush was green and yellow daisies were blooming. The people said that even in the driest years nobody could ever remember a time when the spring had dried up.

Josiah had told him about the spring while they waited for the water barrels to fill. He had been sitting on the wagon seat, taken from a '23 Chrysler that wrecked near Paraje, and after all those years the springs poked through the faded mouse-fur fabric like devil claws. Tayo used to stand in the big sandstone cave and hold the siphon hose under the water in the shallow pool where the spring water splashed down from the west wall of the cave. The water was always cold, icy cold, even in the summer, and Tayo liked the way it felt when he was sweating and took off his shirt: the splashing water made an icy mist that almost disappeared before it touched him.

"You see," Josiah had said, with the sound of the water trickling out of the hose into the empty wooden barrel, "there are some things worth more than money." He pointed his chin at the springs and around at the narrow canyon. "This is where we come from, see. This sand, this stone, these trees, the vines, all the wildflowers. This earth keeps us going." He took off his hat and wiped his forehead on his shirt. "These dry years you hear some people complaining, you know, about the dust and the wind, and how dry it is. But the wind and the dust, they are part of life too, like the sun and the sky. You don't swear at them. It's people, see. They're the ones. The old people used to say that droughts happen when people forget, when people misbehave."

Tayo knelt on the edge of the pool and let the dampness soak into the knees of his jeans. He closed his eyes and swallowed the water slowly. He tasted the deep heartrock of the earth, where the water came from, and he thought maybe this wasn't the end after all.

  ❧ AYI KWEI ARMAH,
    Excerpt from *The Beautyful Ones Are Not Yet Born*—GHANA

Ayi Kwei Armah was born in 1939 in the harbor city of Sekondi Takoradi, in western Ghana. In 1959 he went on scholarship to the

Groton School in Groton, Massachusetts. He attended Harvard University, received a degree in sociology, and then moved to Algeria and worked as a translator for the magazine *Révolution Africaine.* In 1964, Armah returned to Ghana. There he was a scriptwriter for Ghana Television and later taught English at the Navrongo School. Between 1967 and 1968, he was editor of *Jeune Afrique* magazine in Paris. In 1968–70 Armah studied at Columbia University, obtaining his MFA in creative writing. In the 1970s, he worked as a teacher in East Africa, at the College of National Education, Chamg'omge, Tanzania, and at the National University of Lesotho. In the 1980s, he lived in Dakar, Senegal and taught at Amherst and the University of Wisconsin at Madison.

In Armah's first novel, *The Beautyful Ones Are Not Yet Born* (1968), the narrator reflects on memories of the recent violence in Ghana and "how even the worst happenings of the past acquire a sweetness in the memory. Old harsh distresses are now merely pictures and tastes which hurt no more, like itching scars which can only give pleasure now." Yet despite this acknowledgment the rest of the excerpt examines the violence in detail and suggests that the narrator may also still be very disturbed by these memories.

Why do we waste so much time with sorrow and pity for ourselves? It is true now that we are men, but not so long ago we were helpless messes of soft flesh and unformed bone squeezing through bursting motherholes, trailing dung and exhausted blood. We could not ask then why it was necessary for us also to grow. So why now should we be shaking our heads and wondering bitterly why there are children together with the old, why time does not stop when we ourselves have come to stations where we would like to rest? It is so like a child, to wish all movement to cease.

And yet the wondering and the shaking and the vomiting horror is not all from the inward sickness of the individual soul. Here we have had a kind of movement that should make even good stomachs go sick. What is painful to the thinking mind is not the movement itself, but the dizzying speed of it. It is that which has been horrible. Unnatural, I would have said, had I not stopped myself with asking, unnatural according to what kind of nature? Each movement and each growth, each such thing brings with itself its own nature to frustrate our future judgment. Now, whenever I am able to look past the beauty of the first days, the days of birth, I can see growth. I tell myself that is the way it should be. There is nothing that should break the heart in the progressive movement away from the beauty of the first days. I see growth, that is all I see within my mind. When I can only see, when there is nothing I can feel, I am not troubled. But always these unwanted feelings will come in the end and disturb the tired mind with thoughts that will not go away. How horribly rapid everything has been, from the days when men were not ashamed to talk of souls and of suffering and of hope, to these low days of smiles that will never again be sly enough to hide the knowledge of betrayal and deceit. There is something of an irresistible horror in such quick decay.

When I was at school, in Standard Five, one of us, a boy who took a special pleasure in showing us true but unexpected sides of our world, came and showed us something I am sure none of us has forgotten. We called him Aboliga the Frog. His eyes were like that. Aboliga the Frog one day brought us a book of freaks and oddities, and showed us his favorite among the weird lot. It was a picture of something the caption called an old manchild. It had been born with all the features of a human baby, but within seven years it had completed the cycle from babyhood to infancy to youth, to maturity and old age, and in its seventh year it had died a natural death. The picture Aboliga the Frog showed us was of the man-child in its gray old age, completely old in everything save the smallness of its size, a thing that deepened the element of the grotesque. The man-child looked more irretrievably old, far more thoroughly decayed than any ordinary old man could ever have looked. But of course, it, too, had a nature of its own, so that only those who have found some solid ground they can call the natural will feel free to call it unnatural. And where is my solid ground these days? Let us say just that the cycle from birth to decay has been short. Short, brief. But otherwise not at all unusual. And even in the decline into the end there are things that remind the long-ing mind of old beginnings and hold out the promise of new ones, things even like your despair itself. I have heard this pain before, only then it was multiplied many, many times, but that may only be because at that time I was not so alone, so far apart. Maybe there are other lonely voices despair-ing now. I will not be entranced by the voice, even if it should swell as it did in the days of hope. I will not be entranced, since I have seen the destruction of the promises it made. But I shall not resist it either. I will be like a cork.

It is so surprising, is it not, how even the worst happenings of the past acquire a sweetness in the memory. Old harsh distresses are now merely pictures and tastes which hurt no more, like itching scars which can only give pleasure now. Strange, because when I can think soberly about it all, without pushing any later joys into the deeper past, I can remember that things were terrible then.

When the war was over the soldiers came back to homes broken in their absence and they themselves brought murder in their hearts and gave it to those nearest them. I saw it, not very clearly, because I had no way of understanding it, but it frightened me. We had gone on marches of victory and I do not think there was anyone mean enough in spirit to ask whether we knew the thing we were celebrating. Whose victory? Ours? It did not matter. We marched, and only a dishonest fool will look back on his boyhood and say he knew even then that there was no meaning in any of it. It is so funny now, to remember that we all thought we were welcoming victory. Or perhaps there is nothing funny here at all, and it is only that victory itself happens to be the identical twin of defeat.

There was the violence, first of all. If that was not something entirely new, at any rate the frequency and the intensity of it were new things. No one before had told me of so many people going away to fight and coming back with blood and money eating up their minds. And afterward, those who might have answered me if I had asked them before would not take any notice of me, so busy were they all with looking and wondering what it was all about, and when it would end, and if it would end at all. There were no answers then. There never will be any answers. What will a man ever do when he is called to show his manhood fighting in alien lands and leaving his women behind with the demented and the old and the children and the other women? What will a man ever do but think his women will remain his even though he is no longer there with them? And what will a woman do for absent men who send back money not to be spent but to be kept for unknown times when they hope to return, if return they ever will? What new thing is money if it is not to be spent? So there were men who, against the human wishes of some women they had married in their youth, did not die in foreign lands but came back boldly, like drunken thieves in blazing afternoons and cold nights, knowing before they had even drunk the water with the lying smile of welcome that they had been betrayed. Their anger came out in the blood of those closest to themselves, these men who had gone without anger to fight enemies they did not even know; they found anger and murder waiting for them, lying in the bosoms of the women they had left behind. All that the young eye could see then was the truth; that the land had become a place messy with destroyed souls and lost bodies looking for something that could take their pain and finding nothing but those very people whose pain should have been their pain, and for whose protection they should have learned to fight, if there had been any reason left anywhere. It was also the time of the fashion of the jackknife and the chuke, the rapid unthinking movement of short, ugly iron points that fed wandering living ghosts with what they wanted, blood that would never put an end to their inner suffering. A lot found it impossible to survive the destruction of the world they had carried away with them in their departing heads, and so they went simply mad, like Home Boy, endlessly repeating harsh, unintelligible words of command he had never understood but had learned to obey in other people's countries, marching all the day, everywhere, and driving himself to his insane exhaustion with the repetition of all the military drill he had learned, always to the proud accompaniment of his own scout whistle with its still-shiny metal sound. Some went very quietly into a silence no one could hope to penetrate, something so deep that it swallowed completely men who had before been strong: they just plunged into this deep silence and died. Those who were able picked up the pieces of shattered worlds and selves, swallowed all the keen knowledge of betrayal, and came with us along the wharves to search for some humiliating work that could give meaning to the continuing passage of unwelcome days; a hundred or so men waiting with eyes that had gotten lost in the past or in the future, always in some faraway place and time, any faraway place and time, provided it was not the horrible now and here, a hundred men waiting too quietly to fill places enough for seven.

Kofi Billy was one of the lucky ones, picked to do work that was too cruel for white men's hands. He did his work well. At the end of a day he was always tired, but he had found some sort of happiness in all of this, and that was something very valuable indeed. He was one day moving cargo, pushing it with his giant hands across some deck when somewhere some fresh young Englishman sitting at some machine loaded too much tension into even the steel ropes on board and one of them snapped. The free rope whipped with all that power through the air and just cut Kofi Billy's right leg away beneath the knee. He said for a long while he felt nothing at all, and then he felt everything a man could ever feel, and the world vanished for him. The Englishman said he deserved it: he had been playing at his work. Had he moved faster, he would not have been there when the steel rope snapped. Before him I had never actually known anybody with a wooden leg like that, and he himself was unwilling ever to talk about it. He just sat looking at the space which the wood-and-metal limb could never fill, and said nothing. Sister Maanan found refuge in lengthening bottles, and the passing foreigner gave her money and sometimes even love. The wharves turned men into gulls and vultures, sharp waiters for weird foreign appetites to satisfy pilots of the hungry alien seeking human flesh. There were the fights, of course, between man and man, not so much over women as over white men asking to be taken to women, and the films brought the intelligent mind clever new fashions in dress and in murder. There were the more exciting, far more complete fights between large groups of violent men, when soldiers for some reason no one cared to know would be fighting policemen, or solid Kroo men would stand and fight the returned warriors. These were acts of violence directed outward. I do not believe that even this was fully half the horror we all felt. I know that my friends felt the way I felt. And what I felt inside was the approach of something much like death itself. The thing that would have killed us was that there was nothing to explain all this, nothing outside ourselves and those near us or those even weaker than ourselves that we could attack. There was no way out visible to us, and out on the hills the white men's gleaming bungalows were so far away, so unreachably far that people did not even think of them in their suffering. And for those who did, there were tales of white men with huge dogs that ate more meat in a single day than a human Gold Coast family got in a month, dogs which could obey their masters' voices like soldiers at war, and had as little love for black skins as their white masters.

∾ EDMOND JABÈS,
  "The Desert"—EGYPT

Edmond Jabès was born in Cairo in 1912 and was one of three children of a French-speaking Italian couple. He began to write poetry in his late teens, and he published it, first in Cairo and shortly afterwards in Paris. Jabès served as an officer in the British army in Palestine during World War II and wrote a collection of poems at that time called *Chansons Pour Le Repas de L'ogre*. By 1948, however, the Egyptian political climate changed for the worse in reaction to the creation of the State of Israel. Jabès continued to write and was named Chevalier de la Legion d'Honneur in 1952 by the then ambassador of France to Egypt, Maurice Couve de Murville. In 1956, Jabès, his wife, and two daughters were obliged to leave the country as a result of the Suez Crisis. By 1957 they settled in Paris, and in 1967 Jabès obtained French citizenship. After his immigration to France he never returned to Egypt. Jabès was shocked by the amount of anti-Semitism he encountered in France. He had been preoccupied with the idea of foreignness while he was living in Egypt, but the question took on a new, troubling meaning for him in France, his newly adopted home. Edmond Jabès died in 1991.

In his poem "The Desert" (1987), here translated by Rosmarie Waldrop, Jabès asks, "Does forgetting have a color?" For him, memories of war are tinged with yellow—the yellow, dusty sand in which he fought. Jabès also writes of the fragments of memory, which seem like the grains of sand, difficult to clutch without losing many individual details that slip through the sieve.

Hidden language, not that of hands or eyes, a language beyond gesture,
beyond looks, smiles or tears that we had to learn! Ah, what desert
    will revive it now?
We thought we were done with crossing the desolate stretch of land
    where the word had dragged us, making us and our wanderings
    bear amazed witness to its perennial nature.
And here silence leads us into its glass kingdom, vaster yet at first
sight, breaking all trace of our passage.
. . . primal silence which we cannot escape.

Do not confuse *hothouse* and *desert*, *plant* and *speech*. Silence shelters,
    sand shifts.
Princely, the plant; the word, a particle of dust.

Image stripped of its verbal eloquence—don't we speak of a telling
    likeness?—representing nothing. Yellowed. Does forgetting have a
    color? Ah, this yellow, color of awakened sand.
There lies the better part of my past. What persists, writing recovers in
    fragments.
Write, write, write in order to remember.

You only understand what you destroy.

∾ Joyce Carol Oates,
"Words Fail, Memory Blurs, Life Wins"—United States

Joyce Carol Oates was born in 1938 in Lockport, New York,
attending a one-room schoolhouse up until high school. While a
scholarship student at Syracuse University, she won *Mademoiselle*
magazine's fiction contest. She graduated as valedictorian, then
earned an MA at the University of Wisconsin. In 1968, she began
teaching at the University of Windsor. In 1978, she moved to
New Jersey to teach creative writing at Princeton University,
where she is now the Roger S. Berlind Distinguished Professor
of the Humanities. Joyce Carol Oates has written over fifty
novels and many more short stories and has edited several
anthologies. She has won the National Book Award, has thrice
been a finalist for the Pulitzer prize, and has won the O'Henry
Short Story Prize seventeen times. She has also received awards
from the Guggenheim Foundation, the National Institute of Arts
and Letters, and the Lotus Club and is a member of the American
Academy and Institute of Arts and Letters. She won the 1996
PEN/Malamud Award for lifetime achievement in the short
story form.

   In her *New York Times* essay written soon after September 11,
2001, Oates recalls a violently turbulent plane ride that is the
closest she has come to a "senseless" violent death as experienced
by those who died in 9/11. She explores the story-telling techniques
that people use after brushes with death to help tame terror.
She focuses on the anecdote and how it can "extract from the
helpless visceral sensation some measure of intellectual summary
or control." "Amnesia seeps into the crevices of our brains, and
amnesia heals."

Since Sept. 11, what might be called the secondary wave of the terrorist
attacks has been nearly as traumatic to some of us as the attacks themselves: our discovery that we have been demonized and that because we
are Americans, we are hated; because we are Americans, we are seen to
be deserving of death. "Words fail us" was the predominant cliché in the
days immediately after the attacks, but for some, even intellectuals in other
secular democracies, words have been too easily and cheaply produced;
they matter-of-factly declared, "The United States had it coming."

The closest I've knowingly come to a "senseless" violent death was during an airline flight from New Orleans to Newark, when turbulence so rocked, shook, rattled the plane that it seemed the plane could not endure and would break into pieces. White-faced attendants were strapped into their seats, and the rest of us, wordless, very still except for the careenings and lurchings of the plane, sat with eyes fixed forward and hands clenched into fists. In the earlier, less alarming stages of turbulence, the passenger beside me had remarked that turbulence "per se" rarely caused plane crashes, that crashes were caused by "mechanical failure" or bad takeoffs or landings. But now he was silent, for we'd passed beyond even the palliative value of words.

If I survive this, I vowed, I will never fly again. No doubt every passenger on the flight was making a similar vow. *If—survive!—never again.*

The utterly physical—visceral—adrenaline-charged—sensation that you may be about to die is so powerful that it invests the present tense with an extraordinary lucidity and significance. To imagine the next stage as it has been experienced by countless fellow human beings—when the plane actually disintegrates, or begins to fall, or, in the case of hijacked planes, nears the targets chosen by "martyrs" in the holy war—is to re-experience symptoms of anxiety that culminate in the mind simply blanking out: as words fail us in extremis, so do coherent sensations fail us.

We flew through the turbulence. If there was a narrative developing here it was not to be a narrative of tragedy or even melodrama but one that lends itself to a familiar American subgenre, the anecdote.

As soon as such an experience—whether anecdotal or tragic—is over, we begin the inevitable process of "healing": that is, forgetting. We extract from the helpless visceral sensation some measure of intellectual summary or control. We lie to ourselves: we revise experience to make it lighthearted and amusing to others. For in what other way is terror to be tamed, except recycled as anecdotes or aphorisms, a sugary coating to hide the bitter pellet of truth within?

How many airplane flights I've taken since that day I vowed I would never fly again, I can't begin to estimate. Dozens, certainly. Perhaps more than 100. The promise I'd made to myself in extremis was quickly broken, though it was a reasonable promise and perhaps my terror-stricken mind was functioning more practically than my ordinary mind, uncharged by adrenaline.

Yet the fact is: Words fail us. There is the overwhelming wish to "sum up"— "summarize"—"put into perspective." As if typed-out words

possessed such magic and could not, instead, lead to such glib summa-
tions as "The United States had it coming."

Admittedly, having survived that rocky airplane flight, I could not long
retain its significance in my mind, still less in my emotions. Amnesia seeps
into the crevices of our brains, and amnesia heals. The present tense is
a needle's eye through which we thread ourselves—or are threaded—and
what's past is irremediably past, to be recollected only in fragments. So,
too, the collective American experience of trauma has begun already to
fade and will continue to fade, like previous collective traumas: the shock
of Pearl Harbor, the shock of President John F. Kennedy's assassination.

The great narrative of our planet isn't human history but the history
of evolving life. Environments alter, and only those species and individuals that alter with them can survive.

"Hope springs eternal in the human breast" may be a cliché, but it is
also a profound insight. Perhaps unfairly, the future doesn't belong to those
who only mourn, but to those who celebrate.

The future is ever-young, ever forgetting the gravest truths of the past.

Ideally we should retain the intellectual knowledge that such traumas
as the terrorist attacks have given us, while assimilating and moving beyond the rawness of the emotional experience. In this season of unease,
as ruins continue to smolder, we celebrate the fact of our existence, which
pity, terror and visceral horror have made more precious, at least in our
American eyes.

OBJECTS OF MEMORY

Gerald McMaster, a Canadian Cree artist, recently described a poignant moment in Washington, D.C., when a group of Native Americans from Northern Alaska arrived at the Smithsonian National Museum of the American to take home a mask central to their spirituality. The spokesman picked up the mask and started to speak to it as a person. In a certain way, the man was giving back voice and restoring a face to an absent ancestor. In a broader sense he was speaking to past generations—each full of individual voices and faces—who had been erased in the large-scale slaughter of indigenous people in North America, their spiritual relics such as the mask often stolen in the process. At a conference in Lower Manhattan, New York, McMaster said, "Museum objects and artifacts become ventriloquists on behalf of the people that are dead and no longer there."

Memorial museums often use personal objects—such as the piles of suitcases in the U.S. Holocaust Museum in D.C. or the broken spectacles from Buchenwald in artist Naomi Tereza Salmon's work "Twelve Spectacles"—as visual markers or placeholders for those people killed in mass violence. A shoe, or pile of shoes, reminds the viewers of the individual people and bodies who inhabited these objects before they disappeared. Colombian artist Doris Salcedo further develops the theme of objects of memory in her installation *Altabriarios.* Three-dimensional rectangular boxes are cut into a white plaster wall. These niches hold the shoes of people who disappeared in the violent maelstrom that has devastated Columbia. The families of the victims donated the shoes, showcased in the cut-outs in the wall, sealed with a membrane of animal caul, sutured into the plaster of the wall. A faint light glows in the background and the shoes—barely visible—are a particularly haunting evocation of their absent owners. In the case of Columbia, the disappearances were a deliberate political strategy to demoralize and terrify a people in order to ensure their silence. Constructing memorials is an attempt to reclaim some trace of these individuals in history.

This chapter brings together the Polish writer Tadeusz Rózewicz, writing about the Holocaust; the Greek Socialist Yannis Ritsos, writing about violence in Greece; Günter Eich, a poet who served in the German army in World War II and was interned in an American prisoner of war camp; Anna Akhmatova, the Russian poet who lived through World War I and wrote her work "Requiem" as World War II was just beginning; Khaled Mattawa, writing about the Middle East; and Michael Ondaatje, reflecting on violence in Sri Lanka.

↶ Tadeusz Rózewicz,
"Pigtail"—poland

Poet, playwright, and novelist Tadeusz Rózewicz was born in 1921 in Radomsko, Poland, and is considered one of the most influential Polish writers of his generation. He studied art history in Cracow at the Jagiellonian University and joined the Resistance movement during World War II. During the war, he began to write, striving to put into words the violence he witnessed firsthand. He published his first work, *Niepokoj* (Anxiety), in 1947 and since then has become famous for his stark and honest style and tone. In the early 1960s, Rózewicz became a leading figure in Polish avant-garde theater. His work has been translated into numerous languages, including English, German, French, Serbian, Serbo-Croatian, Danish, Finnish, and Swedish, and his plays continue to be performed throughout the world. Rózewicz currently lives and works in Wroclaw, Poland.

Rózewicz's poem "Pigtail" (1948) looks closely at the hair of female Holocaust victims. Very cinematic in style, the poem first focuses on the shaven heads of women being ferried off to a concentration camp and the workmen sweeping up their hair. Next the hair is stored in glass containers as the original owners are suffocated in the gas chambers. Rózewicz focuses on the hair in its present state: "not touched by any hand, or rain or lips." The

final verse of the poem conveys a tragic image: one faded plait, tied
with a ribbon. However, by ending the poem with a description
of human hands—young boys—pulling on this plait, Tadeusz
Rózewicz leaves the reader with the impression not of a victim,
but of a healthy, normal child. It is as if through poetry, he tries
to reverse what was done to the owner of this plait—to preserve
her in memory in a way that overlays the brutal specifics of her
death. We are to remember her vital and alive—to identify her by
more than a severed plait and a savagely curtailed life.

When all the women in the transport
had their heads shaved
four workmen with brooms made of birch twigs
swept up
and gathered the hair

Behind clean glass
the stiff hair lies
of those suffocated in gas chambers
there are pins and side combs
in this hair

The hair is not shot through with light
is not parted by the breeze
is not touched by any hand
or rain or lips

In huge chests
clouds of dry hair
of those suffocated
and a faded plait
a pigtail with a ribbon
pulled at school
by naughty boys

∾ YANNIS RITSOS,
   "Underneath Oblivion"—GREECE

   Yannis Ritsos was born in Monemvassia, Greece, in May 1909.
   During his youth, his father was interned for mental illness and

his mother and elder brother died. Ritsos lived in a sanitarium between 1927 and 1931 because he suffered from tuberculosis. These years fueled Ritsos's desire to become a poet and a revolutionary and formed some of the fodder of his writing. A committed socialist, Ritsos saw his books burned by the Fascist government of Greece in 1936. Ritsos was unable to join the partisans during World War II due to his tuberculosis, but he was still active politically. During the civil war after World War II, Ritsos was forced to go into hiding. He was captured in 1948 and spent four years in concentration camps. Released in 1952, he then began receiving official recognition for his work. After the coup of 1967, he was imprisoned again and was only released again because of his health. Yannis Ritsos is one of the most widely translated modern Greek poets and died in Athens, Greece, in 1990.

In his poem "Underneath Oblivion," translated by Kimon Friar and Kostas Myrsiades, Ritsos writes eloquently of a coat that is all that is left of a loved one, executed during the Civil War. On this coat the speaker sees "the wall of the execution with four holes, and around it our memories." People often speak of the texture of memory, and Ritsos fashions memory into the material of a signature coat. Just as the substance of the coat around the bullet holes makes death visible, so too the whole coat literally outlines the absent body of its owner.

The only evidence remaining from his existence was his coat.
They hung it there in the large closet. It was forgotten,
shoved deeper by our own clothes, summer, winter,
new clothes each year for our fresh needs. Until,
one day, it caught our eye—perhaps because of its strange color,
perhaps because of its old-fashioned cut. On its buttons
there remained three circular, identical scenes:
the wall of the execution with four holes, and around it our memories.

GÜNTER EICH,
"Inventory"—GERMANY

Günter Eich was born in 1907 in Lebus, Germany, on the Oder River, and educated in Leipzig, Berlin, and Paris. After being held as a prisoner of war, he was one of the founders in 1947 of *Gruppe 47*, a literary association in Germany after World War II. In 1950, he received the national literature prize for young writers for a collection of poems. Eich published prose, poetry, and radio plays throughout the rest of his life. In 1953, he married the Austrian writer Ilse Aichinger. They lived in Germany, but Eich died in Salzburg in 1972. His collected works were published in four volumes in *1991*.

In his poem "Inventory," (1947) Eich catalogs the simple belongings of a solider, from the critical physical items he needs such as his cap and coat and his tin cup, with his name inscribed upon it with a nail, to the items which keep him spiritually alive: his pencil and journal in which he writes down the verses he dreams up at night. The poem's final, compelling image of thread could be meant literally—perhaps a spool of thread in his kit of belongings—but it also conveys the notion that his writing is the thread that helps him to maintain his sanity and connects him with other human beings and his audience, just as considering his sparse possessions enables him to remain in touch with a sense of his own humanity.

This is my cap,
this is my coat,
here's my shaving gear
in a linen sack.

A can of rations:
my plate, my cup,
I've scratched my name
in the tin.

Scratched it with this
valuable nail
which I hide
from avid eyes.

In the foodsack is
a pair of wool socks
and something else that I
show to no one.

It all serves as a pillow
for my head at night.
The cardboard here lies
between me and the earth.

The lead in my pencil
I love most of all:
in the daytime it writes down
the verses I make at night.

This is my notebook,
this is my tarpaulin,
this is my towel,
this is my thread.

~ ANNA AKHMATOVA,
Excerpt from "Requiem"—RUSSIA

Anna Andreyevna Akhmatova was born as Anna Gorenko in 1889
into an upper-class family in Odessa in the Ukraine. She attended
law school in Kiev and married Nikolai Gumilev, a poet and
critic, in 1910. After the publication of her first collection of
poems, *Evening*, in 1912, Akhmatova became a cult figure among
the intelligentsia and part of the literary scene in St. Petersburg.
With her husband, she became a leader of Acmeism, a movement
which praised the virtues of lucid, carefully crafted verse and
reacted against the vagueness of the Symbolist style which
dominated the Russian literary scene of the period. She and
Gumilev divorced in 1918. Akhmatova married twice more, to
Vladimir Shileiko in 1918, whom she divorced in 1928, and to
Nikolai Punin, who died in a Siberian labor camp in 1953. The
writer Boris Pasternak, who was already married, reportedly also
proposed to Akhmatova numerous times. Akhmatova's most
accomplished works, "Requiem" (which was not published in
its entirety in Russia until 1987) and *Poem without a Hero*, are
reactions to the horror of the Stalinist Terror. At this time her
writing was repressed and she suffered tremendous personal
loss. Akhmatova also translated the works of Victor Hugo,

Rabindranath Tagore, Giacomo Leopardi, and various Armenian and Korean poets, and she wrote memoirs of fellow Acmeist Osip Mandelstam. In 1965 she was awarded an honorary doctorate from Oxford University. Akhmatova died in 1966 in Leningrad, where she had spent most of life.

Akhmatova's "Requiem" was written in 1940 as World War II was gathering force. She writes of remembering those who are gone and weaving them a garment out of her words. She evokes the image of being a ventriloquist for the countless silenced as she writes, "If a gag should blind my tortured mouth, / through which a hundred million people shout." At the end of her poem, she speaks of being turned into a silent object herself, a monument: "And from my motionless bronze-lidded sockets / may the melting snow, like teardrops, slowly trickle."

I

I have learned how faces fall to bone,
how under the eyelids terror lurks,
how suffering inscribes on cheeks
the hard lines of its cuneiform texts,
how glossy black or ash-fair locks
turn overnight to tarnished silver,
how smiles fade on submissive lips,
and fear quavers in a dry titter.
And I pray not for myself alone . . .
for all who stood outside the jail,
in bitter cold or summer's blaze,
with me under that blind red wall.

II

Remembrance hour returns with the turning year.
I see, I hear, I touch you drawing near:
the one we tried to help to the sentry's booth,
and who no longer walks this precious earth,
and that one who would toss her pretty mane
and say, "It's just like coming home again."
I want to name the names of all that host,
but they snatched up the list, and now it's lost.

I've woven them a garment that's prepared
out of poor words, those that I overheard,
and will hold fast to every word and glance
all of my days, even in new mischance,
and if a gag should blind my tortured mouth,
through which a hundred million people shout,
then let them pray for me, as I do pray
for them, this eve of my remembrance day.
And if my country ever should assent
To casting in my name a monument,
I should be proud to have my memory graced,
but only if the monument be placed
not near the sea on which my eyes first opened—
my last link with the sea has long been broken—
nor in the Tsar's garden near the sacred stump,
where a grieved shadow hunts my body's warmth,
but here, where I endured three hundred hours
in line before the implacable iron bars.
Because even in blissful death I fear
to lose the clangor of the Black Marias,
to lose the banging of that odious gate
and the old crone howling like a wounded beast.
And from my motionless bronze-lidded sockets
may the melting snow, like teardrops, slowly trickle,
and a prison dove coo somewhere, over and over,
as the ships sail softly down the flowing Neva.

∽ KHALED MATTAWA,
   "Letter to Ibrahim"—LIBYA

Khaled Mattawa was born in Libya and came to the United
States in his teens. He studied at the University of Tennessee
and Indiana University and has taught at California State University,
Northridge. He is the author of *Zodiac of Echoes* and *Ismailia
Eclipse* and the translator of three volumes of contemporary
Arabic poetry. He has received a Guggenheim Fellowship, a
Hodder Fellowship at Princeton, and a National Endowment for
the Arts translation grant.

Mattawa's poem "Letter to Ibrahim" (1995) is a letter from the speaker, based in Tennessee, to a friend living in the Netherlands. The poem starts with a joke the boy shared about a man who wanted to build a future but ran out of bricks and cement. It moves to a somber scene in the past, as the friends buried a bird that had died in the speaker's hands. The end of the poem loops back to the joke at the beginning and articulates how futures may not be made of concrete but past memories have a tangible quality to them, like the leaves of trees: "We all raise memories like trees / to live under their shadows, / to be sheltered by their magnificent, / leaking roofs."

You remember the joke, right?
About the guy who wanted
to build a future
but ran out of cement,
ran out of bricks, tossed around
by the wheels of fortune,
crushed under the concrete of neglect
like the bird we found
in the middle of a street
downtown, head nodding,
wings barely flapping,
drowning in automobile exhaust.
I held it, felt the warm clay
cooling in my hands.
I could almost see all its flights
returning to nest forever
in the grayness of its down.
You watched me make
a place for it under a tree.
At least it'll die
in the shade, you said.
And death will come
slowly riding the coattails
of a breeze.

It's morning where you live now.
In your room in Leiden,

you're calling friends
in London, Cairo and D.C.
There's a windmill
in the distance. The old woman
whose basement you rent
plants tulips because they,
like the Turk cycling to deliver
fresh milk and cheese,
are predictable, on time.
Your notebooks are crowded
with cob webs and pigeons
and the angels for whom you wait
build houses on the ocean floor.
Half drunk in Tennessee,
I think of you. I'm happy here
laughing at white lies and curses,
running out of bricks, but not embraces.
Listen brother, it's the same everywhere.
We all raise memories like trees
to live under their shadows,
to be sheltered by their magnificent,
leaking roofs.

ᇋ MICHAEL ONDAATJE,
   Excerpt from *Anil's Ghost*—SRI LANKA

Michael Ondaatje was born in 1943 in Colombo, Ceylon (now
Sri Lanka). He was educated in Ceylon, London, Quebec, and
Ontario and is now a Canadian citizen. Ondaatje has taught for
many years at York University, in Toronto, Canada, and received
many awards including the Booker Prize in 1992. He is the author
of ten collections of poetry and four works of fiction. His 1992
novel, *The English Patient,* was adapted into an Academy
award–winning film in 1996. He and his wife, Linda Spalding, live
in Toronto and edit the literary journal *Brick.*

   In the excerpt from *Anil's Ghost* (2000), the narrator describes
how household rags can become sacred objects when they are
linked to missing relatives. Then the speaker touches on the

skeleton of one man, a "representative of all those lost voices," a mystery the narrator is trying to uncover.

We are often criminals in the eyes of the earth, not only for having committed crimes, but because we know that crimes have been committed. Words about a man buried forever in a prison. *El Hombre de las Máscara de Hierro. The Man in the Iron Mask.* Anil needed to comfort herself with old friends, sentences from books, words she could trust. *"This is the dead-room," said Enjolras.* Who was Enjolras? Someone in *Les Misérables.* A book so much a favorite, so thick with human nature she wished it to accompany her into the afterlife. She was working with a man who was efficient in his privacy, who would never unknot himself for anyone. A paranoid is someone with all the facts, the joke went. Maybe this was the only truth here. In this rest house near Bandarawela with four skeletons. *You're six hours away from Colombo and you're whispering—think about that.*

In her years abroad, during her European and North American education, Anil had courted foreignness, was at ease whether on the Bakerloo line or the highways around Santa Fe. She felt completed abroad. (Even now her brain held the area codes of Denver and Portland.) And she had come to expect clearly marked roads to be the source of most mysteries. Information could always be clarified and acted upon. But here, on this island, she realized she was moving with only one arm of language among uncertain laws and a fear that was everywhere. There was less to hold on to with that one arm. Truth bounced between gossip and vengeance. Rumour slipped into every car and barbershop. Sarath's daily path as a professional archaeologist in this world, she guessed, involved commissions and the favours of ministers, involved waiting politely for hours in their office lobbies. Information was made public with diversions and subtexts—as if the truth would not be of interest when given directly, without waltzing backwards.

She loosened the swaddling plastic that covered Sailor. In her work Anil turned bodies into representatives of race and age and place, though for her the tenderest of all discoveries was finding, some years earlier, of the tracks at Laetoli—almost-four-million-year-old footsteps of a pig, a hyena, a rhinoceros and a bird, this strange ensemble identified by a twentieth-century tracker. Four unrelated creatures that had walked hurriedly over a wet layer of volcanic ash. To get away from what? Historically more significant were other tracks in the vicinity, of a hominid assumed to be approximately five feet tall (one could tell by the pivoting heel impressions). But it was the quartet of animals walking from Laetoli four million years ago that she liked to think about.

The most precisely recorded moments of history lay adjacent to the extreme actions of nature or civilization. She knew that. Pompeii. Laetoli. Hiroshima. Vesuvius (whose fumes had asphyxiated poor Pliny while he recorded its "tumultuous behaviour"). Tectonic slips and brutal human violence provided random time-capsules of unhistorical lives. A dog in Pompeii. A gardener's shadow in Hiroshima. But in the midst of such events, she realized, there could never be any logic to the human violence without the distance of time. For now it would be reported, filed in Geneva, but no one could ever give meaning to it. She used to believe that meaning allowed a person a door to escape grief and fear. But she saw that those who were slammed and stained by violence lost the power of language and logic. It was the way to abandon emotion, a last protection for the self. They held on to just the coloured and patterned sarong a missing relative last slept in, which in normal times would have become a household rag, but now was sacred.

In a fearful nation, public sorrow was stamped down by the climate of uncertainty. If a father protested a son's death, it was feared another family member would be killed. If people you knew disappeared, there was a chance they might stay alive if you did not cause trouble. This was the scarring psychosis in the country. Death, loss, was "unfinished," so you could not walk through it. There had been years of night visitations, kidnappings or murders in broad daylight. The only chance was that the creatures who fought would consume themselves. All that was left of law was a belief in an eventual revenge towards those who had power.

And who was this skeleton? In this room, among these four, she was hiding among the unhistorical dead. *To fetch a dead body: what a curious task! To cut down the corpse of an unknown hanged man and then bear the body of the animal on one's back . . . something dead, something buried, something already rotting away?* Who was he? This representative of all those lost voices. To give him a name would name the rest.

BUILDING BRIDGES

Galway Kinnell, a Pulitzer prize–winning American poet, was a professor at New York University living on Bleecker Street facing downtown during the fall of 2001. About a week after 9/11, NYU creative writing faculty gathered with students so that each could read something written in response to the terrorist attacks. Kinnell had scribbled a short poem. In a conversation with the Legacy Project years later, Kinnell described how he started to write the poem by describing the various types of people who had died. In this process he remembered a poem by François Villon, a famous fifteenth-century French poet who lost his father at a very young age. Kinnell said Villon had "written it better than I could have written it, so I will just put it in there." And as he wrote the poem, the words of several other writers—Paul Célan and Walt Whitman—writing about firsthand experiences of the Holocaust and working in a hospital during the American Civil War also came to mind. Why? They were apt descriptions of what he was trying to write. So he excerpted their words as well. "I reflected this might be a good thing to do because it indicated a universality to this pain and suffering, how this event resembles, in one way or another, other events," he said. The students and faculty met again a few weeks later, by which time Kinnell's poem had grown to a page and a half. Kinnell finished the poem a week before the first anniversary of 9/11 and it was published in the *New Yorker*. Reflecting on the violence of 9/11, Kinnell referenced various cataclysms from slavery to the Holocaust. He said, "This is not a comparison but a corollary, not a likeness but a lineage."

The writers of the selections in this chapter both overtly and implicitly make links to other events, whether by quoting them directly or by suggesting that knowing about other events somehow helps them get through the duress of their specific tragedies. Dunya Mikhail, an Iraqi poet who lived through the Iraq-Iran war, spoke with the Legacy Project about how writings from South Africa and South America were a source of support to her while living in Iraq during fighting in her country. The Libyan American Khaled Mattawa has a speaker in a poem called "The Mail from Tunis" who asks why knowing about someone else's history can help. The speaker says, "I understand your desire for this kind of history. It lets you live again in a place from which you're far removed. But what good will it do you to live so many lives until your sadness is not yours alone?"

In conversation with the Legacy Project, Khaled Mattawa answered the question posed in his poem: "When your sadness is not yours alone, maybe there's a kinship in the experience. It's good to have your sadness in a compound; it might dissolve more easily. Patterns of recognition may not remove all the symptoms, but it's good to know where you are. That expression *knowing where you are*, Robert Duncan said that when he had lung cancer. He said, 'Well at least I know where I am.'"

This chapter brings together Polish Lithuanian writer Czeslaw Milosz, who watched the Holocaust unfold around him; poet Ion Caraion, who lived through fascist and communist dictatorships in Romania; American poet Galway Kinnell, who witnessed 9/11; Victor Serge, the Belgian writer who lived through repression in Russia; Fadhil Al-Azzawi, an Iraqi writer living in Germany; Adonis, a Syrian writer; and Pablo Neruda, a South American writer. All reflect on both the violence they have witnessed firsthand in their own lives and the violence of the past century.

The writer Cynthia Ozick captured the link between literature and empathy when she addressed a group of doctors. She described metaphor, so frequently used by writers, as a building block for empathy. Through metaphor, "Those who have no pain can imagine those who suffer. Those at the center can imagine what it is to be outside. The strong can imagine the weak."

∾ GALWAY KINNELL,
  "When the Towers Fell"—UNITED STATES

Galway Kinnell was born in Providence, Rhode Island, in 1927. He received his BA from Princeton University in 1948 and his MA

from the University of Rochester in 1949. He served in the U.S.
Navy. He later worked for the Congress on Racial Equality and
then travelled widely in the Middle East and Europe. He has taught
at several colleges and universities, in California, Pittsburgh, and
New York. Galway Kinnell held a MacArthur fellowship from 1984
to 1989, and in 1982 he won the Pulitzer Prize for Poetry and the
National Book Award for Poetry for *Selected Poems.* He has also
published translations of works by Yves Bonnefroy, Yvanne Goll,
François Villon, and Rainer Maria Rilke. Kinnell divides his time
between Vermont and New York City, where he is the Erich Maria
Remarque Professor of Creative Writing at New York University.
He is currently a chancellor of the Academy of American Poets.

In a conversation with the Legacy Project, Kinnell likened
writing "When the Towers Fell" to describing World War I.
"I wrote a poem about World War I, which my father had been
in. He didn't really know why he was in it or who did what to
whom and for what reason. It was a strangely pointless war, but
totally ruthless and murderous. The aftermath of 9/11 felt the
same way."

From our high window we saw the towers
with their bands and blocks of light
brighten against a fading sunset,
saw them at any hour glitter and live
as if the spirits inside them sat up all night
calculating profit and loss, saw them reach up
to steep their tops in the until then invisible
yellow of sunrise, grew so used to them
often we didn't see them, and now,
not seeing them, we see them.

The banker is talking to London.
Humberto is delivering breakfast sandwiches.
The trader is already working the phone.
The mail sorter has started sorting the mail.
　　. . . *povres et riches*
　　. . . poor and rich
Sages et folz, prestres et laiz
Wise and foolish, priests and laymen

Nobles, villains, larges et chiches
Noblemen, serfs, generous and mean
Petiz et grans et beaulx et laiz
Short and tall and handsome and homely

The plane screamed low down lower Fifth Avenue,
lifted at the Arch, someone said, shaking the dog walker
in Washington Square Park, drove for the north tower,
struck with a heavy thud, releasing a huge bright gush
of blackened fire, and vanished, leaving a hole
the size and shape a cartoon plane might make
if it had passed harmlessly through and were flying away now,
on the far side, back into the realm of the imaginary.

Some with torn clothing, some bloodied,
some limping at top speed like children
in a three-legged race, some half dragged,
some intact in neat suits and dresses,
they straggle out of step up the avenues,
each dusted to a ghostly whiteness,
their eyes rubbed red as the eyes of a Zahoris,
who can see the dead under the ground.

Some died while calling home to say they were O.K.
Some died after over an hour spent learning they would die.
Some died so abruptly they may have seen death from within it.
Some broke windows and leaned out and waited for rescue.
Some were asphyxiated.
Some burned, their very faces caught fire.
Some fell, letting gravity speed them through their long moment.
Some leapt hand in hand, the elasticity in last bits of love-time letting—
    I wish I could say—their vertical streaks down the sky happen
    more lightly.

At the high window, where I've often stood
to escape a nightmare, I meet
the single, unblinking eye
lighting the all-night sniffing and lifting
and sifting for bodies, pieces of bodies, anything that is not nothing,
in a search that always goes on
somewhere, now in New York and Kabul.

She stands on a corner holding up a picture
of her husband. He is smiling. In today's
wind shift few pass. Sorry sorry sorry.
She startles. Suppose, down the street, that headlong lope . . .
or, over there, that hair so black it's purple . . .
And yet, suppose some evening I forgot
The fare and transfer, yet got by that way
Without recall,—lost yet poised in traffic.
Then I might find your eyes . . .
It could happen. Sorry sorry good luck thank you.
On this side it is "amnesia," or forgetting the way home;
on the other, "invisibleness," or never in body returning.
Hard to see clearly in the metallic mist,
or through the sheet of mock reality
cast over our world, bourne that no creature ever born
pokes its way back through, and no love can tear.

The towers burn and fall, burn and fall—
in a distant, shot, smokestacks spewing oily earth remnants out of
        the past.
Schwarze Milch der Frühe wir trinken sie abends
Black milk of daybreak we drink it at nightfall
wir trinken sie mittags und morgens wir trinken sie nachts
we drink it at midday at morning we drink it at night
wir trinken und trinken
We drink it and drink it
This is not a comparison but a corollary,
not a likeness but a lineage
in the twentieth-century history of violent death—
black men in the South castrated and strung up from trees,
soldiers advancing through mud at ninety thousand dead per mile,
train upon train headed eastward made up of boxcars shoved full to the
        corners with Jews and Gypsies to be enslaved or gassed,
state murder of twenty, thirty, forty million of its own,
atomic blasts wiping cities off the earth, firebombings the same,
death marches, starvations, assassinations, disappearances,
entire countries turned into rubble, minefields, mass graves.
Seeing the towers vomit these black omens, that the last century dumped
        into this one, for us to dispose of, we know

they are our futures, that is our own black milk crossing the sky: *wir*
      shaufeln ein Grab in den Lüften da liegt man nicht eng we're digging
      a grave in the sky there'll be plenty of room to lie down there

Burst jet fuel, incinerated aluminum, steel fume, crushed marble,
      exploded granite, pulverized drywall, mashed concrete, berserked
      plastic, gasified mercury, cracked chemicals, scoria, vapor
of the vaporized—wafted here
from the burnings of the past, draped over
our island up to streets regimented
into numbers and letters, breathed across
the great bridges to Brooklyn and the waiting sea:
astringent, miasmic, empyreumatic, slick,
freighted air too foul to take in but we take it in,
too gruesome for seekers of the amnesiac beloved
to breathe but they breathe it and you breathe it.

A photograph of a woman hangs from a string
at his neck. He doesn't look up.
He stares down at the sidewalk of flagstone
slabs laid down in Whitman's century, gutter edges
rasped by iron wheels to a melted roundedness:
a conscious intelligence envying the stones.
Nie staja sie, sa.
They do not become, they are.
Nic nad to, myslalem.
Nothing but that, I thought,
zbrzydziwszy sobie
now loathing within myself
wszystko co staje sie
everything that becomes.

And I sat down by the waters of the Hudson,
by the North Cove Yacht Harbor, and thought
how those on the high floors must have suffered: knowing
they would burn alive, and then, burning alive.
and I wondered, Is there a mechanism of death
that so mutilates existence no one
gets over it not even the dead?
Before me I saw, in steel letters welded

to the steel railing posts, Whitman's words
written as America plunged into war with itself: *City of the world! . . .*
Proud and passionate city—mettlesome, mad, extravagant city!
—words of a time of illusions. Then I remembered
what he wrote after the war was over and Lincoln dead:
I saw the debris and debris of all the dead soldiers of the war,
But I saw they were not as was thought.
They themselves were fully at rest—they suffer'd not,
The living remain'd and suffer'd, the mother suffer'd
And the wife and the child and the musing comrade suffer'd . . .

In our minds the glassy blocks
succumb over and over into themselves,
slam down floor by floor into themselves.

They blow up as if in reverse, exploding
downward and outward, billowing
through the streets, engulfing the fleeing.

As each tower goes down, it concentrates
into itself, transforms itself
infinitely slowly into a black hole

infinitesimally small: mass
without space, where each light,
each life, put out, lies down within us.

 CzesLaw Milosz,
    "On Prayer"—POLAND

Czeslaw Milosz's biography is included in "Setting the Record
Straight."
    In "On Prayer" (1986), Milosz paints a compelling picture
of "compassion for others entangled in the flesh." He writes
how prayer, and the same can be said of poetry, "constructs a
velvet bridge" connecting those in this world with those who no
longer exist. While the title, "On Prayer," has obvious religious
connotations, Milosz ends the poem on an interesting note, raising
the possibility that there is nothing after what we know now.

If that is the case, we are bound even more tightly by the fact that
we will all have to die and that is the basis for compassion.

You ask me how to pray to someone who is not.
All I know is that prayer constructs a velvet bridge
And walking it we are aloft, as on a springboard,
Above landscapes the color of ripe gold
Transformed by a magic stopping of the sun.
That bridge leads to the shore of Reversal
Where everything is just the opposite and the word *is*
Unveils a meaning we hardly envisioned.
Notice: I say we; there, every one separately,
Feels compassion for others entangled in the flesh
And knows that if there is no other shore
We will walk that aerial bridge all the same.

ᕲ ION CARAION,
"Tomorrow the Past Comes"—ROMANIA

Poet and essayist Ion Caraion was born in a Romanian village in
1923. He was an active journalist and defender of democratic causes
during World War II. He was arrested with his wife in 1951; his
outspoken poetry brought him into conflict with the Communist
authorities. He was sentenced to death but after two years the
sentence was changed to eleven years in labor camps. He was
eventually freed in 1964. He wrote eighteen books of poetry and
seven books of prose. He died in exile in 1985 in Lausanne,
Switzerland. In his poem, Caraion explores how the blood of
violent centuries flows everywhere, "like a subway through capitals,"
since it is like the past which we must live with in our present.

No longer for me is there anything late. All is late.
The blood runs like a subway through capitals.
And the past is everywhere like the blood.
　In the sunrise of the rivers red
　With lightning and groups of centaurs
　There was a kind of light—I don't know what kind of light that was.
In the fog much becomes clear.

∾ VICTOR SERGE,
  "Constellation of Dead Brothers"—BELGIUM

Victor Lvovich Kibalchich (Serge) was born in Belgium in
December 1890. His parents were émigré Russian intellectuals
who fled repression following the assassination of Czar Alexander
II by Narodnik terrorists in 1881. Under the pseudonym Valentin,
he edited the French newspaper *Anarchie.* He was arrested for
terrorism in 1912 and served five years in prison. As a "Bolshevik
agent" he was interned in France again in 1917. This same year he
adopted the name Serge. In the early 1930s, when he became
critical of Stalin, he was arrested for sending his literary works
abroad and was sent into internal exile. He was expelled from
Russia in 1936 and settled in Paris, but left when the Nazis invaded.
Unable to enter the United States because of his Communist past,
he lived in extreme poverty in Mexico until his death in 1947.

    In Serge's poem "Constellation of Dead Brothers," (1935) the
speaker lists the names of various friends who are dead. They
have all died violently—many have been killed—and through this
commonality, they have become connected to the speaker and one
another like brothers or a constellation of stars. Serge's speaker is
reminiscent of Erich Maria Remarque's character in *All Quiet on
the Western Front,* who feels a kinship with all the young men of
the war and the world who meet their deaths before they reach
even middle age. This kinship ends Serge's poem on a modestly
hopeful note.

André who was killed in Riga,
Dario who was killed in Spain,
Boris whose wounds I dressed,
Boris whose eyes I closed.

David my bunk mate,
dead without knowing why
in a quiet orchard in France—
David, your astonished suffering
—six bullets for a 20-year-old heart . . .

Karl, whose nails I recognized
when you had already turned to earth,

you, with your high brow and lofty thoughts,
what was death doing with you!
Dark, tough human vine.

The North, the waves, the ocean
capsize the boat, the Four, now pallid,
drink deeply of anguish,
farewell to Paris, farewell to you all,
farewell to life, God damn it!

Vassili, throughout our sleepless midnights
you had the soul of a combatant
from Shanghai,
and the wind effaces your tomb
in the cornfields of Armavir.

Hong Kong lights up, hour of tall buildings,
the palm resembles the scimitar,
the square resembles the cemetery,
the evening is sweltering and you are dying,
Nguyên, in your prison bed.

And you my decapitated brothers,
the lost ones, the unforgiven,
the massacred, René, Raymond,
guilty but not denied.

O rain of stars in the darkness,
constellation of dead brothers!
I owe you my blackest silence,
my resolve, my indulgence
for all these empty-seeming days,
and whatever is left me of pride
for a blaze in the desert.

But let there be silence
on these lofty figureheads!
The ardent voyage continues,
the course is set on hope.

When will it be your turn, when mine?
The course is set on hope.

∿ FADHIL AL-AZZAWI,
"Feast in Candlelight"—IRAQ

Fadhil Al-Azzawi was born in 1940 in Kirkuk, in northern Iraq. He studied English at Baghdad University and journalism at the University of Leipzig in Germany. He spent three years in an Iraqi jail and in 1977 settled in then East Germany. In 1983 he moved to East Berlin, where he went to work as a freelance writer and critic. Besides poetry and criticism he writes novellas and translates English and German literature into Arabic. Excerpts from his work have been translated into German, English, Italian, Hebrew, Kurdish, Dutch, and other languages. Al-Azzawi has published seven volumes of poetry, six novels, three books of criticism and memoir, and several translations of German literary works. He lives in Berlin.

Al-Azzawi's poem "Feast in Candlelight" (2003) looks back at the violence of the twentieth century and likens it to a debauched feast, where "parades of drunken soldiers wave their bloody flags and march down the street." Yet the reader looking back in time on this scene cannot escape the legacy of violence: "When they finish their feast/ we will sit at that same table/ and drink the same wine too."

Here is the twentieth century
in its long, dim hall
with murderers and conjurers
sitting at its table
in the flickering candlelight
of their victory,
waiting for their meal.
The waiters come out
one by one
from their hidden corners,
balancing dishes of darkness
on their heads
to serve their guests.

They will all drink from the same bottle
watch the evening fall among the trees.

Parades of drunken soldiers
wave their bloody flags
and march down the street.

Through the window
the moon will soon shine.

When they finish their feast
we will sit at that same table
and drink the same wine too.

  ∽ ADONIS,
     "A Mirror for the Twentieth Century"—SYRIA

Adonis is the pen name of Ali Ahmad Said, one of the most
prominent Arab writers in the post–World War II period. He was
born in 1930 in Qassabin, a small mountain village in western Syria
close to the Mediterranean. He studied at Damascus University
and completed a philosophy degree in 1954. In 1955, he was
imprisoned for six months because of his political activities and
membership in the Syrian National Socialist Party. But he escaped
to Lebanon. He settled there in 1956, becoming a Lebanese national.
He received a scholarship to study in Paris from 1960 to 1961. From
1970 to 1985, Adonis taught subjects including Arabic literature at
the Lebanese University, at Damascus University, and at the
Sorbonne in Paris. He has also taught and lectured in a number
of other Western universities. He returned to Paris to live in 1985.
    Adonis's "A Mirror for the Twentieth Century" is a short but
poignant poem that distills the twentieth century down to a few
key images, some more opaque, and others gutting, like the
"coffin bearing the face of a boy."

A coffin bearing the face of a boy
A book
Written on the belly of a crow
A wild beast hidden in a flower
A rock
Breathing with the lungs of a lunatic:
This is it
This is the Twentieth Century

∾ PABLO NERUDA,
"The Sadder Century"—CHILE

Pablo Neruda's real name is Neftalí Ricardo Reyes Basoalto. He
was born in 1904 in the town of Parral, Chile. At thirteen his first
poem was published. Alongside his literary activities, Neruda
studied French and pedagogy at the University of Chile in Santiago. Between 1927 and 1935, he served as a consul and traveled to
Burma, Ceylon, Java, Singapore, Buenos Aires, Barcelona, and
Madrid. The Spanish Civil War and the murder of his friend
García Lorca affected him strongly. He joined the Republican
movement, first in Spain, and later in France. In 1939, Neruda
was appointed consul for the Spanish emigration and resided in
Paris; shortly afterwards, he lived in Mexico, where he was the
consul general. In 1943, Neruda returned to Chile, and in 1945 he
was elected senator of the Republic. He also joined the Communist
Party of Chile. Due to his protests against President González
Videla's policies, he had to live underground in his own country
for two years. He managed to leave in 1949. After living in different
European countries he returned home in 1952. In 1971, he won the
Nobel Prize for Literature. He died in 1973.

In "The Sadder Century" (1969), Neruda writes of the twentieth
century as a black book, tinted with the spilled blood of many. He
gives voice to the killed and homeless but ends with a call to life,
as he talks of celebrating with those who are still there.

The century of émigrés,
the book of homelessness—
gray century, black book.
This is what I ought to leave
written in the open book,
digging it out from the century,
tinting the pages with spilled blood.

I lived the abundance
of those lost in the jungle:
I counted the cutoff hands
and the mountains of ash
and the fragmented cries

and the without-eyes glasses
and the headless hair.

Then I searched the world
for those who lost their country,
pointlessly carrying
their defeated flags,
their Stars of David,
their miserable photographs.

I too knew homelessness.

But as a seasoned wanderer,
I returned empty-handed
to this sea that knows me well.
But others remain
and are still at bay,
leaving behind their loved ones, their errors
thinking maybe
but knowing never again
and this is how I ended up sobbing
the dusty sob
intoned by the homeless.
This is the way I ended celebrating
with my brothers (those who remain)
the victorious building,
the harvest of new bread.

PERMISSIONS

Two: Isolated and Apart

Three: Coping Mechanisms

translation copyright © 1983 by Alfred A. Knopf, a division of Random House, Inc. Used by permission of Alfred A. Knopf, a division of Random House, Inc.

Excerpt from *The Island,* by Athol Fugard (New York: Viking Press, 1974), 68–72 (Act II, Scene Three). Reprinted by permission of Athol Fugard.

Excerpt from *The Stone Virgins,* by Yvonne Vera (New York: Farrar, Straus and Giroux, 2003), 81–86; copyright © 2002 by Yvonne Vera. Reprinted by permission of Farrar, Straus and Giroux, LLC.

Excerpt from *The Anecdotes of Section Chief Maimaiti: Uighur "Black Humor,"* by Wang Meng, translated with an annotated introduction by Philip F. Williams, *Journal of Asian Culture* 8 (1984): 1–30. Reprinted by permission of Wang Meng.

Excerpt from *Ways of Dying,* by Zakes Mda (New York: Picador, 2002), 95–98; copyright © 1995 by Zakes Mda. Reprinted by permission of Farrar, Straus and Giroux, LLC.

Excerpt from *Decision,* in *Three Short Novels,* by Kay Boyle (New York: Penguin Books, 1982), 242–251; copyright © 1948 by Curtis Publishing Co. Reprinted by permission of New Directions Publishing Corp.

Excerpt from *Fatelessness,* by Irme Kertész, translated by Tim Wilkinson (New York: Vintage International, 1996), 245–262; copyright © 2004 by Random House, Inc. Used by permission of Vintage Books, a division of Random House, Inc.

Four: Writing the Unspeakable and the Pressure of Emptiness

"We All Saw It, or the View from Home," by A. M. Homes, in *110 Stories: New York Writes after September 11,* edited by Ulrich Baer (New York: New York University Press, 2002), 151–153. Reprinted by permission of Ulrich Baer.

"A View of Mountains," from *The Gift of Time: The Case for Abolishing Nuclear Weapons* by Jonathan Schell (New York: Owl Books, 1998), 221–223; copyright © 1998 by Jonathan Schell. Reprinted by permission of Henry Holt and Company, LLC.

"Personae Separatae," from *Collected Poems 1920–1954* by Eugenio Montale, translated and edited by Jonathan Galassi (New York: Farrar, Giroux and Strauss, 2000); Translation copyright © 1998 by Jonathan Galassi. Reprinted by permission of Farrar, Straus and Giroux, LLC.

"The Dead of September 11," by Toni Morrison. Reprinted by permission of Toni Morrison.

"What's Not in the Heart," from *My Little Sister and Selected Poems 1965–1985,* by Abba Kovner, translated by Shirley Kaufman (Oberlin: Oberlin College Press, 1986); copyright © 1986 by Oberlin College. Reprinted by permission of Oberlin College Press.

"O," from *The War Works Hard,* by Dunya Mikhail, translated by Elizabeth Winslow (New York: New Directions, 2005); copyright © 1993, 1997, 2000, 2005 by Dunya Mikhail. Reprinted by permission of New Directions Publishing Corp.

COMMANDING OBLIVION

Five: Surviving Survival

Excerpt from *Double Vision: Reflections on My Heritage, Life, and Profession,* by Ben H. Bagdikian (Boston: Beacon Press, 1995), 88–94; copyright © 1999. Reprinted by permission of Beacon Press, Boston.

Excerpt from *We Wish to Inform You That Tomorrow We Will Be Killed with Our Families: Stories from Rwanda* by Philip Gourevitch (New York: Picador, 1999), 227–235; copyright © 1998 by Philip Gourevitch. Reprinted by permission of Farrar, Straus and Giroux, LLC.

Excerpt from *Hiroshima Notes* by Kenzaburo Oe, translated by David L. Swain and Toshi Yonezawa (New York: Marion Boyars Publishers, 1995), 125–132; copyright © 1965 by Kenzaburo Oe. Reprinted by permission of Marion Boyars Publishers, London and New York.

Excerpt from *Days and Memory* by Charlotte Delbo, translated by Rosette Lamont (Evanston: Northwestern University Press, 2001), 1–4. Reprinted by permission of Northwestern University Press.

"Earlier Winter," by Alex Molot from *110 Stories: New York Writes after September 11*, edited by Ulrich Baer (New York: New York University Press, 2002), 213–215. Reprinted by permission of Ulrich Baer.

Six: Landscape and Memory

"Nineteen Thirty-Seven," from *Krik? Krak!*, by Edwidge Danticat (New York: Soho Press, 1995), 33–41; copyright © 1995 by Edwidge Danticat. Reprinted by permission of Soho Press, Inc.

Excerpt from *Blame Me on History*, by Bloke Modisane (New York: Simon and Schuster, 1990), 5–16; copyright © 1986. Reprinted by permission of Jonathan Ball Publishers, Ltd.

"Recalling War," from *Poems About War*, by Robert Graves, edited with a commentary by William Graves (Kingston, R.I.: Moyer Bell, 1990); copyright © The Trustees of the Robert Graves Copyright Trust. Reprinted by permission of Moyer Bell.

Excerpt from "Toba Tek Singh," published in *Words Without Borders* [www.wordswithoutborders.org], by Saadat Hasan Manto, translated by Richard McGill Murphy (September 2003). Reprinted by permission of *Words Without Borders*, an online magazine for international literature hosted by Bard College and supported by the National Endowment for the Arts.

"A Jar of Rain," from *Anticipate the Coming Reservoir* by John Hoppenthaler (Pittsburgh: Carnegie Mellon University Press, 2008); copyright © by John Hoppenthaler. Reprinted by permission of John Hoppenthaler.

Seven: Fading Memory and the Role of Art

"Graphite," from *Dying*, by Varlam Shalamov, translated by John Glad (New York: W.W. Norton & Company, 1981), 283–287; copyright © 1981 by John Glad. Reprinted by permission of W. W. Norton & Company, Inc.

"New York, 12 September 2001," by Breyten Breytenbach, in *110 Stories: New York Writes after September 11*, edited by Ulrich Baer, copyright © 2002; 2004 (New York: New York University Press, 2002), 49–50; copyright © 2002 by Breyten Breytenbach. Reprinted by permission of Anderson Grinberg Literary Management, Inc.

"The Walls Do Not Fall [1], [6], [9–10]," by HD (Hilda Doolittle), from *Trilogy* (New York: New Directions Publishing Corporation, 1998), 3–4, 11–12, 16–17; copyright © 1944 by Oxford University Press; copyright renewed 1972 by Norman Holmes Pearson. Reprinted by permission of New Directions Publishing Corp.

"Shadow," from *Calligrammes: Poems of Peace and War (1913–1916),* by Guillaume Apollinaire, translated and edited by Anne Greet (Berkeley: University of California Press, 1980); copyright © 1980 by The Regents of the University of California. Reprinted by permission of University of California Press.

Eight: Beating Back the Ghosts of the Past

Excerpt from *Rise the Euphrates,* by Carol Edgarian (New York: Random House), 131–140; copyright © 1994. Reprinted by permission of Carol Edgarian.

Excerpt from *The Shawl,* by Cynthia Ozick (New York: Vintage, 1990), 8–10 and 92–96; copyright © 1980, 1983 by Cynthia Ozick. Used by permission of Alfred A. Knopf, a division of Random House, Inc.

"Hut on the Mountain," from *Dialogues in Paradise,* by Can Xue, translated by Ronald Janssen and Jian Zhang (Evanston: Northwestern University Press, 1989), 47–53. Reprinted by permission of the publisher.

Excerpt from *Pnin,* by Vladimir Nabokov (New York: Vintage, 1957), 96–101. Reprinted by arrangement with the Estate of Vladimir Nabokov. All rights reserved.

Excerpt from *Beloved,* by Toni Morrison (New York: Knopf, 1987), 50–53 and 183–185; copyright © 1987 by Toni Morrison. Used by permission of Alfred A. Knopf, a division of Random House, Inc.

REMEMBRANCE

Nine: Setting the Record Straight

Excerpt from *The Other Side of Silence: Voices from the Partition of India,* by Urvashi Butalia (Durham: Duke University Press, 2000), 284–293. All rights reserved. Used by permission of the publisher.

Excerpt from "This Past Must Address Its Present," by Wole Soyinka; copyright © 1986 by The Nobel Foundation. Reprinted by permission of The Nobel Foundation.

Excerpt from "The Chinese Amnesia," by Fang Li Zhi, translated by Perry Link, in *New York Review of Books,* September 27, 1990; copyright © 1990 NYREV, Inc. Reprinted with permission from *The New York Review of Books.*

"Speaking of Courage," from *The Things They Carried,* by Tim O'Brien (New York: Broadway Books, 1998), 137–161; copyright © 1990 by Tim O'Brien. Reprinted by permission of Houghton Mifflin Company. All rights reserved.

"Under Foreign Rain (Footnotes to Defeat): XXV," from *Unthinkable Tenderness: Selected Poems,* by Juan Gelman, edited and translated by Joan Lindgren (Berkeley: University of California Press, 1997); copyright © 1997 Juan Gelman and Joan Lindgren. Reprinted by permission of University of California Press.

Excerpt from "Who Killed India," by Khwaja Ahmad Abbas from *India Partitioned: The Other Face of Freedom,* edited by Mushirul Hasan (New Delhi: Roli Books, 2005), 233–235. Reprinted courtesy of Roli Books.

"Dedication," from *The Collected Poems, 1931–1987,* by Czeslaw Milosz (New York: Penguin Books, 1988); copyright © 1988 by Czeslaw Milosz Royalties, Inc. Reprinted by permission of HarperCollins Publishers.

Ten: Rose-Colored Memory

"Memories of a Battle," from *The Road to San Giovanni* by Italo Calvino, translated by Tim Parks (New York: Pantheon Books, 1993), 77–89; copyright © 1993 by Tim Parks. Reprinted by permission of Pantheon Books, a division of Random House, Inc.

Excerpt from *Ceremony,* by Leslie Marmon Silko (New York: Viking Penguin, 1986), 38–46; copyright © 1986 by Leslie Marmon Silko. Reprinted with the permission of The Wylie Agency.

Excerpt from *The Beautyful Ones Are Not Yet Born,* by Ayi Kwei Armah (London: Heinemann, 1969), 72–78. Reprinted by permission of Harcourt Education.

"The Desert," from *The Book of Dialogue* by Edmond Jabès, translated by Rosmarie Waldrop (Middletown, C.T.: Wesleyan University Press, 1987); © 1987 by Rosmarie Waldrop. Reprinted by permission of Wesleyan University Press.

"Words Fail, Memory Blurs, Life Wins," by Joyce Carol Oates, in the *New York Times,* December 31, 2001. Reprinted by permission of Joyce Carol Oates.

Eleven: Objects of Memory

"Pigtail," from *Tadeusz Rózewicz: They Came to See a Poet* by Tadeusz Rózewicz, translated by Adam Czerniawski (London: Anvil Poetry Press, 1991). Reprinted by permission of the publisher.

"Underneath Oblivion," from *Yannis Ritsos: Selected Poems, 1938–1988* by Yannis Ritsos, edited and translated by Kimon Friar and Kostas Myrsiades (Brockport, N.Y.: BOA Editions, 1989). Reprinted by permission of the publisher.

"Inventory," from *Valuable Nail: Selected Poems* by Günter Eich, translated by Stuart Friebert, David Walker, and David Young (Oberlin, O.H.: Oberlin College Press, 1981), 40–41; copyright © 1981 Oberlin College. Reprinted by permission of Oberlin College Press.

Excerpt from "Requiem," in *Poems of Akhmatova* by Anna Akhmatova, translated by Stanley Kunitz and Max Hayward (Boston: Houghton Mifflin/Mariner Books, 1973); copyright © 1973 by Stanley Kunitz and Max Hayward. Reprinted by permission of Darhansoff, Verrill, Feldman Literary Agents.

"Letter to Ibrahim," by Khaled Mattawa from *Ismailia eclipse: Poems* (Riverdale-on-Hudson: Sheep Meadow Press, 1995); copyright © 1995. Reprinted by permission of Khaled Mattawa.

Excerpt from *Anil's Ghost,* by Michael Ondaatje (New York: Knopf, 2000), 54–56; copyright © 2000 by Michael Ondaatje. Used by permission of Alfred A. Knopf, a division of Random House, Inc.

Twelve: Building Bridges

"When the Towers Fell," by Galway Kinnell in the *New Yorker,* September 16, 2002, 53–55; copyright © 2002 by Galway Kinnell. Reprinted by permission of Galway Kinnell.

"On Prayer," from *The Collected Poems, 1931–1987,* by Czeslaw Milosz (New York: Penguin Books, 1988); copyright © 1988 by Czeslaw Milosz Royalties, Inc. Reprinted by permission of HarperCollins Publishers.

"Tomorrow the Past Comes," from *Ion Caraion: Poems* by Ion Caraion, translated by Marguerite Dorian and Elliott Urdang (Athens: Ohio University Press, 1991). Reprinted by permission of Elliott B. Urdang.

"Constellation of Dead Brothers," from *Resistance* by Victor Serge, translated by James Brook (San Francisco: City Lights Books, 1989); copyright © 1989 by James Brook. Reprinted by permission of City Lights Books.

"Feast in Candlelight" from *Miracle Maker: The Selected Poems of Fadhil Al-Azzawi* by Fadhil Al-Azzawi, translated by Khaled Mattawa (Rochester, NY : BOA Editions, 2003); English translation copyright © 2003 by Khaled Mattawa. Reprinted by permission of BOA Editions, Ltd.

"A Mirror for the Twentieth Century," by Adonis from *Modern Poetry of the Arab World*, translated and edited by Abdullah al-Udhari (New York: Penguin Books, 1986).

"The Sadder Century," by Pablo Neruda, translated by Illan Stavans. Originally published in *The Poetry of Pablo Neruda* by Pablo Neruda, edited by Ilan Stavans (New York: Farrar, Straus, and Giroux, 2003); Copyright © 2003 of the English translation by Ilan Stavans. Used by permission of the translator.

ABOUT THE EDITORS

CLIFFORD CHANIN is founder and president of the Legacy Project (www .legacy-project.org), a nonprofit organization dedicated to documenting contemporary responses—in visual art, literature, film, and public debates about memory—to historical traumas in societies around the world. Previously, he spent a decade as associate director of Arts and Humanities at the Rockefeller Foundation. He has also worked as a journalist and as a spokesman for the mayor of New York.

AILI MCCONNON is the literary editor of the Legacy Project. Upon graduating from Princeton University in 2002, she was awarded a Princeton Reach Out '56 fellowship to co-author this anthology. She is also a recipient of a Commonwealth Scholarship and a graduate of Cambridge University and Columbia University's Graduate School of Journalism. Her writing has appeared the *New York Times,* the *Guardian, Business Week Magazine,* the *Wall Street Journal,* and *New York Magazine.*